Identity Transformation and Identity Politics under Structural Adjustment in Nigeria

Edited by

Attahiru Jega

Nordiska Afrikainstitutet, Uppsala
in collaboration with
The Centre for Research and Documentation, Kano

DEDICATION

This book is dedicated to the ever-lasting memory of Claude Ake, scholar, patriot and activist, who died in a plane crash on 4 November, 1996.

This book was commissioned and published within the framework of the Nordic Africa Institute's programme on *The Political and Social Context of Structural Adjustment in Sub-Saharan Africa*.

Programme Co-ordinator:
Adebayo O. Olukoshi

Indexing terms
Economics
Structural Adjustment
Identity
Nigeria

Language checking: Elaine Almén
Cover photo: Pressens Bild

© Nordiska Afrikainstitutet and Centre for Research and Documentation

ISBN 91-7106-456-7

Printed in Sweden by Elanders Gotab, Stockholm, 2000

Table of Contents

FOREWORD..7
PREFACE AND ACKNOWLEDGEMENTS...........................9

1. GENERAL INTRODUCTION. IDENTITY TRANSFORMATION AND
THE POLITICS OF IDENTITY UNDER CRISIS AND ADJUSTMENT....11
Attahiru Jega

2. THE STATE AND IDENTITY TRANSFORMATION UNDER
STRUCTURAL ADJUSTMENT IN NIGERIA 24
Attahiru Jega

3. THE TRANSFORMATION OF ETHNO-REGIONAL IDENTITIES
IN NIGERIA 41
Jibrin Ibrahim

4. RELIGIOUS IDENTITY IN THE CONTEXT OF STRUCTURAL
ADJUSTMENT IN NIGERIA 62
Ibrahim Mu'azzam and Jibrin Ibrahim

5. TRANSFORMATION OF MINORITY IDENTITIES IN
POST-COLONIAL NIGERIA 86
Abdul Raufu Mustapha

6. NATIONAL COUNCIL OF WOMEN'S SOCIETIES AND THE STATE,
1985–1993: THE USE OF DISCOURSES OF WOMANHOOD
BY THE NCWS 109
Charmaine Pereira

7. ADJUSTMENT AND THE TRANSFORMATION OF LABOUR
IDENTITY: WHAT'S NEW AND DOES IT MATTER? 134
Jimi O. Adesina

8. THE YOUTH, ECONOMIC CRISIS AND IDENTITY
TRANSFORMATION: THE CASE OF THE *YANDABA* IN KANO 161
Yunusa Zakari Ya'u

9. YOUTH CULTURE AND *AREA BOYS* IN LAGOS..............181
Abubakar Momoh

10. STRUCTURAL ADJUSTMENT, STUDENTS' MOVEMENT AND
POPULAR STRUGGLES IN NIGERIA, 1986–1996 204
Said Adejumobi

CONTRIBUTORS 234

List of Tables and Figures

Tables

Table 1. Industrial Relations 1980–1995 149
Table 2. Registered Unemployed and Vacancies Declared
       (Lower Grade Workers) 152
Table 3. Registered Unemployed and Vacancies Declared
       (Professionals and Executives) 153
Table 4. Crime in Lagos State 183
Table 5. Standard Score on Violent Crime in Lagos Metropolis
       (1990–1992) 189
Table 6. Educational Enrolments in Nigeria 1969/70–1983/84 210
Table 7. Rates of Return on Investments in Education
       in Sub-Saharan Africa 211

Figures

Figure 1. Strike Trend in Nigeria (1980–1995) 150
Figure 2. Trend in Number of Workers Going on Strike (1980–1995) 150

List of Abbreviations

ABU	Ahmadu Bello University
AFRC	Armed Forces Ruling Council
AG	Action Group
ASUU	Academic Staff Union of Universities
BLP	Better Life Programme
BYM	Bornu Youth Movement
CAN	Christian Association of Nigeria
CBN	Central Bank of Nigeria
CD	Campaign for Democracy
CRD	Centre for Research and Documentation
CDHR	Committee for the Defence of Human Rights
CLO	Civil Liberties Organisation
CODESRIA	Council for the Development of Social and Economic Research in Africa
COR	Calabar Ogoja and Rivers Movement
CRP	Constitutional Rights Project
DA	Democratic Alternative
DFFRI	Directorate of Food, Roads and Rural Infrastructure
ECWA	Evangelical Church of West Africa
FNWS	Federation of Nigerian Women's Societies
FOS	Federal Office of Statistics
GDP	Gross Domestic Product
GNP	Gross National Product
ICWA	Igbo Community Welfare Association
IDB	Islamic Development Bank
IMF	International Monetary Fund
ING	Interim National Government
JMI	Jama'at Nasril Islam
LGA	Local Government Area
MAN	Manufacturers' Association of Nigeria
MOSOP	Movement for the Survival of the Ogoni People
MSS	Muslim Student Society
NACOMYO	National Council of Muslim Youths' Organisation
NADECO	National Democratic Coalition
NAK	National Archives Kaduna
NANS	National Association of Nigerian Students
NAOWA	Nigerian Army Officers Wives' Association
NBA	Nigerian Bar Association
NCNC	National Council of Nigerian Citizens
NCW	Nigerian Council of Women
NCWS	National Council of Women's Societies
NDLEA	National Drug Law Enforcement Agency
NEPU	Northern Elements' Progressive xUnion
NGO	Non-Governmental Organisation
NLC	Nigeria Labour Congress
NPC	Northern People's Congress
NPN	National Party of Nigeria
NRA	National Reformation Army
NRC	National Republican Convention
NRM	National Reformation Movement
NUJ	Nigeria Union of Journalists

NUNS	National Union of Nigerian Students
NUPENG	National Union of Petroleum and Natural Gas Workers
OIC	Organisation of Islamic Conference
PENGASSAN	Petroleum and Natural Gas Senior Staff Association of Nigeria
PRP	People's Redemption Party
RPF	Rwandan Patriotic Front
SAP	Structural Adjustment Programme
SDP	Social Democratic Party
UAC	United Africa Company
UDD	Universal Defenders of Democracy
UMBC	United Middle Belt Convention
UN	United Nations
UNPO	Unrepresented Nations' and Peoples' Organization
UNRISD	United Nations Research Institute for Social Development
UPN	Unity Party of Nigeria
WDF	World Development Fund
WID	Women in Development
WIN	Women in Nigeria
YOUMBAS	Young Muslim Brothers and Sisters

Foreword

One of the innovations which the Nordic Africa Institute has attempted to promote as part of its networking mandate with African researchers and their institutions is the extension of funding support to groups of scholars based in Africa to undertake collaborative work on a mutually agreed subject. This study on identity politics in Nigeria falls within this category of co-operation between the Institute and African scholars and it was promoted within the framework of the Institute's research programme on *The Political and Social Context of Structural Adjustment in Sub-Saharan Africa*. It is particularly gratifying that the collaborative effort has not only stimulated close interaction among the African researchers concerned but also demonstrated the full workability of that mode of co-operation with the African academic community. For this and other reasons, I would like to extend both my personal gratitude and that of the Institute to Dr. Attahiru Jega who was the co-ordinator of the Nigerian research group, and the Centre for Research and Documentation in Kano which was the institutional host in Nigeria for the project, for all the effort which they put into ensuring the production of this manuscript.

The book itself represents the first systematic effort to undertake a detailed, case study-based analysis of the dynamics of identity politics in contemporary Nigeria. The study was initiated and undertaken at a time of great political turmoil and continuing economic decline which was conditioned by an adjustment programme of sorts and the most brutal experience of military dictatorship in Nigeria's history. This broad context was to have a direct role in shaping and re-shaping identity politics in Nigeria during the 1980s and 1990s but many students of Nigeria's contemporary political economy were to feel a great sense of frustration at the absence of a properly-researched and historically-grounded analysis of the shifts which were taking place in the contours of identity politics. This study, therefore, represents a major contribution to an understanding of contemporary Nigerian politics, economy and society and is highly recommended to readers for this reason in the hope that it will be found to be insightful and stimulating.

Adebayo Olukoshi
Co-ordinator,
NAI Research Programme on The Political and Social Context of Structural Adjustment in Sub-Saharan Africa.

Preface and Acknowledgements

This book is the product of research conducted by a group of scholars who, in February 1995, formed a national working group to undertake a study of the transformation of popular identities in Nigeria, especially in the context of structural adjustment and the Babangida regime's programme of transition to civil rule (1986–1993). A small group of those of us associated with the Ahmadu Bello University, Zaria and Bayero University, Kano, political economy programmes conceived of the project which has resulted in this book for two basic reasons. First, it was designed to serve as a follow-up to previous collaborative efforts to study and explain contemporary trends in Nigerian politics, society and economy from the political economy perspective. These previous efforts had resulted in the publication of *The Politics of Structural Adjustment in Nigeria* (1993), edited by Adebayo Olukoshi, and *Expanding the Nigerian Democratic Space* (1996), edited by Jibrin Ibrahim. Second, we have been increasingly concerned with the phenomenon of the resurgence of negative forms of identity politics in contemporary Nigeria, as well as dissatisfied with the growing inability of conventional theoretical frameworks to explain the emerging trend. We, therefore, set out with the aim of investigating this phenomenon fairly rigorously and throwing more light on its dynamics in the contemporary Nigerian political economy.

The work of the national working group was greatly facilitated by a grant offered by the Nordic Africa Institute (NAI), Uppsala, through its programme on *The Political and Social Context of Structural Adjustment in Sub-Saharan Africa*. The grant enabled us to hold a methodology workshop preparatory to field research in December 1995, defray part of the research expenses incurred by the researchers, and then hold a national seminar in January 1997, at which the result of the research conducted by each of the individual contributors was presented and discussed extensively by a select group of Nigerian scholars and representatives of a number of non-governmental organisations and civil society groups. It is the revised and edited versions of the papers presented at that national seminar that constitute the chapters in this book.

I wish to acknowledge, with gratitude, the encouragement and assistance given to us by the Nordic Africa Institute, both in conducting the research and in the final publication of this book. Our special thanks go to Adebayo Olukoshi, the Director of the programme on *The Political and Social Context of Structural Adjustment in Sub-Saharan Africa*. The personal interest he showed in the project, as well as his patience, understanding and prodding, contributed greatly to the completion of this book.

The Centre for Research and Documentation (CRD), Kano, of which the majority of the contributors are members, also offered generous support to the project and the preparation of this book. It co-sponsored the methodology workshop and the national seminar together with NAI, and also provided a tremendous amount of administrative and secretarial assistance to the contributors, and especially to me as the project co-ordinator. We gratefully acknowledge this assistance, and wish to particularly thank Dr. Yahaya Hashim, the Director of CRD for his enthusiastic support and encouragement.

Many other people contributed in different ways and at various stages of the preparation of this book and they deserve special thanks. They include Omafume Onoge, Eskor Toyo, Akin Fadahunsi, Björn Beckman, Ogban Ogban-Iyam, Peter Ozo-Eson, Usman Bugaje, Judith-Ann Walker, Issa Aremu, Kate Meagher, Adagbo Onoja, Haruna Wakili, Emma Ezeazu, Abdullahi Sule Kano, Salihu Lukman, and Nasiru Kura, who participated either in the methodology workshop, or the seminar, or both, and who made very useful comments on earlier drafts of the chapters in this book. Similarly, Abdallah Uba Adamu, Hadiza Jega and Abubakar Hussaini read the first draft of the manuscript and made useful comments, and generally offered tremendous assistance in the final stage of the preparation of the manuscript, for which I am profoundly grateful.

Finally, I wish to thank all the contributors for their commitment to the project and for their valuable contributions to this book. Their perseverance and sacrifices, in spite of the stifling intellectual atmosphere in the Nigerian universities and the competing demands on their time, are highly appreciated, for they went a long way to ensure that this collaborative effort was made both possible and worthwhile.

Attahiru Jega

Chapter 1

General Introduction
Identity Transformation and the Politics of Identity under Crisis and Adjustment

Attahiru Jega

Introduction

There has been growing global sensitivity and concern with regards to the resurgence of identity politics, especially negative forms of identity politics, in many countries in the contemporary international system. The promise and prospects of the so called new world order which came in the wake of the collapse of Soviet communism in the late 1980s seem to have been swiftly replaced in the 1990s with anxiety about the rising tide of ethnic conflicts in Eastern Europe, especially in the former Yugoslavia, and the phenomenon of genocide and ethnocide, especially in Rwanda and Burundi on the African continent.

At the level of policy makers, this anxiety was recently articulated by Kofi Annan, Secretary General of the United Nations Organisation in his 1997 Annual Report. He lamented the rise of negative forms of identity politics and their potentially explosive consequences. He stated, among other things, that:

> This particularistic and exclusionary form of identity politics has intensified in recent years within and among nations... It is responsible for some of the most egregious violations of international humanitarian law and, in several instances, of elementary standards of humanity... Negative forms of identity politics are a potent and potentially explosive force. Great care must be taken to recognise, confront and restrain them lest they destroy the potential for peace and progress that the new era holds in store (*The Guardian*, 1997:8).

At the academic level, although many conventional political scientists, sociologists and social anthropologists, especially those of the modernisation theoretical orientation, have undertaken extensive studies on the role of religion, ethnicity and communalism in the politics of the so called emergent nation-states (e.g. Melson and Wolpe, 1971; Paden, 1973; Young, 1976), their focus had not been on the subject of identity and identity politics as such.

Similarly, studies on identity politics have long largely been ignored by radical and neo-Marxist scholars and researchers of the African political economy. Thus, as Calhoun has aptly noted in general terms, for quite some time "we had managed to maintain for the most part theories that obscured the importance of identity politics from our analyses..." (1994:4). This was partly because of a phobia among a certain category of scholars about undertaking any intellectual work perceived as capable of "undermining the process of nation-state formation", and the post-colonial state's national integration project (Mustapha, 1992:1), and also partly because of a preoccupation with what can be termed as excessive "class-determinism" in most of radical scholarship's attempts to explain the dynamics of African politics and development.

However, this situation is now changing as attested to by the increasing attention which is being paid to the identity issue. As Bangura has noted, "the subject of identity has gained prominence in recent years as dominant theoretical frameworks prove inadequate in explaining the crisis of development and the complexities of present day conflicts" (1994:1). What many used to dismiss as primordial sentiments are fast becoming significant elements of political organisation in the contemporary worlds, including crisis-ridden African countries. They are increasingly creating, recreating and reinforcing a centrifugal form of politics, often check-mating and decisively overcoming those few unifying tendencies engendered by the post-colonial state. This seems to be especially so in the period of economic crisis and structural adjustment, although rigorous empirical research is yet to concretely establish the causal relationship between SAP and this phenomenon. Under the circumstances, there is the need to devote greater attention to the comprehension of the dynamics of these processes, especially their linkage to patterns and processes of accumulation, by employing alternative and all-encompassing theoretical frameworks such as those offered by radical political economy. It is necessary to investigate how the resurgence of the politics of identities relates to, or feeds into, the democratisation processes of plural, peripheral and dependent capitalist societies such as Nigeria, especially under conditions of economic crisis and structural adjustment, and in this era of the much celebrated global resurgence of democracy (Diamond and Plattner, 1993).

Evidently, in many African countries, the state is embroiled in an acute crisis of legitimacy, at the same time as it struggles to cope with crises in the areas of production and consumption. The myth of the strong, authoritarian state lording it over civil society has been shattered and identities that were previously suppressed by the state and, perceived as politically irrelevant by several scholars are now being reasserted and are becoming politically significant. Some have been, or are being, recomposed in new dynamics and with added significance, and in some cases suggesting the imminent collapse of the post-colonial nation-state. Seemingly perplexing, if not paradoxical socio-economic and political dynamics have been rapidly unfolding across the African continent with profound (actual and potential) consequences that are as yet insufficiently comprehended. This is especially so in plural societies such as Nigeria with complex, multiple and competing ethnic, religious, communal and other sorts of identities and loyalties. There is now, perhaps more than ever, the pressing need for more comprehensive, empirical and multi-disciplinary studies with an unconventional theoretical framework to explain and provide a better understanding of these unfolding dynamics.

Although numerous studies have been conducted on the impact of Structural Adjustment Programmes on a number of socio-economic and political processes in African countries using the radical political economy framework of analysis (e.g. Havnevik, 1987; Olukoshi, 1990 and 1993; Gibbon, et al., 1992; Olukoshi, et al., 1994), researchers are just beginning to focus attention on the politics of identities in African societies, with special reference to the market reform context. Indeed, this volume represents the first serious attempt to do so in the Nigerian context. Thus, the contributions in this volume represent a modest attempt to analyse the resurgence of the politics of identities in Nigeria, with particular reference to ethnic, religious, communal, gender, labour and youth identities. Special focus has been placed on the dynamics of this situation in the period of economic crisis and structural adjustment. The period also covers the rule of the Babangida military regime during which SAP was introduced and "consolidated" and a Transition to Civil Rule Programme was simultaneously implemented. Also partly covered was the period of the Abacha regime during which "guided deregulation" was said to have replaced SAP, and another political transition programme was implemented.

Contributors to this volume have attempted to answer a number of pertinent questions, which are relevant to the different issues addressed in all the chapters. What has been the nature, extent, magnitude and character of identity transformation and identity politics in contemporary Nigeria? How do identities play a formative role? Which projects have they been concerned with, and which discourses are being used? What has been the role of economic crisis and structural adjustment in this process? In particular, how has SAP facilitated the resurgence of identities, both in their positive and the negative forms, and their use as rallying grounds for collective political organisation and or action? Or, how do identity actions interact with socio-economic conditions, and with what consequences?

Similarly, the contributors have tried to understand and explain how SAP has refocused political participation, political struggles and political conflicts, making them increasingly predicated on the politics of identity, not only in the context of the Babangida and Abacha regimes' politics of transition, but also in the Nigerian democratisation process in general. Class based struggles and conflicts appear to be in a dynamic interaction with socio-cultural and other non-class based identities with interesting outcomes.

At one level, this volume is generally aimed at providing useful insights into recent political developments and trends in Nigeria, and the place or role of identities in such developments. At another level, it is also aimed at complementing previous works conducted by a network of researchers associated with the Ahmadu Bello University, Zaria, and the Bayero University, Kano political economy programmes, on the politics of structural adjustment (Olukoshi, 1993) and on popular struggles for the expansion of democratic space in Nigeria (Ibrahim, 1997). Through these and similar collaborative efforts, we hope to promote political economy studies based on inter-disciplinary research and networking.

Identity Transformation and the Resurgence of Politics of Identities

The concept of identity has long been used in social anthropology and psychology, especially by structuralists and post-structuralists, and has gained particular currency in the post-modernist literature. As a socio-political concept, "identity" has both an individualist and a collective meaning. In any case, it can simply be defined as "a person's sense of belonging to a group if (it) influences his political behaviour" (Erickson, 1968:57). It is said to be "always anchored both in physiological 'givens' and in social roles..." (ibid.:63). Its attributes comprise "commitment to a cause", "love and trust for a group", "emotional tie to a group", as well as "obligations and responsibilities" relating to membership of a group with which a person identifies. According to Pye, "those who share an interest share an identity; the interest of each requires the collaboration of all" (1962:124). Thus, ordinarily, identities serve as rallying and organising principles of social action within the civil society, and in state-civil society relations. They inform and guide political behaviour, and they add dynamism to political conduct in the context of plural societies (Parry and Moran, 1994). In the context of state-civil society relations, they also serve as a check on the potential excesses of the state. Hence, Parry and Moran have observed that "in advanced societies...what is as significant as overriding national identities are the multiple identities which go to make up plural societies" (1994:275). Such physiological givens as gender and age, and sociological characteristics as ethnicity, nationality, religion, kinship relations, or even workplace affiliations can, and often do, create a basis for identity. Identity is not only about individuality and self-awareness, but also and especially about identification with, and commitment to, shared values and beliefs, in a social collectivity into which a person belongs. At any given time, a person may have multiple identities, each of which may always have some bearing on his or her political conduct and social roles in society. Thus, as Adesina noted, where identities are concerned, an individual is Janus-faced.

However, the question of which sort of identity has the most significant impact or bearing on a person's behaviour is the critical issue, and a subject of theoretical speculation. It is significant that while identities are more or less fixed, identity consciousness is dynamic. Hence, mobilisation, provocation and agitation are central to the formation of a requisite identity consciousness which, in turn, is critical to identity-based politics.

The formation or construction of identity space, according to Larsh and Friedman, is the "dynamic operator linking economic and cultural processes" in modern societies (1992:336). In competition or struggles over societal resources, especially in situations of scarcity, collective demands tend to be predicated and organised on shared interests, which in turn tend to be hinged on either physiological 'givens' or, as is more often the case, on shared sociocultural identities. Thus, what can be termed as identity politics is nothing more than, to use Joseph's phraseology, "the mutually reinforcing interplay between identities and the pursuit of material benefits within the arena of competitive politics" (1987:52).

Identity politics, in other words, is basically "politics either starting from or aiming at claimed identities of their protagonists" (Calhoun, 1994) in national political struggles over access to the state and to avenues of accumulation. It involves the mobilisation of identity consciousness in order to create a mass base of support for the ruling classes, and the elite generally, in their factional struggles in the accumulation process. Also, identity politics connotes a relatively high degree of the subjective entering into politics.

Identity transformation is conceived here, not as an end product, but rather as a continuous process which suggests the changing role of identities and the heightening or increasing magnitude and consequences of identity politics. In other words, the concept of identity transformation is different from that of changed nature of identities, which implies the creation of completely new forms of identities and politics. A broad definition of transformation is favoured in order to achieve a wide ranging understanding of the dynamics of identity politics under situations of crisis and adjustment, since we are not so much concerned with a rigorous empirical testing of the causal relationships.

The Nigerian Context: Identity Transformation and Politics of Identity under SAP

Identities have historically been significant in the Nigerian political process, under colonial rule as well as in the post-colonial dispensation. Under colonialism, administrative exigencies warranted "the invention of traditions", and the nurturing and exacerbation of an "us" *versus* "them" syndrome: Muslim *versus* Christian; Northerner *versus* Southerner; Hausa-Fulani *versus* Yoruba *versus* Igbo, and so on. Religious, regional and ethnic differences were given prominence in conceiving and implementing social, educational and economic development policies and projects under the indirect system of colonial administration favoured by the British. Thus, the differential impact of colonialism set the context of the regional educational, economic and political imbalances which later became significant in the mobilisation or manipulation of identity consciousness in order to effectively divide and rule, as well as in the politics of decolonisation and in the arena of competitive politics in the post-colonial era. For example, the differential impact of colonial education policies ensured that the Northern region was educationally backward relative to the Southern region. Similarly, the differential impact of colonial economic policies ensured that the Southern region, especially the Lagos seaport area, was relatively more advanced economically than the Northern region, while Southern cities became the hub of the country's commercial and industrial activities. The differential political impact came about as a result of the deliberate colonial political policy which used population as a criterion for representation to give the Northern region a greater chance of controlling political power nationally as a counterveiling factor to Southern economic and educational dominance. The end-result was that the political elite in the Northern region capitalised on fears of domination by the Southerners, in view of their region's economic and educational disadvantages, to mobilise a Northern identity to ensure control of political power with which they hoped to check-mate the perceived threat of Southern domination. On the other hand, the Southern elite detested "the use of numbers" for perpetual control of political power by the Northern elite despite the economic and educational backwardness of the Northern region, and felt aggrieved by the inverse relationship between political power and socio-economic advancement. Hence, they also mobilised a Southern identity to oppose and struggle against a perceived injustice in the national power equation. However, the mobilisation of a Southern identity seemed ineffective compared to that of a Northern identity largely because of the different competing ethnic compositions in the western and eastern parts of Southern Nigeria.

But, significantly, underlying all of these elite perceptions and struggles and the mobilisation of identities to garner popular support for their political projects is the imperative of capital accumulation dependent on the character and role of the Nigerian state in capitalist development as nurtured and conditioned by its colonial origin and the mono-cultural and rentier nature of the modern, post-colonial Nigerian economy.

The colonial state pursued a capitalist development strategy initially through the promotion of primary commodity production for export, through which foreign commercial interests established a firm footing in the Nigerian economy, facilitating the rise of an indigenous commercial comprador class and the introduction of capitalist relations of production. Subsequently, in the post-second world war period, manufacturing enterprises controlled by foreign capital burgeoned, with the growing comprador classes playing a supporting role. With this came an accelerated process of urbanisation and proletarianisation, and the development and consolidation of capitalist production processes and relations.

The role of the indigenous comprador class in the capitalist production processes and accumulation increased in the era of decolonisation, as foreign capital sought willing partners to protect its investments, and then even more swiftly in the post-independence period when the post-colonial state became a prime mover of capitalist development. For some time thereafter, foreign capital still controlled the industrial and manufacturing sector, but it had increasingly to accommodate the emergent and fast growing indigenous capitalists who were backed by the power of access to the state that they enjoyed. Indeed, by the late 1970s, the burgeoning capitalist classes comprised not only those whose source of accumulation originated in their collaboration with colonial trading and manufacturing firms, but also those recruited from the critical organs of the state, such as the bureaucracy, the military, the police, the legislature and the cabinet. And, the state itself has been the major source, facilitator and protector of their wealth, either through deliberate policies, such as indigenisation, or through corruption.

Thus, given the critical role of the state in capital accumulation in the post-colonial era, political contests for the capture of state power became intense, more so with the expanded revenue base it came to acquire from petroleum export earnings which rose dramatically and profoundly in the 1970s. In the circumstances, colonially nurtured regional differences combined with historic sociocultural diversity in ethnic and religious terms to crystallise politically significant identities. Mobilised by the ruling classes in particular, and the elite in general, these identities have been transformed into a popular base, employed to garner popular support for the advancement of particularistic interests in state-based accumulation.

However, for most of the decade of the 1970s, the politics of identity although present, remained contained, and its negative features buried, in contrast to what had happened in the decade of the 1960s, and what was to happen in the following decade of economic crisis and structural adjustment. An authoritarian military regime, under General Gowon (1966–75), freshly victorious in a civil war, enjoying some measure of popularity, if not legitimacy, on account of keeping Nigeria one, with an expanded revenue base from petroleum export earnings and rents, and an inclination to spread the wealth around (for example in the form of wage reviews and populist sounding development programmes and projects), sought to promote a pan-Nigerian national identity. This effectively put an apparent hold on the politics of identity based on historic perceptions of inequalities and sociocultural, religious and ethnic differences which had been mobilised in the politics of the First Republic (October 1960 to January 1966). And when the Gowon regime weakened and began to drift by the mid-1970s, its corruption and broken political promises giving rise to popular discontent, a "corrective" and apparently more patriotic and populist regime, the Murtala/Obasanjo regime, took over in July 1975 and also recorded some success in suppressing the tendency towards negative forms of identity politics, until it handed over power to an elected civilian regime, bringing about the commencement of the Second Republic, in October 1979.

The decade of the 1980s opened with a civilian democratic regime and the on-set of economic crisis in Nigeria. The price of petroleum collapsed, export earnings declined, the manufacturing sector experienced a decline in capacity utilisation, and inflation rose dramatically (Olukoshi, 1993). As manufacturing and productive activities collapsed, Nigerian capitalist classes gravitated around the state for patronage to source accumulation through contracts, consultancies and other non-productive services, a situation which has greatly strengthened their compradorial attributes (Fadahunsi, et al., 1996). At the same time, the civilian regime under President Shagari became profoundly licentious, characterised by excessive neo-patrimonialism and prebendalism (Ibrahim, 1992; Joseph, 1987). Politicians saw politics and access to state power as a do or die affair, jettisoning the rules of the game, and personalising public office for selfish gains, for private accumulation, for rewarding of clients and supporters and for punishing opponents. The Nigerian debt burden increased substantially, her credit-worthiness evaporated, and the IMF and the World Bank literally foreclosed on Nigeria, demanding structural adjustment reforms and imposing conditionalities. By the time the Shagari regime attempted a feeble reform through a Stabilisation Act in late 1983, the die had, literally, been cast, for a few days later, in January 1984, it was overthrown by a military Junta led by General Buhari. The General Buhari regime itself was consumed by the contradictions engendered by the politics of crisis and adjustment, as it was overthrown in what came to be known as a "palace coup" led by General Babangida, in August 1985.

By the time the Babangida regime came into power, the economic crisis had become acute in all its manifestations. International pressure had been mounted by the Bretton Woods institutions, and domestic demand for a resolution of the crisis had also heightened. The regime skilfully manœuvred Nigerians into accepting a Structural Adjustment Programme with all the conditionalities without taking the IMF loan. It doggedly implemented the SAP side by side with a Transition to Civil Rule Programme. Meanwhile, according to several studies, the impact of the SAP, combined with that of the economic crisis, has been devastating on the majority of the Nigerian people.

One of the most critical questions addressed by virtually all the contributions in this volume is that of the relationship between SAP and the transformation of identities in the political terrain. What seems clear is that it is difficult to establish a direct causal relationship. Also, if transformation is defined rigidly to mean a complete change in the character or the conventional role of identities, this is not apparent. However, transformation defined broadly as a continuous process of increase in their role as collective platforms of political action is clearly discernible. In other words, there is an increase in the mobilisation of identities and in the resurgence of the politics of identities, with negative or centrifugal tendencies assuming prominence, during the period under study. Clearly, also, this phenomenon is associated with, if not directly caused by, the dynamics of the accumulation process under economic crisis and structural adjustment, as dominant classes and elite compete for access to the state for its power and resources. Beyond this, many of the contributions to this book have also made very interesting revelations about the specificity of the dynamics of the resurgence of the politics of the identities they focused on, as the following section briefly describes.

Outline of Chapters

Chapter 2, which follows the general introduction, focuses on the specific role of the Nigerian state in generating and sustaining the resurgence of identity politics in the period of crisis and adjustment, especially in the context of the Babangida and Abacha regimes' transition to civil rule programmes, drawing upon specific examples and illustrations. The historical specificity of the Nigerian state, its colonial origin and role in the development of capitalist production processes and relations, it is argued, largely defined its role and impact in the accumulation process in the post-colonial dispensation. The ruling class derived both its origin and wealth from the state, around which it gravitates, using every available means to secure power and access. Hence, in the competition and struggles for state power, especially in the period of economic crisis, identity politics become heightened and tend to assume primacy. The state tends to resort to politics of identity for its legitimation, while those excluded tend to resort to identity politics to contest this exclusion. The state is, thus, projected as the critical variable in identity transformation, and the resurgence of identity politics.

In chapter 3, Jibrin Ibrahim focuses on the transformation of ethno-regional identities. He relates this phenomenon to prolonged military rule and its institutionalisation of "permanent transition", which has led to increased repression and an equally increased disarticulation of the legitimacy of the state, a situation which has "provoked the intensification of different forms of identity mobilisation and consciousness (ethnic, regional, religious, communal etc.) and even conflagration". Identity consciousness and mobilisation are normal features of plural societies. But, he argues, they become counter-productive when they become platforms on which "discriminatory practices and unjustified use of violence are organised". Perceptions of denial of rights and domination by others create the basis of ethno-regional conflicts. Ibrahim sees the character of the state and its relationship with "historically entrenched modes of consciousness", as the central factor in the dynamics of ethno-regional identities.

Ethno-regional identities become highly politicised over the questions of control of political power and economic power. Jibrin identified three historical phases on the unfolding of the dynamics of ethno-regional identities. The first was 1958 to 1965, characterised by the mobilisation of these identities in order to gain access to regional power. The second was 1966 to 1970, characterised by mobilisation of the nation to fight a civil war and resolve national crises. The third phase was the post-civil war era, "characterised by the rise of a unitary state and the consequent weakening of the regional bases of power". In this phase, the mobilisation of ethno-regional identities was solely aimed at conquering federal power. Such mobilisation intensified under structural adjustment "due to the enhanced *centralisation, concentration* and *reduction* of the resources available to be accessed even at the centre". In this situation, struggles for access became a zero-sum game, characterised by the need to block the access of others, or to displace those who have access.

Chapter 4 is a joint contribution by Mu'azzam and Ibrahim on the transformation of religious identities. It reviews the phenomenal growth of religious revivalism under SAP, and explores the major dimensions of the rise of religious identities occasioned by this phenomenon. They argue that increased economic hardship under SAP accounts in many respects for the sharp rise in religious activities and the mobilisation of religious identities in competitive politics. The significance of religious identity is in the fact that religion is not just a source of identity but also an ideological system of values and beliefs.

The chapter analyses how the Babangida regime, while silencing all sources of popular organised opposition, went out of its way to dispense patronage to organised religious bodies, a situation which on the one hand created competition amongst the established religions to gain favour from the state, and on the other, heightened the politicisation of religious identities.

The phenomenon of minority identity is addressed by Abdul Raufu Mustapha in chapter 5. Based on a case study of three of the most problematic areas in the management of minority politics in Nigeria, Mustapha provides an illuminating analysis of the transformations that have occurred in minority identities in Nigeria. The evidence marshalled confirms the postulation that identities are dynamic and constantly changing, especially in periods of great socio-economic crisis. He shows the relationship between colonial policies and the crystallisation of identity consciousness amongst minority ethnic groups. Minority identity is a latter day development, related to the recognition of powerlessness in competitive politics based on the mobilisation of identities. And, significantly, Mustapha argues that "economic and political change, including economic crisis and the military centralisation of power, have tended to alter the contours of minority identity".

Chapter 6 by Charmaine Pereira analyses the use of discourses of womanhood, as exemplified by the case of the National Council of Women Societies (NCWS), under the Babangida regime. These discourses, Pereira argues, have been conditioned by the history and the politics of the NCWS, its relationship with the state, and ideological struggles that relate to the capacity of women to engage in democratisation. It sees itself as a "non-political body", and its definition of what it means to be a woman reinforces hegemonic conceptions of male-dominated gendered relations. It maintains a patron-client relationship with the state, supported by it, and supportive of it. Similarly, the NCWS engaged in the mobilisation of women for participation in the politics of transition engendered by the Babangida regime. It is dominated by elite women, and patronised by wives of federal and state chief executives, playing significant roles "in the development of a highly visible femocracy". In the process, the NCWS "contributes to the legitimation of social and political power". Its role also, essentially, signifies the ways in which privileged women are empowered to access the state and participate in the accumulation process, although generally as unequal partners of their male counterparts, on the platform of mobilisation of women's identities using conservative discourses.

Chapter 7 addresses an important aspect of identity transformation and identity politics under crisis and adjustment, namely that of labour identity. Adesina argues that this aspect of micro-level impact of adjustment is paradoxical. For example, labour militancy, which increased under crisis and adjustment, does not suggest a transformation of labour identity *per se*, as this is still within the purview of the traditional identity of labour. Neither the impact of increased poverty nor the subordination of labour leadership by the state can be said to be new processes that really matter, insofar as the transformation of labour identity is concerned. However, the impact of the mobilisation of ethno-regional identities on the struggles of workers and the structuring of labour relations, has the potential of transforming labour identities, suggesting new dynamics worthy of rigorous empirical investigation. But it seems moot whether it matters, as experience shows that workers seem capable of accommodating class to primordial interests, rather than jettisoning their class identity.

The remaining chapters, namely 8, 9 and 10, address the equally paradoxical process of the transformation of youth identity. In chapter 8 Ya'u analyses the phenomenon of the *'Yan daba* urban youth gangs in Kano, showing the ways in which conditions under crisis and adjustment have transformed their conventional sociocultural roles, from macho-showy age-grade associations, to increasingly violent and criminal gangs. In chapter 9, Momoh examines the role of the Lagos *Area Boys*, also revealing how their traditional roles, socially acceptable if not desirable, became criminalised under crisis and adjustment. He highlights the role of the military authoritarian state in this transformation, as well as how the criminalised *Area Boys* have responded to, and have been coping with, this 'new' identity.

In Chapter 10, Adejumobi examines another aspect of the transformation of youth identity, using as a case study the role that the students' movement has played in popular struggles between 1986 and 1996. The impact of SAP on education seems to have pushed students into organised struggles to contest relations of domination in the education sector, as well as confront the state in struggles over a wide ranging agenda, which often goes beyond the narrow confines of education.

In addressing the dynamics of identity formation and identity politics in Nigeria in this volume, we may have raised more questions than we have been able to satisfactorily answer. However, we shall consider our goal achieved if this modest pioneering attempt inspires other like-minded scholars and researchers who will feel encouraged to engage in further debates and inquiries on similar phenomena not only in Nigeria, but in other equally pluralistic societies. In this way, we shall have contributed in opening up an area of study which has largely been ignored or merely taken for granted in conventional scholarship.

Bibliography

Bangura, Y., 1994, "The Search for Identity: Ethnicity, Religion and Political Violence", mimeo.

Calhoun, C. (ed.), 1994, *Social Theory and the Politics of Identity*. Oxford: Blackwell.

Diamond. L., and M. F. Plattner (eds.), 1993, *The Global Resurgence of Democracy*. Baltimore and London: The Johns Hopkins University Press.

Fadahunsi, A., A. Olukoshi, A. Momoh and T. Babawale, 1996, "Nigeria Beyond Structural Adjustment: Towards a National Popular Alternative Development Strategy", in Fadahunsi, A., and T. Babawale, (eds.) *Nigeria Beyond Structural Adjustment*. Lagos: Panaf Publishing Inc.

Gibbon, P., Y. Bangura and A. Ofstad (eds.), 1992, *Authoritarianism, Democracy and Adjustment. The Politics of Economic Reform in Africa*. Uppsala: Nordic Africa Institute.

Havnevik, K. J., (ed.), 1987, *The IMF and the World Bank in Africa. Conditionality, Impact and Alternatives*. Uppsala: Scandinavian Institute of African Studies.

Ibrahim, J., 1992, "The State, Accumulation and Democratic Forces in Nigeria", in Rudebeck, L., (ed.) *When Democracy Makes Sense: Studies in the Democratic Potential of Third World Movements*. Uppsala: AKUT.

Ibrahim, J., (ed.), 1997, *Expanding the Nigerian Democratic Space*. Dakar: CODESRIA Books.

Joseph, R., 1987, *Democracy and Prebendal Politics in Nigeria*. Cambridge: Cambridge University Press.

Larsh, S. and J. Friedman (eds.), 1992, *Modernity and Identity*. Oxford: Blackwell.

Melson, R. and H. Wolpe (eds.), 1971, *Nigeria: Modernization and the Politics of Communalism*. East-Lansing: Michigan State University Press.

Mustapha, A. R., 1992, "Identity Boundaries, Ethnicity and National Integration in Nigeria", paper to CODESRIA Seminar on Ethnic Conflicts in Africa, Nairobi, November 16–18.

Olukoshi, A., 1990, *Crisis and Adjustment in the Nigerian Economy*. Lagos: JAD Publishers.

Olukoshi, A., (ed.), 1993, *The Politics of Structural Adjustment in Nigeria*. London and Ibadan: James Currey and Heinneman.

Olukoshi, A., R. O. Olaniyan and F. Aribisala (eds.), 1994, *Structural Adjustment in West Africa*. Lagos: Nigerian Institute of International Affairs.

Paden, J. N., 1973, *Religion and Political Culture in Kano*. Berkeley: University of California Press.

Pye, L., 1962, *Politics, Personality and Nation-Building: Burma's Search for Identity*. New Haven. Conn.: Yale University Press.

Vail, L., (ed.), 1989, *The Creation of Tribalism in Southern Africa*. London: James Currey.

Young, C., 1976, *The Politics of Cultural Pluralism*. Madison: University of Wisconsin Press.

Newspapers and Magazines

The Guardian, September 9, 1997, "Annan Worried over Identity Politics", p. 8.

Chapter 2

The State and Identity Transformation under Structural Adjustment in Nigeria

Attahiru Jega

Introduction

One of the most prominent features of contemporary politics world-wide is what can be termed identity politics. Indeed, throughout the world, and in Africa in particular, there is what can be called the resurgence of the politics of identities. Personal, 'given', chosen and shared identities are fast becoming rallying points for collective action in crises-ridden post-colonial African states. This came about especially in the decade of the IMF and World Bank-inspired Economic Recovery and Structural Adjustment Programmes of the 1980s. Traditional forms of identities, dubbed as primordial and for long trivialised, have proved to be resilient and, in a wave of resurgence, are fast becoming popular and of political significance in the contemporary political economy, with all sorts of outcomes and consequences. Even new forms of identities have emerged and become quite significant. All of these are competing effectively with, often surpassing, post-colonial conceptions of national identity. Other forms of identities, earlier hailed by radical scholars and progressives as primary in shaping the dynamics of politics, such as class, are seemingly proving to be not as decisive; they seem at best elusive, if not contradictory. What is responsible for this situation? What accounts for the emergence and persistence of identity politics? How can this be concretely explained? These are some of the questions which are beginning to engage the attention of scholarly research on the dynamics and the contemporary manifestations of the politics of identity. I have addressed these questions in this chapter in the general context of the unfolding situation in Nigeria. But I focus particularly on the role of the Nigerian state in this process of the rise of identity politics under situations of a generalised socio-economic crisis and structural adjustment. I analyse the role of the state in generating identity crisis, facilitating the transformation of identities and nurturing the conditions for the resurgence of identity politics in Nigeria.

Nigeria has experienced a profound socio-economic and political crisis from the early 1980s. The Nigerian state, through its major organs and functionaries, has been busily managing (or mismanaging) the crisis which it has, itself, greatly engendered. The dynamics of the management of this crisis accelerate the process of the transformation of identities and the politics of identities in Nigeria. Identity transformation, in general, and the consequent politicisation of identities, may not have been solely and directly caused by the state. But there is certainly a profound relationship between the role of the state and the transformation of identities, and especially with the growing intensity of the politics of identities. Specifically, the role of the state in the accumulation process and the way in which it makes politics and political struggles for office a 'do or die' affair has given rise to what Claude Ake has termed as the primacy of politics (see Mittleman, 1997), a phenomenon which can be said to have facilitated both the politicisation, as well as, the transformation of identities.

Under conditions of economic crisis, and subsequently structural adjustment, there has been a swift decline in the ability of the Nigerian state to provide for the basic socio-economic needs of the people. Similarly, there has been increased exclusion of a segment of the elite and the bourgeoisie in the distribution of the spoils of office, and an acute marginalisation of the majority of the population from the benefits of development projects and social provisioning. All of these have led to an increased crisis of legitimacy of the state (Amin, 1996). As the state experiences what some observers have termed as a process of decomposition and recomposition (Beckman, 1996), and disengages from critical, basic social provisioning, only the constituencies and clients of those who control state power actually continue to have access to state resources through patronage. Thus, under these conditions, groups have tended to rely on identity-based politics to struggle for access to the state and the resources that it controls, or in order to protest exclusion and oppression, as well as to demand basic rights and socio-economic provisioning.

It is argued that the state is the critical variable in understanding the dynamics of identity transformation and the resurgence of an intensified form of identity-based politics in Nigeria. The state has, historically, shaped and conditioned the arena for competition over scarce societal resources and for expanded accumulation. In the period of the "oil boom", under relatively popular, if not populist military regimes, the state's legitimacy was hardly seriously questioned or challenged in terms of the ways in which it managed the huge petroleum based revenues. But, confronted with a generalised socio-economic crisis in the decade of the 1980s, the Nigerian state, under prolonged, and increasingly authoritarian and unpopular military rule, came to experience an acute crisis of legitimation, in the context of which national identity became increasingly threatened and undermined, particularly as previously suppressed or relegated identities gained in ascendancy.

In the circumstances, ethnic, religious, regional, communal and other identities have become central modes of political organisation, on account of, as well as aided and abetted by, the actions and or inactions of the state.

Identity politics is not a new phenomenon in Nigeria. But its recent manifestations and trends are much more profound and consequential on the Nigerian political economy than has ever been the case previously. The ways and manner by which the Nigerian state, under military rule, introduced and consolidated SAP seemed to have re-focused political participation, political struggles and political conflicts, making them increasingly predicated on the politics of identity. This has been amply illustrated by the unfolding of events in the politics of transition under the Babangida and Abacha transition to civil rule programmes (1987–1996).

The Nigerian State: An Overview

The Nigerian state is, first and foremost, a colonial creation. Historically, it came into being as a super-imposed and, arguably, over-developed (à la Alavi, 1972), colonial structure attending to the requirements of British conquest and imperial domination. Since independence in 1960, segments of the Nigerian elite associated with the critical organs of the state, such as the military officer corps, the so called political class and the bureaucratic-technocratic elite, have come to assume and play a prominent role in the Nigerian political economy, a role that has been profoundly facilitated as well as conditioned by the phenomenon of prolonged military rule. They do so, however, in close alliance and collaboration with other segments of the dominant classes in the Nigerian society.

Partly on account of its colonial origin, the Nigerian state has acquired certain characteristics with remarkable impact on the manner in which the Nigerian society has been transformed. For example, it seems detached from, and relatively autonomous of, the Nigerian society. But this is only partly so, for as Vincent (1987) has observed, virtually all states derive from society but operate more or less over and above it. This relative autonomy has been significant in the ways in which the state has directed capitalist development, especially the processes of class formation, conflicts and struggles and accumulation.

As a facilitator of capitalist development processes, the Nigerian state has been both a major owner of the means of production and a stake holder in several capitalist enterprises (Beckman, 1982). It collaborates with both domestic and foreign capitalist interests in playing this role. As Beckman has noted, sometimes it tends to serve as an agent of imperialism, at other times it may tend to serve the interests of foreign bourgeoisie, and at other times, it may tend to serve the interests of the domestic bourgeoisie, but at all times, it serves the interest of capital in general.

However, in facilitating capitalist development, the Nigerian state is, paradoxically, shaped and conditioned by intense competition, conflict and struggles by contending classes in the Nigerian civil society, and particularly by incessant factionalism and in-fighting amongst the active and dominant forces in the political economy. This factionalism and in-fighting has been nurtured and sustained by the mobilisation of regional, ethnic and religious sentiments. This phenomenon substantially accounts for the military intervention in politics, the culture of *coup d'état* and counter *coup d'état*, and the prolonged nature of military rule as well as its domineering control of and influence on the Nigerian state. But it especially accounts for the mobilisation of all sorts of sentiments by the dominant classes in order to garner popular support in their struggles to capture and control political power and access to state revenues for expanded accumulation.

Thus, the role of the post-colonial state in Nigeria has been drastically affected and conditioned by essentially three major factors: its colonial origin, excessive factionalism amongst a multi-ethnic, multi-religious, and regionally segmented elite, and prolonged military authoritarian rule. These define the pattern and the character, as well as the essence, of its role in the capitalist development processes, in state-civil society relations, in international relations, and in the dynamics of resource utilisation and accumulation in the Nigerian political economy. For example, the Nigerian state's supposed patrimonial and prebendal character (Diamond, 1988; Joseph, 1987; Graf, 1988) is accounted for by these three conditioning factors. A regionally segmented elite struggles for political power by mobilising religion, regionalism and ethnicity. The faction that gains power also relies on these to establish hegemony and to perpetuate its control on state power. This means that, historically, identity-based politics has been significant in struggles for political power and control of the state. Obviously, that led to conflictual and crisis-ridden politics. However, it can be argued that it was only in the period of economic crisis and structural adjustment that the most negative and damaging aspects of identity mobilisation and identity politics, with serious consequences on the political economy, came to prominence. For, in the preceding periods, expanded oil based revenues cushioned the damaging impact of conflicts and struggles as the state embarked on profligate public expenditures which somewhat spread the benefits from oil revenues, until the country moved from oil boom to burst.

For instance, for the first two decades of independence, 1960–1980, the Nigerian state relied on its expanded revenue base from petroleum exports to strengthen its domineering influence over the civil society. For example, oil revenues rose from N166 million in 1970, to N12,353 million in 1980 (Forrest, 1995:134). Consequently, public expenditure rose fairly dramatically, from 19 per cent of GDP in 1973, to 54 per cent in 1977/8 (Forrest, 1995:143 and 147). Thus, through this expanded revenue base and massive public expenditure, the state effectively established its presence in virtually all aspects of the political economy, especially in critical sectors such as construction, commerce, industry and banking, and in the delivery of goods and services, especially in education, health and social welfare. Access to the state, thus, became a major avenue for accumulation, especially through contracts, patronage and corruption, or abuse of public office. Under the circumstances, the Nigerian state assumed the stature of an ideological canopy of power in some fundamental respect, propped up by a relatively strong technocratic class, bureaucracy and institutions of law and order (military, police and judiciary). It expanded the horizon of capital accumulation for a nascent capitalist class dependent on the state. And, significantly, under this situation, also, state power, as Ake noted, became pervasive:

> the state is everywhere and its power appears boundless. There is hardly any aspect of life in which the state does not exercise power and control. That makes the capture of state power singularly important (Ake, 1996a:23).

Thus, those who had captured state power were able, first, to use and manipulate identity politics, and then, paradoxically, to reduce, trivialise, ignore, or otherwise suppress the real significance of identity politics in their public and official utterances. Deliberate state policies, symbolically represented by such slogans as "One Nigeria" and "One Nation, One Destiny" in the 1970s and 1980s, sought to bring about national integration and forge an all-embracing and all-encompassing Nigerian identity as a substitute for those traditional forms of identity dubbed as primordial, centripetal and counter-productive to the objective of maintaining one united and indivisible nation. Successive Nigerian constitutions sought to legally prevent such identities as religion, ethnicity and regionalism from being the basis of political organisation and contest for state power by, for example, insisting on a "federal character" in organising political parties and in the distribution of public offices. The post-independent Nigerian state ostensibly pursued a project of nation-building, which entailed the relegation, if not destruction, of other identities considered as primordial, and their substitution with a "Nigerian" identity.

The reality of the situation was, however, far from its outward appearance. The underlying current in the management of national resources or even in the sharing of the so called national cake remained that of the politics of identities. For, the actual role of the state in the management of the petroleum based revenues, particularly its crass patrimonialism in the use of state power in the dispensation of federal revenues from its rentier-economy, reinforced perceptions of relative deprivation which found accommodation in, and became organised around, resilient traditional forms of identities. This situation also heightened factionalism within the dominant power elite, and went a long way to eroding the power and the efficacy of the state, initiating what can be appropriately termed as the process of the decomposition of the state, and the subsequent resurgence of identity politics in state-civil society relations, in the period of economic crisis and structural adjustment.

The State, SAP and Identity Transformation

By the middle of the 1980s, Nigeria came to be afflicted by a devastating economic crisis, manifested in declining revenues from oil (e.g. from N10,915 million in 1985 to N8,107 million in 1986), a heavy debt burden, of about 20 billion US dollars, and a generalised crisis of production and the rapidly declining purchasing power of the incomes of the Nigerian workers due to inflation and a general decline in the production of goods and services in the Nigerian economy (see Olukoshi, 1993; Oluyemi-Kusa, 1994). In this situation, the Nigerian state also came to be confronted by an intense crisis of legitimation.

In order to cope with these crises, the Babangida regime introduced the Structural Adjustment Programme (SAP), which it said would halt economic stagnation and revitalise growth. General Babangida affirmed repeatedly and quite vigorously that SAP would indeed bring about the needed self-reliance and self-sustenance of the Nigerian economy. The SAP introduced by the Babangida regime was a package of neoliberal economic reforms primarily aimed at strengthening market forces and "rolling back the state". It consisted of stabilisation policies targeted at restoring price stability and balance of payments equilibrium. Its expressed goals were to increase efficiency and productivity in the economy by reducing wastage, and promoting entrepreneurship in the society (Olukoshi, 1993).

Specifically, the essential elements of SAP included currency devaluation and exchange rate deregulation; cuts in public expenditure especially in the social services sector and so called removal of subsidies on state provided goods and services; and privatisation and commercialisation of public enterprises and services.

The Babangida regime pursued the implementation of the SAP ardently, with rapid and dramatic, if not profoundly devastating, consequences for the Nigerian political economy. The result was little, if any, curbing of waste in the management of the economy and in the operation of the government, with the manufacturing sector experiencing persistent decline in capacity utilisation, and the economy recording large overall fiscal deficits. The economic growth rate was inconsequential, falling to 1.5 per cent in 1993 while GDP growth virtually stagnated (World Bank, 1995:149). Similarly, the country continued to be pressed down by a heavy external debt burden which rose from $19.5 billion in 1985 to around $30 billion by the end of 1994 (World Bank, 1995:151). In addition, the period witnessed a phenomenal rise in inflation, reaching triple digits in 1994, as well as increased job losses and insecurity. The cost of education and healthcare sky-rocketed. In short, SAP resulted in a generalised and acute immiseration of the majority of the

Nigerian people, with GNP per capita falling from $1,160 in 1980 to $300 in 1993. Indeed, as a World Bank report noted:

> With GDP growing at 5 per cent a year and population at 3 per cent, per capita income grew at 2 per cent over the period 1987–92. Continuing that growth rate would take about 30 years for Nigeria to recover its peak living standard achieved in 1981. In real per capita terms, consumption and income are now little higher than they were in the early 1970s, before the oil boom (1995:149–150).

Thus, the impact of the SAP-based economic policies has been very devastating on most sectors of the economy, such as industry and agriculture, and especially on the majority of the Nigerian people. The Nigerian state systematically disengaged from social provisioning, leading, for example, to dramatic and unbearable increases in the cost of education, medical and healthcare services. Devaluation worsened the purchasing power of the incomes of the working classes and poor peasants, heightening the cost of living and pushing a significant percentage of the members of the working classes below the poverty line (Jega, 1993a; Olukoshi, 1993; Adejumobi, 1995). Whatever indicators are used to assess the impact of SAP, the picture invariably looks grim and disconcerting.

Clearly, the combined impact of the socio-economic crises and SAP exposed the Nigerian state as reckless, insensitive, and irresponsible, if not structurally weak and incapable of meeting its basic obligations to the Nigerian people. The prebendal, patrimonial as well as authoritarian manner by which the state tried to suppress and contain popular agitations against its management of the economic crisis, rather than strengthen it, objectively further eroded its legitimacy and efficacy. The reaction, or response, of civil society to the state, in turn, contributed to the acceleration of the process of the decomposition of the state. For example, a national, Nigerian, civic identity, imbued with patriotism and accepted, uncontested obligations to the state, virtually disappeared. As the state itself became lawless, so too did the citizens increasingly rely on lawlessness in state-civil society relations and in inter-personal relations. Increasingly, virtually every actor in the political process, including even functionaries of the state came to rely on factors other than patriotism and pan-Nigerian nationalism as the critical elements of popular mobilisation. In this context, the stage was appropriately set for the transformation of traditional forms of identities, as well as for the emergence of new forms of identities, into open platforms for political organisation either in order to cope with the demands of livelihood under crisis and adjustment, or in order to check-mate the excesses of the state in the sphere of accumulation, or both.

Quite significantly, the increased incapacity and inadequacy of the state in meeting the fundamental needs of the Nigerian people under the period of economic crisis, combined with the negative effects and damaging impact of the implementation of the World Bank and IMF inspired Structural

Adjustment Programme, had pushed many Nigerians into increasingly vibrant civil society groups, with many of these gravitating around the politics of identity. The suppressive and authoritarian manner by which the state pursued SAP alienated many Nigerians and gravitated them towards questioning, not only the efficacy, but also the legitimacy of the state. From then on, the Nigerian state has become, as Khilnani has observed in respect of India, "an arena of combat populated by indivisible and non-negotiable identities" (Dunn, 1992:202). But much more than has been the case in India, the Nigerian state seems to be increasingly incapable of a credible mediation and arbitration between these conflicting and potentially explosive identity-based interests. Those dominant elite who used identity politics to access and control the state and its resources turned around to use state power to suppress or weaken other identity-based agitations against, and challenges to, their power. The more this happened, the greater the intensity of the resurgence of the negative forms of identity politics.

Thus, the period beginning from June 1986 when the Structural Adjustment Programme (SAP) was introduced in Nigeria, marked a water-shed in the accelerated process of the transformation of identities into distinctly manifest expressions of popular sentiments in national politics. Even new forms of identities emerged to be significant such as gender and youth-based identities.

In essence, therefore, the process of decomposition of the state, characterised by chaotic management of the economy, institutional decay, and the inability of the state to provide the basic socio-economic and security needs of the people, was simultaneously accelerating the emergence of contending loci of power organised around identity politics. The crisis of legitimacy which has engulfed the Nigerian state has forced citizens to increasingly retreat from their "Nigerian" identity which the post-colonial state had sought to promote, into communal, ethnic, religious and other forms of identities. The goal of constructing a citizen with a solid "Nigerian" identity, a de-tribalised, secular, patriotic identity, proved elusive. Contradictory state policies and the dynamics of politics of state-based accumulation made nonsense of the post-colonial state project. On the contrary, these reinforced incipient identities and gave them a critical role in national affairs. It was not only fashionable, but also logical, in the accumulation process, that virtually everything makes sense only if perceived from the prism of communal, ethnic, regional or religious contexts.

Prolonged military rule, it should be noted, institutionalised a culture of authoritarian rule and reinforced acute patrimonial and prebendal dispositions in the use of public office and state resources. State functionaries increasingly became unresponsive and unaccountable to the people, dispensing federal largesse to patrons and clients, and withholding public projects and programmes to punish opponents. In this context, especially during the period of economic crisis and structural adjustment, politics, as

Ake observed, assumed primacy and political struggles for access to the state and its revenue became, in many respects, a matter of life and death. As Ake noted:

> The state is in effect privatised: it remains an enormous force but no longer a public force; no longer a reassuring presence guaranteeing the rule of law but a formidable threat to all except the few who control it, actually encouraging lawlessness and with little capacity to mediate conflicts in society (1996b:73).

Thus, as the majority of the people become alienated from the state, they increasingly tend to question its legitimacy, and they increasingly congregate around "whatever can be the way they could express, not only their discontent but their solidarity" (Amin, 1996). Hence, religion, ethnicity and other forms of identity become convenient platforms of organised political action. Given the general culture of intolerance nurtured under authoritarian military rule, religious, ethnic, and communal struggles and conflicts increased greatly.

Identities are not static, although some can be enduring and long-lasting. Such identities based on religion, ethnicity, regionalism and communalism, which are essentially 'given', rather than 'chosen', have existed since the creation of modern Nigeria by the British colonialists. As noted earlier, they have also been the underlying, even if latent, currents of political engagements in post-colonial Nigeria, as they combined with, as Joseph observed, "the pursuit of material benefits within the arenas of competitive politics" (1987:52). Similarly, as Forrest has noted, "[a]ccess to resources and strategies of accumulation were very often dependent on ties of kinship, lineage, and friendship and on reciprocal ties of clientele. Community identities were strong, shaping economic participation and conditioning social differentiation." (1995:24).

At the initial stages of the implementation of SAP, some organised civil society groups, notably the labour movement, the students, and professionals, were able to mobilise and struggle using brands of nationalist and patriotic, if not class-based, 'chosen' identities (Jega, 1993b; Beckman and Jega, 1995). Hence, university students organised under their national association, NANS, to agitate for collective demands and to oppose state education and other economic policies perceived as detrimental to the Nigerian people. Similarly, workers organised under the Nigeria Labour Congress (NLC) to advance collective economic and political interests, while professionals such as lawyers and university lecturers, under the Nigeria Bar Association (NBA) and the Academic Staff Union of Universities (ASUU), respectively, struggled, agitated against, or otherwise impacted upon state policies.

However, as the crisis intensified and the impact of the adjustment measures became rooted, the fabric of these collective solidarities, under 'chosen' identities, were literally torn apart by a combination of state strategies of co-optation, intimidation, harassment and suppression, and individualist survival methods on the part of some of the leading activists. Increasingly, the politics and the struggles of many of these organisations came to be constrained by state-sponsored factionalism and the mobilisation of sentiments associated with traditional identities, giving rise to a situation in which the struggles of these groups and organisations came to be characterised by a rising trend of religious, regional and ethnic factionalism. As an illustration, the case of the 1988 and 1994 internal crises in the NLC can be cited, which led to its virtual break-up and the emergence of state-sponsored candidates in the contest for its leadership, under the direction of a state-appointed sole administrator and the Minister of Labour. There was also the attempt to balkanise ASUU into North *versus* South groups in order to sabotage the struggles led by the association in 1994 and 1996.

Thus, in general, the Nigerian state can be said to have contributed to the transformation of traditional forms of identities into popular platforms of political organisation and agitation in a number of fundamental respects. First, given its patrimonial and prebendal character, the state utilised and allocated federal resources selectively, favouring in the first instance the military, which has been the dominant force controlling state power, and, in the second instance, those factions and sections to which the ruling junta belonged, together with their clients and allies from amongst the dominant classes in society. For as long as the military has ruled, this dominant faction has been generally perceived as of Northern origin. This situation has in turn been creating and deepening or otherwise reinforcing additional perceptions of Northern or Hausa-Fulani domination, and organised reactions to this, based on identity politics. Thus, the Babangida and Abacha regimes have been repeatedly accused of committing a disproportionate amount of public resources, especially through extra-budgetary spending, for the development of the Northern part of Nigeria at the expense of the Southern part. Similarly, they have been accused of using their control of state power to promote Islam, at the expense of Christianity, and to provide federal jobs and contracts to Northerners and or Hausa-Fulanis, at the expense of Southerners, and or Yorubas, Igbos, and so on (see for example, *Spectrum International*, October 1992; *The African Guardian*, October 18, 1993; Awa, 1994; The Democratic Forum, 1994; *Newswatch*, January 16, 1995). Indeed, leading functionaries of the State have generally acted in such a non-transparent manner in public conduct as to reinforce perceptions of deliberate exclusion of certain groups (Jega, 1996a; Ayagi, 1994). As this has continued to happen under situations of shrinking public revenues from the petroleum-based economy in the period of economic crisis and structural adjustment, it has heightened recourse to the politics of identities to articulate, as well as challenge both the actual, as well as the perceived, injustices.

Second, and perhaps most significantly, in this process of transformation of identities, has been the state's increasing abnegation of its social responsibilities and obligations to the citizens. The collapse of state institutions, structures and agencies, and the services which these are supposed to provide, in short, what has been termed as the decomposition of the state, confronted many citizens with one of two alternatives: either 'exit' and alienation or 'voice' and expressed discontent, if not effective challenge of the prevailing situation. Evidently, many have taken the 'exit' option, characterised by despondency and political apathy. But the phenomenon of the transformation of identities is largely accounted for by the fact that a substantial majority of those who have taken to the 'voice' option have chosen to do so by recourse to traditional identities or other forms of identity that were hitherto suppressed.

The processes of state decomposition, combined with the devastating impact of SAP on the livelihood of Nigerians, can be said to have been actually transforming the Nigerian people's multiple identities and narrowed them into a single focus, resulting in "deeper and more rigid social divisions" gravitating around the politics of identity (UNRISD, 1995:95). Thus, although at any time individuals may simultaneously share multiple identities, they tend to use one, or at most a few, of these as platforms of political organisation and action. This has increasingly become so in the Nigerian context, as is evidenced by the manifestations of identity politics in the Babangida and, subsequently, Abacha regimes' transition to Civil Rule Programmes.

The Politics of Identity under Transition to Civil Rule Programmes

The Babangida regime launched a Transition to Civil Rule programme in July 1987, barely one year after it had introduced the far-reaching Structural Adjustment Programme. It was ostensibly aimed at a gradual transfer of power to civilians from the local government to the state and national levels, in a phased programme over six years. In reality, it turned out to be a strategy of regime legitimation with guided political liberalisation, rather than democratisation and popular empowerment. It sought to induce acceptance of the regime and its economic policies, by the political class especially, on the assumption that the regime was transitional and on its way out of power. But even as a strategy of legitimation, the IBB transition programme, as it came to be known, failed woefully, albeit with dramatic consequences (Jega, 1995). For example, it was characterised by inconsistencies and contradictions, and 'shifting goal-posts' insofar as the terminal date of handing-over of power to an elected civilian federal government was concerned. For example, after an elaborate process, inducing the political class to form associations from which political parties would be registered, the regime dissolved all the political associations and created two parties, the Social Democratic Party (SDP) and the National Republican Convention (NRC), in May 1989. Then, it sought to promote "a new breed" of politicians by banning the so called "old brigade", which was later unbanned, and then banned again. The Transition to Civil Rule Programme was supposed to terminate with the election of a civilian President in 1990 according to the recommendation of the Political Bureau set up by the regime. However, the regime rejected this date and fixed a new one for October 1992, but this was later shifted to January 1993, and then to August 1993. In the end, in June 1993, the Babangida regime exposed its hidden agenda of wanting to extend military rule, if not to entrench General Babangida himself in power, with the annulment of an evidently free and fair presidential election. It took a generalised political crisis following the annulment of the June 12 election, to compel General Babangida to hurriedly "step aside" from power and hand over to a hand-picked Interim National Government, in August 1993. (See Oguibe, 1993; International Forum for Democratic Studies, 1995.) But the ING proved to be so ineffectual, if not illegitimate, that by 18 November, 1993, it was pushed aside and replaced by a new junta under General Abacha.

The manner in which the Babangida regime executed its Transition to Civil Rule Programme, and particularly the ways in which the regime handled the post-June 12 crisis in the wake of the annulment of the presidential elections, went a long way to destroying whatever little legitimacy both the regime and the state had retained since the introduction of SAP in 1986. These generated tremendous discontent in the civil society, giving a boost to the resurgence of the politics of identity, induced essentially in the first instance by the impact of the Structural Adjustment Programme.

The Abacha regime which came to power on 18 November, 1993, in the wake of the June 12 crisis, purportedly "as a child of necessity", also unfolded its own transition programme, phased and crafted very much like its predecessor's, scheduled to terminate in October 1998. The regime's preoccupation with stability, its slow pace of implementing its own political programme, and the containment measures it uses to deal with its opponents, have all cast doubts about its commitment to genuine popular democratisation. These combine with its apparent inability to significantly assuage the acute immiserisation of the Nigerian people engendered by the SAP introduced by Babangida, to heighten the politics of identity. For example, GDP growth rate has stagnated at about 3 per cent, a far cry from the projected annual rate of over 5 per cent; inflation has remained acute; social services and infrastructure have collapsed in spite of a Petroleum Trust Fund created to resuscitate these; and the manufacturing sector has remained crippled by lack of basic raw materials and policy constraints and disincentives. Meanwhile, a small class that has controlled access to the state and its resources, has become fantastically rich through unbridled personalisation of office, theft and graft (see Gboyega, 1996; Transparency International, 1996; Okigbo, 1994). The ways in which they conduct state policies, site projects, execute programmes, and distribute patronage reinforce traditional perceptions of injustices, domination and exploitation, giving rise to a conducive atmosphere for the resurgence of negative forms of identity politics.

Thus, in these circumstances, much more so than at any other time in the Nigerian post-independence history, political organisations based on ethnic, regional and even religious identities, such as the Northern Elders Forum, the *Egbe Afenifere*, the Eastern Mandate Union, the Western Elders Meeting, the Middle Belt Forum, the Christian Association of Nigeria, the Supreme Council for Islamic Affairs, to mention a few, have become openly active, either in challenging or in supporting state policies and programmes, aggressively mobilising sentiments to prop up their partisan positions. Indeed, the state itself has become much more visibly partial and partisan, and actively involved in the politics of identity, as usual dispensing patronage and largesse to allies and supporters, and intimidating, harassing or suppressing perceived opponents. This contributed in no small way in heightening the politics of identity.

For example, the state's dabbling in religious matters, while Nigeria is supposed to be secular, opened it up to criticism of partisanship (see Kukah, 1993). The apparent disproportionate channelling of state resources into Muslim and Christian monuments in the federal capital, Abuja, and in annual pilgrimages, perceived to be in favour of the Muslims, as well as the secretive manner by which Nigerian membership of the Organisation for Islamic Conference (OIC) was handled, heightened religious intolerance and the mobilisation of contending and opposed religious positions in national politics (see CAN, 1989; Gumi, 1992). Consequently, even the composition of the regime's cabinet after a reshuffle was invariably accompanied by a vigorous debate on religious domination and the religious preferences of the state. For example, when General Babangida reshuffled his cabinet in December 1989, and appointed 27 Muslims out of the total of 35, CAN publically condemned this as evidence of Muslim domination over Christians, and even organised a public demonstration to express its discontent (Falola, 1995). On their part, Muslim activists and organisations felt that Babangida was playing Christians against Muslims in order to divert attention away from his personal rule, and that he filled his Armed Forces Ruling Council with Christians; and that "even Christian governors were posted to predominantly Muslim states apparently in order to destabilise and displace Muslims from governance" (Bako, 1994:28–29). Muslim organisations, such as the Muslim Students Society, MSS and the Council of Ulama, also publically condemned the state under the Babangida regime based on their perception that it was favouring Christians at the expense of Muslims.

Similarly, the manner in which the Babangida regime handled the June 12 1993 election crisis conveyed the impression of state partisanship in favour of a Northern Presidential candidate, thus reinforcing perceptions of a grand design to consolidate Hausa-Fulani hegemony on national politics and, thereby, generating counter-regionalist and ethnic reactions from such groups as the *Egbe Afenifere*, who saw the annulment of Abiola's mandate in the election as a deliberate attempt to rob the Yorubas of their chance to rule Nigeria. The ways in which the *Egbe Afenifere* and other pan-Yoruba political groupings pursued the annulment of the June 12 election generated counter- , often insidious, reactions by other ethno-regional groups, such as the Northern Elders Forum, the Eastern Mandate Union, and so on. While the former accused the "Sokoto Caliphate" and the Hausa-Fulani for the annulment, as part of their grand design to consolidate their political control and domination, the latter accused the Yorubas of behaving "like a rain-beaten chicken", and of "tribalising" the agitations against the annulment. In the wake of these accusations and counter-accusations, the post-annulment political dispensation became highly ethnicised and regionalised, in spite of the Abacha regime's attempts to make Nigerians forget the June 12 crisis, through the Constitutional Conference Committee and the unfolding of a transition programme.

Even more significant, as an example of the state's partisan role in reinforcing the negative trends of identity politics in Nigeria, is the manner in which the office of the Minister for Special Duties, occupied by Alhaji Wada Nas, under the Abacha regime, came to be used for the whipping up of regional, religious and ethnic sentiments, both to galvanise support for the regime and to intimidate, harass or weaken perceived opponents of the regime. Periodic press statements emanating from this office tended to incite regional, religious or ethnic sentiments, and to generate equally inciting counter-tendencies. (See *The News*, 1997.)

Clearly, therefore, since 1986, especially under SAP, Nigeria has witnessed a more heightened, contentious and violent politics of identities than has ever been the case previously. The impact of the economic crisis on the dynamics of state-based accumulation, and the ways in which social classes and groups have related with one another in the accumulation process, have largely accounted for this. This may not be the sole determinant of identity transformation and the resurgence of identity politics, but it certainly is a very strong contributing factor that cannot be discountenanced.

Conclusion

The Nigerian situation presently reflects an acute crisis of identity, characterised by heightened identity politics. This situation has been largely occasioned by the character and the role of the post-colonial Nigerian state under prolonged authoritarian military rule. It is essentially attributable to the ways and manner in which the military-controlled state has managed, or mismanaged, the political economy in the period of economic crisis and structural adjustment. Both the political and economic programmes initiated by the state from the middle of the 1980s contributed significantly and decisively in bringing about the prevailing identity crisis and politics of identity. In some fundamental respects, both the identity crisis and politics of identity are paradoxically manifestations of, as well as facilitating elements in, the decomposition of the Nigerian state.

What is the implication of this phenomenon for the future of the democratisation process in Nigeria? What role, in other words, can the politics of identity be expected to play in bringing about the desired civilian democratic governance in Nigeria? The answers may be highly speculative, but we can hazard a guess. Firstly, it would seem that in societies such as Nigeria where identity politics seems to gravitate essentially around sharply focused ethnic, regional, and religious cleavages, its entrenchment, especially under situations of acute economic crisis and immiserisation, would tend to create conditions for perpetual political instability, the ready excuse that military juntas seize upon to capture power and entrench themselves. Secondly, politics of identity may make civil society groups vibrant and active in their inter-personal relationships, as well as in the context of state-civil society relations, but such vibrancy may not necessarily be a catalyst for popular democratisation. On the contrary, it may indeed pose serious obstacles to democratisation by raising the stakes in the competition for political power and the mobilisation of negative forms of identity politics to prop up this competition for power (Jega, 1996b). In such a situation, the colonially created nation-state itself may become a questionable and contested enterprise, seeking a re-definition. Indeed, the clamour by the elite on behalf of their groups, such as in MOSOP and NRM, in the wake of the annulment of the June 12 presidential election, for a Sovereign National Conference where a new federal arrangement is to be worked out, points to this tendency.

Bibliography

Adejumobi, S., 1995, "Adjustment Reform and Its Impact on the Economy and Society", in Adejumobi, S., and A. Momoh, (eds.) *The Political Economy of Nigeria under Military Rule: 1984–1993*. Harare: SAPES Books.

Ake, C., 1996a, "The Political Question", in Oyediran, O., (ed.) *Governance and Development in Nigeria: Essays in Honour of Professor Billy Dudley*. Ibadan: Agbo Areo Publishers.

Ake, C., 1996b, *Democracy and Development in Africa*. Washington, D.C.: The Brookings Institution.

Alavi, H., 1972, "The State in Post-Colonial Societies: Pakistan and Bangladesh", New Left Review, No.74, July/August.

Amin, S., 1996, "Africa Must Adapt", *Tempo*, August 1.

Awa, E., 1994, "Sokoto Caliphate Is Our Problem", in *Democracy*, Vol. 1, No. 1, pp. 12–16.

Ayagi, I., 1994, "Nigeria. An Economy in Ruins", in *Constitutional Rights Journal*, January-March, pp. 10–12.

Beckman, B., 1981, "Oil, State Expenditure and Class Formation in Nigeria", paper to Conference of Nordic Political Scientists, Turku, Finland.

Beckman, B., 1981, "Imperialism and the 'National Bourgeoisie'", *Review of African Political Economy*, No. 22.

Beckman, B., 1982, "Whose State? State and Capitalist Development in Nigeria", *Review of African Political Economy*, No. 23.

Beckman, B., 1996, "The Decomposition and Recomposition of the Nigerian State", Discussion Notes for a Nigerian Seminar, St. Peters College, Oxford, May 28–29, mimeo.

Beckman, B., and A. Jega, 1995, "Scholars and Democratic Politics in Nigeria", *Review of African Political Economy*, No. 64, 167–181.

Calhoun, C., (ed.), 1994, *Social Theory and the Politics of Identity*. Oxford: Blackwell.

CAN, 1989, *Leadership in Nigeria*. Enlightenment Series 1. Kaduna: CAN, Northern Zone.

Coomasie, A., 1994, "National Identity and Nationalities Struggle", in Mahdi, A. *et al.*, (eds.) *Nigeria: The State of the Nation and the Way Forward*. Zaria: Ahmadu Bello University Press.

Diamond, L., 1988, *Nigeria in Search of Democracy*. Boulder Colorado: Lynne Rienner.

Dunn, J., (ed.), 1992, *Democracy: The Unfinished Journey 508 BC to AD 1993*. Oxford: Oxford University Press.

Erickson, E., 1968, *Identity: Youth and Crisis*. New York: Norton.

Falola, T., 1995, "Christian Radicalism and Nigerian Politics", paper to the conference on "The Dilemmas of Democracy in Nigeria", African Studies Center, University of Wisconsin-Madison, 10–12 November.

Forrest, T., 1995, *Politics and Economic Development in Nigeria*. Boulder: Westview Press.

Gboyega, A., (ed.), 1996, *Corruption in Nigeria*. Ibadan: Agbo Areo Publishers.

Graf, W. D., 1988, *The Nigerian State*. London: James Currey and Heinemann.

Gumi, S. A., and S. A. Tsiga, 1992, *Where I Stand*. Ibadan: Spectrum Books.

Hirsch, E., 1982, *The Concept of Identity*. Oxford: Oxford University Press.

International Forum for Democratic Studies, 1995, *Nigeria's Political Crisis: Which Way Forward?* Washington, D.C.

Jega, A. M., 1993a, "Crisis, Adjustment and Poverty in Nigeria", paper to the national conference on "Economic and Social Policy Options for the Third Republic", organized by the Friedrich Ebert Foundation and the African Centre for Development and Strategic Studies, May 4–5, Federal Palace Hotel, Lagos.

Jega, A. M., 1993b, "Professional Associations and Structural Adjustment", in Olukoshi, A. (ed.) *The Politics of Structural Adjustment*. London: James Currey and Heinemann.

Jega, A. M., 1994, *Nigerian Academics under Military Rule*. Stockholm: Department of Political Science, University of Stockholm.

Jega, A. M., 1995, "The Military and Democratization in Nigeria", paper to the conference on "The Dilemmas of Democratization in Nigeria", African Studies Center, University of Wisconsin-Madison, 10–12 November.

Jega, A. M., 1996a, "The Political Economy of Nigerian Federalism", in Elaigwu, I. and R. A. Akindele, (eds.) *The Foundation of Nigerian Federalism 1960–1994. Volume 3*. Abuja: National Council on Inter-Governmental Relations.

Jega, A. M., 1996b, "Democracy in Nigeria: Conceptions, Representations and Expectations", paper to the international workshop on "The Nigerian Democratization Process and the European Union", Centre d'Etude d'Afrique Noire, University of Bordeaux, France, 12–14 September.

Joseph, R., 1987, *Democracy and Prebendal Politics in Nigeria*. Cambridge: Cambridge University Press.

Keith, M., (ed.) 1993, *Place and the Politics of Identity*. London: Routledge.

Khilnani, S., 1992, "India's Democratic Career", in Dunn, J., (ed.) *Democracy: The Unfinished Journey 508 BC to AD 1993*. Oxford: Oxford University Press.

Kukah, M. H., 1993, *Religion, Politics and Power in Northern Nigeria*. Ibadan: Spectrum Books Ltd.

Kukah, M. H., 1996, *Religion and the Politics of Justice in Nigeria*. Lagos: Constitutional Rights Project.

Mamdani, M., 1996, *Citizen and Subject: Contemporary Africa and the Legacy of Late Colonialism*. Kampala, Cape Town and London: Fountain Publishers.

Mittleman, J., 1997, "Tribute to Claude Ake", (Discussion of Ake's "How Politics Underdevelops Africa"), *CODESRIA Bulletin*, 2.

Nnoli, O., 1978, *Ethnic Politics in Nigeria*. Enugu: Fourth Dimension Publishers.

Oguibe, O., (ed.), 1993, *Democracy in Nigeria: The June 12 Mandate*. London: ARIB Papers on Democracy in Africa.

Okigbo, P., 1994, "Abuse of Public Trust", in *Newswatch*, October 24.

Olukoshi, A., (ed.), 1993, *The Politics of Structural Adjustment in Nigeria*. London and Ibadan: James Currey and Heinneman.

Olukoshi, A., R. O. Olaniyan and F. Aribisala (eds.), 1994, *Structural Adjustment in West Africa*. Lagos: Nigerian Institute of International Affairs.

Oluyemi-Kusa, A., 1994, "The Structural Adjustment Programme of the Nigerian State", in Olukoshi, A., R. O. Olaniyan and F. Aribisala, (eds.) *Structural Adjustment in West Africa*. Lagos: Nigerian Institute of International Affairs. pp. 80–93.

Parry, G. and M. Moran (eds.), 1994, *Democracy and Democratization*. London and New York: Routledge.

Poulantzas, N., 1978, *State, Power, Socialism*. London: Verso.

Smith, R. and P. Wexler (eds.), 1995, *After Post-Modernism*. London: The Falmer Press.

The Democratic Forum, 1994, "The Caliphate, An Obstacle to Nigerian Unity", in *Vanguard*, August 29, p. 13.

Transparency International, 1996, *Annual Report*. Berlin-Germany.

UNRISD, 1995, *States of Disarray*. Geneva.

Vincent, A., 1987, *Theories of the State*. Oxford: Blackwell.

Weigert, A. J., et al., 1986, *Society and Identity*. Cambridge: Cambridge University Press-

Williams, C. J. F., 1989, *What Is Identity?* Oxford: Clarendon.

World Bank, 1995, *Trends in Developing Economies: Extracts. Volume 3. Sub-Saharan Africa*. Washington, D.C.: The World Bank.

Newspapers and Magazines

Newswatch, January 16, 1995, "Pandora's Box: Unravelling the Details of How Former President Ibrahim Babangida Spent the Oil Windfall Is 'like peeling an onion'".

Spectrum International, October 1992, "The Babangida Legacy: An Economy in Disarray", and "Aka Bashorun Insists Transition Is '419'".

The African Guardian, October 18, 1993, Cover Story.

The News, 1997, "Dirty Deals", Cover Story, 28 April.

Chapter 3

The Transformation of Ethno-Regional Identities in Nigeria

Jibrin Ibrahim

Introduction

The Nigerian military has been engaged in a programme of transition to democratic rule since 1985 and many scholars now believe that the military have developed a strategy of permanent transition or transitions without end (Oyediran, 1995) as a ruse to prevent democratisation in Nigeria. Under successive so called democratic transitions, the authoritarian grip of the state has become firmer and democratic forces as well as civil society have been receiving a very thorough bashing. As repression increases, there is a marked increase in the rate of the decomposition and/or disarticulation of effective state authority and legitimacy and the coercive apparatus of the state becomes terroristic in its actions, rather than playing its expected role as the organ with the monopoly of the legitimate use of violence in society. This situation has provoked the intensification of different forms of identity mobilisation and consciousness (ethnic, regional, religious, communal etc.) and even conflagration. These forms of consciousness are in themselves not a dangerous feature in plural states. They become problematic when they become, or are perceived as, objects around which discriminatory practices and unjustified use of violence are organised (see Otite, 1990). Ethno-regional conflicts tend to emerge at moments when groups perceive that they are being excluded from access to what they consider to be their right; be they linguistic, political, economic, administrative, commercial, religious etc. The most important question, therefore, is the perception and fear of domination by a group. Violent ethno-regional conflicts, therefore, are usually linked to perceptions of group domination in the absence of channels for articulating demands (Osaghae, 1992:219–220).

Two broad issues are posed when ethno-regional domination emerges as a political issue. The first issue is the control of political power and its instruments such as the armed forces and the judiciary. The second is the control of economic power and resources. Both are powerful instruments that are used to influence the authoritative allocation of resources to groups and individuals. When democratic transition and its manipulation enters the agenda, the question of numbers becomes part of the game. Political forces seek to assemble the largest coalitions that could assure them access to power, and apart from ideology and interest articulation, primordial issues such as ethnicity, regionalism and religion become major instruments for political mobilisation. The largest groups become central forces that are either used to open the gateways of power or are excluded or marginalised from power in one way or another. Our argument in this chapter is that the dynamics of ethno-regional identities is essentially a function of the character of the state and the manner in which it articulates with historically entrenched modes of consciousness.

The "Episode" of Nigerian History and the "Epoch" of Ethno-Regionalism

The Ibadan school of history has always maintained that although what is known as the Nigerian state today was the creation of British colonialism, colonial rule itself was an episode in the long historical march of the Nigerian peoples towards the formation of political systems. Colonial rule, Ajayi reminds us, "was neither profound, nor unique" (1991:60). The little episode of colonialism, however, created a political class that has difficulties with reconciling itself with the long epoch of the historical development of the Nigerian peoples in forging a modern nation-state. According to Ade Ajayi, nationalism and the creation of the nation-state were a question of fitting people with the same language and culture into the new nation while in Africa, nationalism was confronted with fitting people with different languages and cultures into one nation-state. History therefore became a problem in the African case and the nationalist elite developed:

> A fear of localism .... they feared that history and culture would highlight local peculiarities and identities, thus becoming factors of division and serving the ends of tribalism or ethnicity more than the ends of nationalism (1991:14).

Rather than seeking the ways through which the histories of the Nigerian peoples could be used to build the new nation, most of the nationalists simply focused on getting political power, and assumed the establishment of government run by Nigerians would suffice in building the nation. The few nationalists that had a wider and more far reaching vision such as the members of the Zikist Movement were marginalised by the mainstream nationalists (see Okoye, 1979).

Since the achievement of self-government, however, we have been repeatedly reminded by varying forms of identity affirmations and conflicts that there has, indeed, been a long epoch of regional histories of the various peoples in the territory now known as Nigeria and a much shorter history of the Nigerian nation. That history is composed of two parts—the colonial and the post-colonial. What was the content of the Nigerian nation during colonial times? What has been the content of the Nigerian nation since independence in 1960?

The histories of the groups occupying the Nigerian area have involved considerable exchange of people, trade, crafts, religions and other aspects of social interactions. These interactions were, however, regional and partial and did not, therefore, involve all the peoples. In addition, it involved other peoples currently outside the frontiers of the country. These histories and interactions which predated the colonial conquest were, however, rigidified in space with the advent of colonial rule. In addition, colonial rule led to the development of new social structures, social classes and categories and even new ethnic groups such as the Yoruba and the Igbo. As Peter Ekeh (1983) has argued, what this means is that the impact of colonial rule on Nigerian society has been so profound that it cannot be dismissed as a mere episode; it set forth a new historical epoch. He argues that one of the most important influences of colonialism was the creation of two public realms, the primordial and the civic, which related differentially with the private realm in terms of morality. The primordial public realm was based on cultures and traditions of the people and reflected a high standard of morality derived from peoples' histories. The civic public realm however was associated with illegitimate and exploitative colonial rule and had no moral linkages with the private realm. It was an amoral public realm in which cheating the system was considered a patriotic duty. This position has been expressed more eloquently:

> The unwritten law of the dialectics is that it is legitimate to rob the civic public in order to strengthen the primordial public (Ekeh, 1975:108).

> To many people, the state and its organs were identified with alien rule and were proper objects of plunder and they have not yet been reidentified fully as instruments for the promotion of common interests (Leys, 1965:224).

That attitude has been transferred to the post-colonial state and it defines the parameters of relative non-commitment to the Nigerian nation-state and commitment to other levels of primordial identity. It has been expressed in numerous works and a selection from some of the prose of Chinua Achebe's *No Longer at Ease* (1960) could be a good illustration:

> In Nigeria the government was "they". It has nothing to do with you or me. It was an alien institution and people's business was to get as much from it as they could without getting into trouble (p. 33).

> Many towns have four or five or even ten of their sons in European posts in this city. Umuofia has only one. And now our enemies say that even one is too much for us (p. 6).

> The meeting agreed that it was money, not work, that brought them to Lagos (p. 79).

In reading Achebe, it is made clear that these citations apparently referring to Obi Okonkwo's descent into corruption and the loss of his juicy job are really about the post-colonial state. The real tragic hero is the Nigerian state. No one has any commitment to it, and everybody is seeking for access, not to bake the cake, but to eat it.

To continue with our literary diversion, by the time Chinua Achebe arrives at *A Man of the People* (1966), the struggle for access to the state and its resources had reached what was assumed to be a Hobbesean level:

> A common saying in the country after independence was that it didn't matter what you knew but who you know (p. 19).
>
> Our people must press for their fair share of the national cake (p. 13).
>
> Tell them that this man has used his position to enrich himself and they would ask you—as my father did—if you thought that a sensible man would spit out the juicy morsel that good fortune placed in his mouth (p. 2).
>
> The village had a mind; it could say no to sacrilege. But in the affairs of the nation, there was no owner, the laws of the village became powerless (p. 167).

Achebe then describes the way in which democracy was jettisoned as a diversionary luxury as the struggle for access to the national cake intensified. Rules and regulations were discarded and bribery and thuggery became the order of the day

The question of moral attitudes to the state is an important indication of the placement of political identities. When people consider that the primary objective of access to posts in the structures of the nation-state is the advancement of primordial and personal interests rather than their defined tasks in "nation building", then the state has not yet made its mark among the people. The core content of Nigerian nationalism at its highest level between 1945 and 1960 was a united struggle of the elite and the people against British rule. It was a struggle predicated on the assumption that victory would translate into more prosperity for all the Nigerian people. What happened was that the prosperity was for only a few people and the select few effectively used identities other than the label "Nigerian" to get access to the state machine. Nigeria, as it were, remained a small episode for most of the people who had the label of "Nigerian citizen".

Nigeria was amalgamated into a single political community only in 1914. That act of 1914 had limited objectives—the amalgamation of some aspects of separate colonial administrative mechanisms rather than a political unification of the peoples. Even at the level of the administrative machinery, only the railways, telegraphs, customs and excise and the supreme court were amalgamated. Other aspects of administration including education, public works, health, agriculture, forestry, lands and survey and local government remained separate (Ajayi, 1980:28). The two lieutenant-governors at Enugu and Kaduna wielded real powers and were not just deputies to the governor in Lagos. Twenty-five years later, in 1939, regional autonomy was reinforced with the division of the country into three regions and the appointment of chief commissioners. Not only has commitment to the Nigerian nation-state been shallow for most of our history, even the practice of national governance has not been entrenched in our political norms.

The short Nigerian post-colonial political life has been riddled with calls for secession, confederation or other ways of breaking up the country. The reasons for the calls for separation, Tamuno (1991) correctly argues, have been self-interest of elite groups rather than the national interest. Whenever the interests of a political elite have been threatened, they have floated the secession banner, and all major political groups in the country have resorted to the tactic at some point. It was the Sardauna of Sokoto, leader of the Northern People's Congress, who first referred to the amalgamation of the Nigerian provinces as "the mistake of 1914" in the early 1950s when he floated the secession banner because he felt that Southern politicians were unwilling to understand the attitudes of the Northern elite towards independence—that they would not rush if it meant replacing European domination with Southern domination (Bello, 1962:132). At the 1950 Ibadan Constitutional Conference to review the Richards Constitution, a representational ratio of 45:33:33 for the North, West and East was proposed. Northern politicians felt threatened by this arrangement and the Emir of Zaria had to articulate their position clearly. The North must have 50 per cent of the seats or secede from the country (Tamuno, 1991:402). In May 1953, after Northern politicians had been ridiculed in Lagos for opposing the AG motion for Self Government in 1956, the Northern House of Assembly and the Northern House of Chiefs met and passed an eight point resolution that amounted to a call for confederation and separation (Tamuno, 1991:403). At the 1954 Lagos Constitutional Conference, it was the turn of the AG to demand that a secession clause be inserted in the Constitution but it was then opposed by the NPC and NCNC (Tamuno, 1991:404). In 1964, following the census and election crises, Southern politicians were getting disenchanted with their future in Nigeria. Michael Okpara, Premier of the Eastern Region had threatened in December 1964 that the East would secede and the Sardauna, the Northern Premier had to draw his attention to the absence of a secession clause in our Fundamental Laws:

> Sir Ahmadu Bello's comments went further to blame the attitude of Eastern Nigeria to continued membership of the Nigerian Federation to the discovery and development there of crude oil resources (Tamuno, 1991:407).

After a number of criticisms, Okpara denied that he had opted for secession but, as Tamuno (1991:412) reveals, he went ahead to establish a committee under his Attorney General to work out the modalities for a declaration of secession by Eastern Nigeria. When Ojukwu finally decided to embark on the course of secession three years later, he had a ready made plan waiting for him.

Calls for secession were also being expressed within the regions themselves. In February 1964, Isaac Sha'ahu of the UMBC declared in the Northern House of Assembly that the Tiv people felt unwanted and threatened:

> To pull out of the North and the Federation as a whole. We shall be a sovereign state, we shall be joining nobody. We are 1,000,000 in population, bigger than Gambia and Mauritania (Tamuno, 1991:412).

He was reacting to perceived marginalisation of the Tiv elite from the formal political process and excessive state repression in Tiv land.

The transition from threats to an actual attempt at secession was made on 23 February 1966 when Isaac Boro decided that he was not ready to live in a Nigeria that was ruled by Igbos. He, therefore, declared the independence of the Niger Delta People's Republic following the first coup and the establishment of the Ironsi Regime. Boro had become very disturbed about perceived Igbo domination of Eastern minorities since his days as a student activist at the University of Nigeria, Nsukka. His Republic lasted for only twelve days, the time it took the police to round up his rag-tag army of 159 volunteers. Isaac Boro and two of his colleagues were charged with treason in March and condemned to death in June 1966. Boro was eventually released at the onset of the Nigerian civil war when he joined the Federal side and was killed in battle in 1968, fighting for the liberation of Rivers State from the Igbo on the platform of the Federal Government of Nigeria.

The civil war of 1967 to 1970 was of course the most serious threat to the existence of Nigeria as a country and it led to the loss of over a million lives. The calls for secession or confederation did not stop after the civil war. It should be recalled that just before the war, Western leaders had warned that if the East went, the West would follow. That threat was not put into action and Awolowo, the Western leader was released from jail to serve as Finance Minister and Deputy Leader of the Federal Executive Council. During the Second Republic, Awolowo made two more electoral attempts to get the leadership of Nigeria and when that failed, one of his closest confidants, Governor Bisi Onabanjo declared on 1 October 1983 that: "the time has come to consider a confederation, by which I mean a federation of autonomous states" (Tamuno, 1991:430). This proposition was taken up at the National Executive Council of the UPN until deliberations on it were halted following the December 1983 Buhari coup.

The Buhari coup itself was read by many within the Southern political elite as a further narrowing of the base of political power to a core Hausa-

Fulani oligarchy and Brigadier Benjamin Adekunle and Lt. General Alani Akinrinade continued the calls for a confederation on behalf of the West (Tamuno, 1991:432). Not to be left out, the elite from the other regions also continued with similar calls, some examples being the calls by Dr. Muhammadu Sani Abubakar and Francis Arthur Nzeribe (Tamuno, 1991:431–32). On 22 April 1990, Major Gideon Orkar announced in a national radio broadcast that a group of officers had carried out a coup and had decided to excise the five most northerly states from the rest of the country.

Nigerian post-colonial history could be schematically divided into three major phases. The first phase, 1958 to 1965 was characterised by the mobilisation of ethno-regional identities with the objective of gaining access to regional power. At that time, the real locus of power was in the regions and there were relatively low proportions of elite in the country. Federal power was, however, still significant and the power elite that were already entrenched in the regions were fighting among themselves for what came to be known as the national cake. The second phase was from 1966 to 1970 and it was a period in which efforts were directed towards mobilising the nation to fight the civil war and resolve the national crises that had crippled the First Republic. The third phase which signalled a major transformation in the mobilisation of ethno-regional identities was the post civil war era, characterised by the rise of a unitary state and the consequent weakening of the regional bases of power. The sole question informing political mobilisation then became the conquest of federal power at the centre. This tendency has been exacerbated over the past decade, the years of structural adjustment, due to the enhanced *centralisation, concentration* and *reduction* of the resources available to be accessed even at the centre. This means that groups are obliged to block the access of others or displace those who already have access if they are to eat from the national cake. That process of a permanent strategy of blockage has amplified the expression of fissiparous tendencies because all those who are not in, are out. In other words, politics has been turned into a zero sum game.

The Nigerian State: Generator of Fissiparous Tendencies

The Nigerian state has a patrimonial as well as a rentier character. Patrimonialism means that the distinction between the public and the private domains have become blurred and power, which has become a major source of wealth, has become personalised. Nigeria has gone far in the process of what J.-F. Médard has called the production of a "state patrimonial bourgeoisie" (1982:33). The Nigerian state also has a rentier character. The major characteristic of the rentier state is that its main relationship with the society is mediated through its expenditures on the military and state security, development projects, consumption subsidies, construction, etc. (Skocpol, 1982:269). Rent, it should be recalled, is not merely an income earned by landlords but is in general a reward for the ownership of all natural resources. A rentier economy is one that relies on substantial external rent. The creation of wealth is centred around a small fraction of the society; the rest of the society is engaged mainly in the distribution and utilisation of the wealth so created. In a rentier state, the government is the main recipient of external rent. One of its major features is that production efficiency is relegated to the background and, in fact, there is at best a tenuous link between individual income and activity. Getting access to the rent circuit is a greater preoccupation than attaining production efficiency (Beblawi and Luciani, 1987:13). The importance of access in a rentier economy leads to what has been termed a rentier mentality which embodies a break in the work-reward causation. Reward-income or wealth is not related to work and risk bearing, rather to chance or situation. For a rentier, a reward becomes a windfall gain, an isolated fact, situational or accidental as against the conventional outlook where reward is integrated into a process of the end result of a long, systematic and organised production circuit (Beblawi, 1987:52). There is thus a glaring contradiction between rentier and production ethics. The rentier state is oriented away from the conventional role of providing public goods that have been extracted from the people through taxation; it is a provider of private favours. It becomes what Luciani (1987:70) has called an allocation (as distinct from a production) state. At least 40 per cent of state income must be derived externally (usually from oil). Luciani argues that the fact that rentier states do not have to wrest taxes from their citizens has serious implications for political reform or, rather, the lack of it.

Whenever the state essentially relies on taxation, the question of democracy becomes an unavoidable issue and a strong current in favour of democracy inevitably arises. This is the result of the fact that people will naturally be induced to coalesce according to their economic interests, and those groups that find no way to influence the decision-making process in their favour claim appropriate institutional choice. The state for its part must give credibility to the notion that it represents the common good. That is how state legitimacy is constructed. While it is logical that the necessity for sustained taxation demands the construction of legitimacy in production states, it does not follow that the marginality of taxation in rentier states reduces the importance of legitimacy and democratic reforms. Rentier states are capable of generating a level of legitimacy when they succeed in guaranteeing access to resources to a relatively large cross-section of society. When they are no longer able to do that, due to a shortfall in rent or to the fact that the rent is monopolised by a small oligarchy, or both, they lose their legitimacy and are often able to remain in power only through extreme coercion. They tend to face regime crisis when they experience drastic shortfall in rent and are thus unable to allocate resources at a level they have accustomed their populations to. The tendency is for a ruling elite to exclude more and more people from access to state resources, thereby creating the basis for widening political crisis. This has been the situation in Nigeria.

Nigeria has a rentier economy similar to the Arab rentier economies described by Beblawi and Luciani (1987) which revolve around petroleum revenues. Petroleum exports which accounted for only 10% of export earnings in 1962 rose to account for 82.7% of total export earnings in 1973 and for a period peaked at 90–93%. The price of crude oil jumped from 11 US dollars per barrel to 40 US dollars per barrel in 1980 with output reaching 2.05 million barrels a day in the same year (Olukoshi, 1991:29). The country was turned overnight into an allocation state and there was a dramatic rise in public expenditure. Government spending rose from N1.1 billion in 1970 to N6.5 billion in 1975, thus raising state expenditure as a percentage of GDP from 15.5 per cent to 30.5 per cent (Olashore, 1989:156). The then Head of State, General Yakubu Gowon, declared that "finance was not a problem to Nigeria" (Ayagi, 1990:73) and a spending spree on cement imports, festivals of arts, sports jamborees, universal primary education, and all sorts of public works commenced. The boom did not last long. Indeed, by 1978, an economic crisis was set in motion, due to a decline in oil exports and revenues. Income from petroleum dropped from N7 billion in 1977 to N5.9 billion in 1978 while production plummeted from 2.1 million barrels in 1977 to 1.57 million barrels in 1978 (Olukoshi, 1991:29). Oil revenues rose briefly to a record N10.1 billion in 1979 but collapsed to N5.161 billion in 1982. By 1985, oil prices had fallen to 28 US dollars a barrel and by 1986, a barrel of oil was selling at only 10 US dollars (Olukoshi, 1991:30). The economic crisis was by now at full steam. Meanwhile, the rentier state in Nigeria had lost much of the production capacity of its economy. Agricultural production which was the mainstay of the economy in the colonial period and during the First Republic had gone into decline. Its contribution to the GDP declined from 61 per cent in 1964 to 18 per cent in 1982 as the state lost interest in the extraction of peasant agricultural surpluses. Manufacturing and employment also declined significantly and between 1980 and 1983 over one million workers were retrenched (Olukoshi, 1991:28–33).

As a way of getting out of the economic crisis, the state, under the impulsion of the IMF, adopted a Structural Adjustment Programme (SAP) in 1986, aimed at reducing the staggering external debt that had built up, the chronic balance of payments crisis, hyper-inflation and rising unemployment. The positive effects of SAP are yet to be seen, however. The employment scene has been devastated by mass retrenchment, galloping unemployment and underemployment as well as under-utilisation of installed capacity. The workforce of the UAC, one of Nigeria's biggest conglomerates, has been compressed from 23,850 workers in 1985 to 9,000 in 1988 (Fadahunsi, 1993:93). Capacity utilisation since the introduction of SAP in 1986 has remained low, between 30 and 37 per cent, and income per capita has collapsed from 778 US dollars in 1985 to 108 US dollars in 1989 (Fadahunsi,

1992:91–101). All indices of economic production and efficiency are on the decline, the standard of living has been reduced to a historic low point and the rentier state seems to have given up on the economy. The various sections of the power elite have focused their attention on struggles for access to the declining rent produced by the state. It is therefore not surprising that ethno-regional identities have hardened under SAP, and conflicts, including violent ones have increased.

The Nigerian state has undergone considerable transformation over the past two decades. The First Republic had collapsed after a serious political crisis that led to a long and bloody civil war. Paradoxically, Nigeria came out of the civil war as a much stronger state due mainly to the growth of federal power, enhanced by the creation of smaller states that could not challenge federal power and the significant increase in the revenues accruing to the Federal Government, particularly from petroleum. The Nigerian state was placed on the path of centralisation by the multiplication of states from 4 regions to 12 federated states in 1967, and then to 19 in 1976, 21 in 1987, 30 in 1991 and 36 in 1996. This miniaturisation of the federated states enhanced the power of the central state. The increased power enjoyed by the federal state also benefited from the transformation of the taxation system and the sources of revenue. As from the beginning of the 1970s, rent from petroleum replaced extraction of surplus from cash crops as the principal source of revenue. Towards the end of the 1970s, Nigeria was exporting more than two million barrels of petroleum per day. The centre thus replaced the states as source of funds for development projects. Between 1958 and 1983, revenue from petroleum came to a staggering 101,000,000,000 US dollars (Graf, 1988:218). Since 1974, more than 80 per cent of the revenues accruing to the state have come from petroleum rent. That justifies our characterisation of the Nigerian state as a rentier state. The new capacity of the federal state not only to impose its will on the federated states but also to make its presence felt in the economy, social life and local government areas which was an indication of the significant increase in the despotic power of the state. Indeed, Allison Ayida, who was Secretary to the Federal Government between 1975 and 1977, was right in proclaiming that the state had started an "institutional revolution" characterised by national control of the direction of development and of the allocation of the country's resources (Williams and Turner, 1978). The major transformation under SAP is that the so called institutional revolution has been transformed into a personal revolution as virtually all powers became concentrated in one institution and indeed one person, the Head of State. A situation that cannot but provoke the exacerbation of ethno-regional conflicts directed at that office and what it can offer.

The Transformation of Ethno-Regional Identity Profiles

The mosaic of identity profiles in Nigeria is vast, complex and multi-dimensional. In this section, we shall only attempt a simplistic presentation. In so doing, we shall follow the most common profiles embedded in popular discourses in the country. Ethno-regional identities in Nigeria have developed along a tri-tendential trajectory. The first is the North/South divide that emerged at the beginning of the colonial period. The second is the tripolar framework related to the three colonial regions and the majority groups that dominated each region. The third and maybe the most important tendency in Nigerian politics is a persistent multi-polarity which is continuously repressed with imposed bipolarity and/or tri-polarity but has managed to survive. It encompasses the essence of Nigerian politics which I have described elsewhere as the politics of variable geometry played by the hundreds of ethnic, linguistic and cultural groups in the country (Ibrahim, 1988). In his October 1st 1995 address to the Nation, General Abacha announced the introduction of a modified Presidential system in which six key executive and legislative offices will be zoned and rotated between six identifiable geographical groupings; North-West, North-East, Middle-Belt, South-West, East-Central and Southern-Minority.

As John Paden (1995:6) has argued, Abacha's geographical zones correspond roughly to the six cultural zones (Emirate states, Borno and environs, Middle Belt minorities, Yorubaland, Igboland and Southern minorities which followed the original assessment of British colonialism and became rooted in part because of the Indirect Rule policy that was subsequently adopted. He adds that these component zones have certain cultural and/or historical characteristics which have profoundly affected Nigerians' efforts at unity and democratic rule. The six cultural zones are indeed central poles around which much ethno-regional mobilisation has occurred in the country's recent political history. Fears of domination of one zone over the others played a central role in convincing politicians of the necessity of a federal solution for the First Republic. The First Republic which operated essentially as an equilibrium of regional tyrannies was, however, characterised by the domination of each region by a majority ethnic group and the repression of regional minorities. The relative autonomy enjoyed by the regions has been eroded under military rule and soldiers are now widely perceived as carriers of a hidden agenda set to destroy one cultural zone or the other.

The central problem that has been generating the steady rise of ethno-regional tensions and conflicts has been the supplanting of Nigeria's federal tradition by a Jacobin unitary state that emerged under a long period of military rule. The erosion of multiple poles of political power that have existed in Nigeria by military dictators has exacerbated the spectre of the fear of domination in the country. The Nigerian state is no longer seen as a neutral arbiter. Conflict resolution mechanisms are breaking down and political actors are taking maximalist positions and treating compromise with disdain.

The Hausa Factor

In Nigeria, the Hausa-Fulani oligarchy were maintained in power by the British during colonial rule through the Indirect Rule system of Native Authority administration. During the First Republic, the Northern Peoples' Congress, a party considered as an instrument of the Hausa-Fulani oligarchy won both the Federal and Northern Regional elections. Since then, most succeeding regimes, civilian and military, have been monopolised by the Hausa-Fulani, and there have been serious concerns in the country about the perpetuation of Hausa-Fulani domination. There is a general thesis that posits that if the Hausa control political power, the country's financial sector and bureaucracy is controlled by the Yorubas while the Igbos control commerce and much of the vibrant informal sector. This thesis notwithstanding, the general opinion in most parts of the country is that political power is the most important element, and those who control it, influence or even control the other sectors. The Hausa in this regard, are widely considered as those *ruling* and *ruining* Nigeria.

The Hausa elite are becoming increasingly fed-up with accusations from other parts of the country and are beginning to articulate their own grievances. According to Dahiru Yahaya:

> The Hausa Muslims of the Far-North appear to be the target of the frustration of all other Nigerians. They are hated for the reasons of the political leadership imposed on them by the mutual suspicions of other Nigerians. They are subjected to humiliation by the South-Western Yoruba powerful media by which their culture, religion and leadership are daily treated to insults. They are also excluded from full economic participation by the Yoruba control of the financial institutions. In the private sector they are open to the exploitation of the Ibo control of the modern sector of private business activities. Ibos fix prices unilaterally by which Hausa money is siphoned daily. The Hausa are reduced to utter poverty and a large percentage of them rendered street beggars. The Hausa also feel that they are put at serious disadvantages in the public and social services in the country (Yahaya, 1994:3).

Ado Gwaram (1994) gave extensive statistics that demonstrate that the Hausa-Fulani are systematically under-represented in federal establishments in the country. Another point that has been raised is that in their political practice, the Hausa-Fulani have been much more issue oriented than many of the other competing elite. Ibrahim Mu'azzam's review of the 1959, 1979, 1983 and 1993 elections for example demonstrate that the Hausa-Fulani have never been a voting bloc and that they have consistently been involved in issue voting:

> In 1959, the NPC had to go into coalition with the NCNC to form a Government. In the 1979 elections, Shehu Shagari's NPN votes were higher in the areas

defined as "minority" than in the traditional "Hausa-Fulani" enclave. It was in fact Kano that provided the test case on the legal interpretation of the elections. In June 1993 elections, the Hausa-Fulani from Kano, Jigawa and Kaduna voted for Abiola of the SDP not their son and indigene, Tofa, of the NRC (1994:8).

In addition, the Hausa-Fulani elite argue that it is the serious disunity and mutual distrust between the other groups that has imposed the mantle of leadership on them.

The Bornu Factor: The North-East Pole

Given the common Islamic and cultural traditions between the Hausa states and the Kanuri, a legitimate question that could be posed is why it is Hausa-Fulani and not Hausa-Fulani/Kanuri politics in contemporary Nigeria. Is there a Bornu factor in current Nigerian politics? Indeed, it will be recalled that the Bornu elite had established the Bornu Youth Movement (BYM) in June 1954 because they felt that both the NEPU and the NPC were essentially Hausa-Fulani parties that did not adequately represent their interests. The BYM:

> declared its independent stand in stating that it believed that the interests of Bornu, Adamawa and Plateau provinces could not be adequately served in the existing political set-up unless these provinces were to become a separate state in the Northern Region (Dudley, 1968:89).

In his book *Ahmadu Bello* (1986), John Paden describes an elaborate policy of incorporation and subordination of the future Bornu elite to the Sokoto aristocratic pole at Katsina College under the aegis of the British, a policy that was subsequently pursued by the NPC. (Katsina College was established by the colonial administration as a leadership training school to groom aristocratic emirate children to run the system of Native Authority administration. Graduates of Katsina College were the major political actors in Northern Nigeria.) That policy clearly had its limits and the Bornu factor has remained a major factor in Northern politics.

The Northern Minority Factor

The Northern opposition to Hausa-Fulani hegemony has been most consistent within the Middle Belt—in particular, among the non-Muslim populations in Benue, Niger, Plateau, Bauchi and Zaria provinces. The opposition first took an organisational form with the formation under Birom initiative of the Northern Nigeria Non-Muslim League in 1950, aided by the Christian Missions (Dudley, 1968:92). Immediately after that, a number of political organisations emerged in the area such as the Tiv Progressive Union, Wurkum Tribal Union, Middle Zone League and the Middle Belt People's Party, with the last two merging to form the United Middle Belt Congress (UMBC) in 1955. The UMBC was established as a front to contest Muslim Hausa-

Fulani hegemony (Dudley, 1968:98). Central to the politics of the Middle Belt, therefore, is their relationship with the Hausa-Fulani. According to Tyoden (1993:5), it is a relationship of subordination, oppression and exploitation and he follows Chunun Logams in characterising it as internal colonialism.

The Middle Belt has always had a disproportionate presence in the army. In 1963, 80 per cent of the other ranks in the army were from the North and 90 per cent of that figure was from the Middle Belt, and they have since retained a significant presence. Long repressed, the Northern minorities rose to the limelight through the army in the 1970s and 1980s when they increased their ratio in the officer corps substantially. However, questions are now being posed on their marginalisation from that institution following a number of unsuccessful coup attempts that led to a series of prunings of Middle Belt officers. As discussed earlier, their politics in Northern Nigeria is strongly influenced by the Christian/Muslim divide. At the national level, they vacillate between northern chauvinism and alliance with southern political groups. Their major concern today is that they have participated in many successful coup attempts since the Gowon era but they have not succeeded in attaining the apex of the leadership because as soon as a coup occurs "the true northern leadership emerged from behind the scene to control the affairs of government" (Tyoden, 1993:77).

The Yoruba Factor

The Yoruba factor in Nigerian politics is summarised by the life of Obafemi Awolowo entailing a long, organised and determined attempt to occupy the summit of the Nigerian political hierarchy which culminated in failure. A failure that has now become truly pan-Yoruba with the success of Abiola in the June 12 elections and the so called "Hausa-Fulani checkmate" through the annulment of the election results by the Babangida Military Junta. The Yoruba political elite have a long list of grievances against the Northern political establishment. They include suspicions of rigging in all the elections that Awolowo had lost, federal interference in the Action Group crises and imposition of a state of emergency and federal power over the West in the 1960s, creation of the Mid West, which whittled down their territorial control etc.

As we have argued above, by October 1983, the Yoruba political elite within the Unity Party of Nigeria were so frustrated by the defeat of Awolowo, their leader, that they started once again seriously considering the secession option. Echoes of the establishment of a Yoruba "Oduduwa Republic" re-emerged strongly following the annulment of the June 12 1993 presidential election. The Yorubas have, however, never been politically united since the Yoruba civil wars of the 19th century and a section of the Yoruba elite has been consistently in alliance with the Hausa-Fulani elite since the early 1960s. The Yoruba elite have also been at loggerheads with the Igbo elite since the latter overtook them in educational and social development between 1930 and 1950. Their rivalry has, at least for now, excluded the possibility of a grand Yoruba-Igbo political alliance.

The Igbo Factor

The Igbo factor in Nigerian politics is also one of failure and frustration. A proud and hard-working people that have been forced to play second fiddle to the Hausa-Fulani ruling circles. Following the massacre of Igbos in 1966 in the Northern region, and the subsequent declaration of secession by the Eastern region in May 1967, the Igbo elite had assumed that other Nigerians would not fight to keep them in the Federation, but they did, and the result was a thirty-month civil war in which over a million people were killed. The Igbo elite have developed a concept they call the "Igbo problem". According to Arthur Nwankwo (1985:9) "Nigerians of all other ethnic groups will probably achieve consensus on no other matter than their common resentment of the Igbo", a phenomenon that Chinua Achebe had dubbed "the Igbo problem". They argue that the Igbos are more cosmopolitan, more adapted to other cultures, more individualistic and competitive, more receptive to change and more prone to settle and work in other parts of the country but the myth persists that they are aggressive, arrogant and clannish (Nwankwo, 1985:10). This purported attitude of other Nigerians towards the Igbos they add, has led to the development of a "final solution" aimed at neutralising and marginalising the Igbos after the civil war. This is seen to have occurred in two ways:

- Pauperising the Igbo middle class by:
  - the offer of a twenty pound ex gratia award to all bank account holders irrespective of the amounts they had lodged with the banks before the civil war;
  - routing the Igbos from the commanding heights of the economy by introducing the indegenisation decree at a time when the Igbos had no money, no patronage and no access to loans;
  - declaring Igbo landed property "abandoned property" particularly in Port Harcourt.

- Marginalising the Igbo elite by:
  - refusing to re-absorb most of the Igbos who had attained high positions in the armed forces and the federal public service. For example, at independence in October 1960, 24 of the 52 senior army officers of the rank of major and above were Igbos (Nwanwko, 1985:21).

They therefore feel that the policies of "no victor, no vanquished" and "reconciliation, reconstruction and rehabilitation" announced after the war were not applied.

Igbo politics today is torn between conflicting poles that disagree on how to advance and build on the remarkable Igbo economic and commercial élan that has occurred since the end of the civil war—see Olukoshi and Ahonsi (1994). Should they continue with the politics of second fiddle or revert to the assertiveness and aggressiveness of these so called "Jews of Africa". Okoye (1964:117) reminds us that since C. D. Onyeoma's boastful assertion in the 1930s that "the Ibo domination of Nigeria is a matter of time", other groups have been very apprehensive of the Igbo success story. They are seen as a cohesive and united group even if in reality, they are very divided (Ejionye, 1993:430). Be that as it may, their elite have indeed demonstrated a significant capacity for unity of purpose.

The Southern Minorities

A history of fear and suspicion of the aggressiveness and hegemonic intentions of their Yoruba and Igbo neighbours led to political co-operation between the Southern Minorities and the Hausa-Fulani elite in the 1960s. In 1966, Isaac Boro had attempted the secession option rather than accept what he considered to be an Igbo hegemonic plan on the minorities (see Boro, 1982). The creation of the Mid-West region and subsequently of states liberated the Southern Minorities from the direct political control of the Igbo and Yoruba political elite. Since then, their identity struggles have been re-directed towards the petroleum issue.

Most of the Nigerian petroleum resources are produced in the territory of the Southern Minorities and they have gradually developed a high "oil consciousness" directed at getting more benefits from this mainstay of the Nigerian economy. According to Ben Naanen, the Southern Minorities are also suffering from "internal colonialism" which is not carried out through economic domination but through control of political power which has been used to transfer resources from the numerically weaker groups to the numerically stronger ones, creating in the process "an economically advantaged powerful core and an impoverished and weak periphery" (1995:50). Central to their current politics is the argument that they are the major providers of Nigeria's oil wealth and the major victims of pollution due to oil spillage and gas flaring. Their movement took a radical politically organised form with the declaration of the Ogoni Bill of Rights demanding political autonomy in 1990 and the uprising that has since been going on. Ken Saro-Wiwa, the leader of the Ogoni political struggle and eight of his colleagues were hanged by the state in November 1995 but the Southern Minority struggles have not abated since then. Indeed, struggles over access to oil wealth and protection from pollution have been rapidly spreading to the other oil producing communities.

Conclusion

Over the past four decades, the Nigerian State has evolved from a federal polity characterised by three politically strong regions, each controlled by the elite of a majority ethnic group—Hausa, Yoruba and Igbo, to a highly centralised system in which the so called federating states have no real autonomous powers and are at the beck and call of a strong centre in which enormous powers are vested in the hands of one person and one institution, the president and the presidency. This political transformation was carried out mainly under military rule in a context in which excessive corruption and primordial issues of ethnic, religious and regional political domination have become central elements in the country's political culture. Much of what has been published about Nigerian politics revolves around the issue of ethno-regional identities. Ethno-regional identities have become problematic in the country because they have been associated with perceptions of discrimination and the inability of some groups to exercise certain rights. The main issues have been the control of political power and in particular, control of the armed forces, the judiciary and the bureaucracy. There is also the question of the control of economic power and resources. As Kirk-Greene put it:

> Fear has been constant in every tension and confrontation in political Nigeria. Not the physical fear of violence, not the spiritual fear of retribution, but the psychological fear of discrimination, of domination. It is the fear of not getting one's fair share, one's dessert (1975:19).

It is clear that there has been an intensification of identity mobilisation over the past decade, the ten years of structural adjustment. While the mobilisational themes have not changed much during the SAP years, the major transformation in the country regarding identities and power has been the reduction of the powers of regionally based elite groups. They are now all fighting for the highest office in the land, i.e. that of the president. That was why the June 12 1993 elections became so important.

The June 12, 1993, presidential elections were cancelled mid-way through the announcement of the results just at the moment when it had become clear that M. K. O. Abiola, a Yoruba Muslim had won a landslide victory over Bashir Tofa, a Kano Hausa. Even if the truth of the matter was that Babangida was a dictator who wanted to rule for ever, the Yoruba and indeed, the Southern elite think it was a Hausa-Fulani plot to keep them out of power. The elections themselves were considered relatively free and fair and a good opportunity to start rebuilding confidence in the Nigerian nation-state. The cancellation however led to strong ethnic and regional fears that the Hausa ruling class were not going to allow a Southerner to rule, even if he wins a democratic election. The Southern press has been leading a media campaign over the past few years, the main tenet of which is that the Hausa-Fulani will always sacrifice democratisation so as to maintain themselves in power.

There is a real ambivalence among the Nigerian elite on their attitude to the nation-state. They are dissatisfied by the present arrangement and would like to retreat to their primordial shells, and yet, they frequently realise that they need the country to survive as a protector for their own identities, regions, religions and tribes. Two statements from the same interview granted by Gani Fawehinmi, one of Nigeria's major political and human rights crusaders illustrates this point:

> If I were 30 years younger and I am not Gani Fawehinmi of 56 years of age, enveloped by hypertension, I will do to this government what Taylor did to Sergeant Doe. I will go into the bush.
> If Nigeria breaks, the East will split into at least four or five nation-states. If Nigeria breaks today, there might not be an Oduduwa nation-state. So let us find our fulfillment in a nation called Nigeria (*The News*, 7/3/1994).

Eskor Toyo might, thus, be right in affirming that "The Nigerian nation exists. What it lacks at the moment is a really patriotic, broad-minded, principled, enlightened, humane and honest leadership" *The Guardian* (21/10/1996). But then, isn't that a lot to ask for?

Bibliography

Achebe, Chinua, 1960, *No Longer at Ease*. London: Heinemann.
Achebe, Chinua, 1966, *A Man of the People*. London: Heinemann.
Adamu, Mahdi, 1978, *The Hausa Factor in West African History*. Zaria and Ibadan: Ahmadu Bello University Press/Oxford University Press.
Agbaje, A., 1994, "Twilight of Democracy in Nigeria", *Africa Demos*, Vol. III, No. 3.
Agbese, P. O., 1988, "Defence Expenditure and Private Capital Accumulation in Nigeria", *Journal of African and Asian Studies*, Vol. XXIII, (3–4).
Ajayi, J. F. A., 1980, *Milestones in Nigerian History*. London: Longman.
Ajayi, J. F. A., 1991, *History of the Nation and Other Addresses*. Ibadan: Spectrum Books.
Ake, C., 1985, "The Nigerian State", in Ake, C., (ed.) *Political Economy of Nigeria*, London: Longman.
Aniagolu, A. N., 1993, *The Making of the 1989 Constitution of Nigeria*. Ibadan: Spectrum Books, Ibadan.
Ayagi, Ibrahim, 1990, *The Trapped Economy*. Ibadan: Heinemann.
Bangura, Y., 1991, "Authoritarian Rule and Democracy in Africa: A Theoretical Discourse", UNRISD Discussion Paper, Geneva.
Bangura, Y., 1994, "Intellectuals, Economic Reform and Social Change: Constraints and Opportunities in the Formation of a Nigerian Technocracy", *Development and Change*, Vol. 25, No. 2.
Bayart, J-F., 1989, *L'Etat en Afrique: La Politique du Ventre*. Paris: Fayard.
Beblawi, H.,1987, "The Rentier State in the Arab World", in Beblawi, H. and G. Luciani, (eds.) *The Rentier State*. London: Croom Helm.
Beblawi, Hazem and G. Luciani (eds.), 1987, *The Rentier State*. London: Croom Helm.
Beckman, B., 1987, "The Post-Colonial State: Crisis and Reconstruction", *IDS Bulletin*, No. 19(4).
Bello, Ahmadu, 1962, *My Life*. Cambridge: Cambridge University Press.

Berry, S., 1989, "Social Institutions and Access to Resources", *Africa*, 59(1).
Bonat, Z. A., 1994, "Political Change and Socio-Economic Processes in the Nigerian Middle Belt", in Ibrahim, J., (ed.) *Population, Space and Development in Nigeria*, report for ADB/CINERGIE Project, Abijan.
Boro, I., 1982, *The Twelve-Day Revolution*. Benin City: Idodo Umeh Publishers.
Callaghy, T., 1986, "Politics and Vision in Africa", in Chabal, P., *Political Domination in Africa*. Cambridge: Cambridge University Press.
Diamond, L., 1993, "Nigeria's Perennial Struggle against Corruption: Prospects for the Third Republic", *Corruption and Reform*, No. 7.
Diamond, L., 1995, "Nigeria: The Uncivic Society and Descent into Praetorianism" in Diamond, L., J. Linz and S. Lipset (eds.) *Politics in Developing Countries: Comparing Experiences with Democracy*. 2nd edition, Boulder: Lynne Rienner.
Dudley, B. J., 1968, *Parties and Politics in Northern Nigeria*. London: Frank Cass.
Ejionye, U. A., 1993, *The Abia Dream: Selected Speeches of O. Onu*. Ibadan: Spectrum.
Ekeh, P., 1975, "Colonialism and the Two Publics in Africa: A Theoretical Statement", *Comparative Studies in Society and History*, No. 17.
Ekeh, P., 1983, *Colonialism and Social Structure: An Inaugural Lecture*. Ibadan: Ibadan University Press.
Ekwekwe, E., 1986, *Class and State in Nigeria*. London: Longman.
Fadahunsi, A., 1993, "Devaluation: Implications for Employment, Inflation, Growth and Development", in Olukoshi, A. (ed.) *The Politics of Structural Adjustment*. London: James Currey.
Gwaram, A., 1994, "The Myth of Quota System and the Injustices in Nigeria's Public Services", paper for Kano State Constitutional Conference Workshop, Kano, April.
Ibrahim, J., 1988, "La société contre le bipartisme", *Politique Africaine*, No. 32.
Ibrahim, J., 1991a, "Le Developpement de l'Etat Nigerian", in Medard, J-F,. (ed.) *Les Etats d'Afrique Noire: Formation Mecanism et Crise*. Paris: Karthala.
Ibrahim, J., 1991b, "Religion and Political Turbulence in Nigeria", *Journal of Modern African Studies*, No. 29(1).
Ibrahim, J., 1992, "The State, Accumulation and Democratic Forces in Nigeria", in Rudebeck, L., (ed.) *When Democracy Makes Sense: Studies in the Democratic Potential of Third World Movements*. Uppsala: AKUT.
Ibrahim, J., (ed.), 1997, *Expanding the Nigerian Democratic Space*. Dakar: CODESRIA Books.
Ibrahim, J., forthcoming, "Ethno-Religious Mobilisation and the Sapping of Democracy in Nigeria", in Hyslop, J. (ed.), *Democratic Movements in Contemporary Africa*. London: James Currey.
Ibrahim, J., and C. Pereira, 1993, "On Dividing and Uniting: Ethnicity, Racism and Nationalism in Africa", paper for International Development Research Network, CLACSO, Buenos Aires.
Jega, A., 1993, "Professional Associations and Structural Adjustment" in Olukoshi, A. O., (ed.) *The Politics of Structural Adjustment in Nigeria*, London: James Currey.
Joseph, R., 1995, "The Dismal Tunnel: From Prebendal Republic to Rogue State in Nigeria", paper for "Conference on Dilemmas of Democracy in Nigeria", University of Wisconsin, November.
Kirk-Greene, A. H. M., 1975, *The Genesis of the Nigerian Civil War and the Theory of Fear*. Uppsala: NAI.
Laakso, L. and A. Olukoshi, 1996, "The Crisis of the Post-Colonial Nation-State Project in Africa", in Olukoshi, A. and L. Laakso (eds.) *Challenges to the Nation-State in Africa*. Uppsala: Nordic Africa Institute.

Leys, C., 1965, "What Is the Problem about Corruption?", *Journal of Modern African Studies*, Vol. 3, No. 2.

Luciani, G., 1987, "Allocation vs Production States: A Theoretical Statement", in Beblawi, H., and G. Luciani (eds.) *The Rentier State*. London: Croom Helm.

Mahadi, A. and M. Mangvat, 1986, "Some Remarks on the National Question in Pre-Capitalist Formations: The Case of Nigeria before 1900 A. D", paper for National Seminar on the National Question, Abuja.

Medard, J-F., 1982, "The Underdeveloped State in Tropical Africa: Political Clientelism or Neo-Patrimonialism", in Clapham, C., (ed.) *Private Patronage and Public Power*. London: Pinter.

Mu'azzam, I., 1994, "Voting Pattern and the Myth of Hausa-Fulani Political Domination", Kano State Constitutional Conference Workshop, Kano, April.

Mustapha, A. R., 1986, "The National Question and Radical Politics in Nigeria", *Review of African Political Economy*, no 37.

Naanen, B., 1995, "Oil-Producing Minorities and the Restructuring of Nigerian Federalism: The Case of the Ogoni People", *Journal of Commonwealth and Comparative Politics*, 33, 1.

Nwankwo, A., 1985, *The Igbo Leadership and the Future of Nigeria*. Enugu: Fourth Dimension.

Okoye, M., 1964 and 1981, *Storms on the Niger*. Enugu: Eastern Nigeria Printing Corporation.

Okoye, M., 1979, *A Letter to Dr. Nnamdi Azikiwe*. Enugu: Fourth Dimension.

Olashore, O., 1989, *Challenges of Nigeria's Economic Reform*. Ibadan: Fountain Publication.

Olukoshi, Adebayo (ed.), 1991, *Crisis and Adjustment in the Nigerian Economy*. Lagos: JAD.

Olukoshi A. and B. Ahonsi, 1994, "Population Dynamics and Industrial Development in Eastern Nigeria", in Ibrahim, J. (ed.) *Population, Space and Development in Nigeria*. Abijan: Club du Sahel/Cinergie.

Olukoshi A. and O. Agbu, 1996, "The Deepening Crisis of Nigerian Federalism and the Future of the Nation-State", in Olukoshi, A. and L. Laakso, (eds) *Challenges to the Nation-State in Africa*. Uppsala: Nordic Africa Institute.

Osaghae, E., 1992, "Managing Ethnic Conflicts Under Democratic Transition in Africa" in Caron, B., et al. (eds.), *Democratic Transition in Africa*. Ibadan: CREDU.

Osoba, S., 1977, "The Nigerian Power Elite: 1952–1965", in Gutkind, P. and P. Waterman, (eds.) *African Social Studies*. London: Heinemann.

Othman, S., 1992, "Nigeria: Power for Profit. Class, Corporatism, and Factionalism in the Military", in Cruise O'Brien, D., et. al. (eds.) *Contemporary West African States*. Cambridge: Cambridge University Press.

Othman, S. and G. Williams, forthcoming, "Politics, Power and Democracy in Nigeria", in Hyslop, J. (ed.), *Democratic Movements in Contemporary Africa*. London: James Currey, London.

Otite, O., 1990, *Ethnic Pluralism and Ethnicity in Nigeria*. Ibadan: Shoneson.

Oyediran, O., 1995, "Transitions without End: From Hope to Despair", paper for conference on "Dilemmas of Democracy in Nigeria", University of Wisconsin Madison, November.

Paden, J., 1986, *Ahmadu Bello Saraduna of Sokoto: Values and Leadership in Nigeria*. London: Hodder and Stronghton.

Paden, J., 1995, "Nigerian Unity and the Tensions of Democracy: The Implications of the 'North-South' Legacies", paper for the conference on "Dilemmas of Democracy in Nigeria", University of Wisconsin, Madison, November.

Pryzowski, A., 1991, "Ethnic Conflicts in the Context of Democratising Political Systems", *Theory and Society*, No. 20.
Salomone, F. A., 1976, "Becoming Hausa: Ethnic Identity Change and Its Implications for the Study of Ethnic Pluralism and Stratification" in Sanda, A. (ed.) *Ethnic Relations in Nigeria*. Ibadan: Sociology Department, University of Ibadan.
Soyinka, W., 1996, "The National Question in Africa: Internal Imperative", *Development and Change*, Vol. 27, No 2.
Skocpol, T., 1982, "Rentier State and Shi'a Islam in the Iranian Revolution", *Theory and Society*, Vol. 11, No. 3.
Suberu, R. T., 1993, "The Challenge of Ethnic Conflict: The Travails of Federalism in Nigeria", *Journal of Democracy*, Vol. 4, No. 4.
Tamuno, T. N., 1991, *Peace and Violence in Nigeria*. Nigeria since Independence History Project, Ibadan.
Tyoden, S. G., 1993, *The Middle Belt in Nigerian Politics*. Jos: AHA Publishing House.
Ukwu I. U., (ed.), 1987, *Federal Character and National Integration*. Kuru: National Institute.
Williams, G., 1980, *State and Society in Nigeria*. Idanre: Afrografika.
Williams, G. and T. Turner, 1978, "Nigeria", in Dunn, J. (ed.) *West African States: Failure and Promise*. Cambridge: Cambridge University Press.
Yahaya, Dahiru, 1994, "Key Note Address", Kano State Constitutional Conference Workshop, Kano, April.

Newspapers and Magazines

The Guardian, October 21, 1996.
The News, March 7, 1996.

Chapter 4

Religious Identity in the Context of Structural Adjustment in Nigeria

Ibrahim Mu'azzam and Jibrin Ibrahim

Introduction

In its April 4, 1994 edition with the caption "In God's Name Plc," *The News* magazine, after noting the drastic economic downturn which was exacerbated by Babangida regime's Structural Adjustment Programme (SAP) introduced in 1986, stated that religion in Nigeria is now big business. The new "generation Pentecostal outfits rake in millions of naira weekly" at a time when banks and other financial institutions are becoming cash-strapped or are going under. Apart from the economic crisis, the emergence of over five hundred churches, according to the report, "represents an outward strength for Christianity" and is also partly a response to the "rival pull of other religions, especially Islam, for the membership of today's Christian Mission". The report in general, though quite exaggerated in certain aspects, seemed to provisionally provide a basis for the understanding of the growth of Islamic and Christian fundamentalism in Nigeria, most especially witnessed during the era of the Babangida regime's Structural Adjustment Programme.

This chapter is an attempt to focus on this phenomenon, by mapping out the major dimensions of the explosion of religious identities during the period of SAP. We attempt to account for the sharp rise of religiosity in the context of increased economic hardship. Since our focus is on both Christian and Islamic identities in a comparative sense, we necessarily have to grapple with the "visibility politics" of these two religious groups, especially in situations where, in the perception of their adherents, identity is either personally or collectively challenged or denied.

Identity involves the location of oneself, giving meaning to the self on the political map, both as an individual and as part of a collective. It is a system of social relations which cannot be maintained in isolation and which can be used to mobilise human beings as part of a generation within a system of diverse identities. Religion, as a social and historical phenomenon, is not just an experience of reality, which is both personal and ultimate, but has a vision of reality, and means of articulating that vision expressed in concepts.

In religion, the objective of experience is ultimate and this implies that it is transcendental both theoretically and practically. It provides the ground for all decisions, actions and ultimate explanations in social, political and economic life, giving meaning to human life and action. Religions do not just consist of values, but also cognitions and skills with conceptions and images of the world, the nature of human beings, human society, perspectives of space and time and conceptions of the constitution of nature. Religion is, thus, not only a source of identity, but also an ideological system in itself; its vision incorporates an identity frame which weakens private identity because of its emphasis on the collective.

Politics and the Pulpit

Madeley (1982) used the term "politics and the pulpit" to demonstrate that in Europe, despite secularising tendencies, religious cleavages and issues are important factors in politics. Not only is "God not dead so far as European politics is concerned", as Madeley noted, but also that religious issues operate as "the hidden agenda in the pattern of voting behaviour".

In Nigeria, various scholars (Sulaiman, et al., 1988; Ibrahim, 1989 and 1991; Isiyaku, 1991; Olupona, 1992; Dambazau, 1993; Kukah, 1993) have written on the politicisation of religion and the relationship between the Church and the State in Nigeria. It has in fact been observed that:

> since *the inception of SAP*, the Babangida regime went out of its way to in a systematic and organised manner silence *all popular and democratic organisations* that are capable of challenging its harsh policies. However, the regime had on the other hand, extended support and a lot of its patronage to religious organisations such as the Jama'atu Nasril Islam (JNI) and the Christian Association of Nigeria (CAN) ... a development which has more than ever before, promoted a culture of religious bigotry (Chafe, 1992:19).

But even before SAP, and in fact since the 1970s, Nigeria has witnessed a surge in the phenomena of Christian and Islamic religious revivalism (Ibrahim, 1989 and 1991). Christian fundamentalism, organised under the rubric of the "Born Again" movement involves a struggle against what it considers to be the corrupt Nigerian Church whose spirituality has been destroyed by pagan practices, materialism and hierarchical structures. Thus, every "born again man is two men, the old man and the new man. The old is of the flesh; the new man is of the Spirit. The old person is corrupt and sinful, incapable of any spiritual good; the new man is perfect, incapable of sinning, but holy and sinless" (De Hann, 1972:26).

Islamic fundamentalism is seen to be involved with a frontal attack against remnants of traditional African religious practices still present among Muslim communities, and the struggle against the mystical practices and beliefs of the *Sufi* brotherhoods, mainly *Tijjaniyya* and *Qadiriyya*. The origin of this could, however, be traced to the debate initiated by Dr. Abubakar Imam on the pages of the Hausa Newspaper, *Gaskiya tafi Kwabo* in the late 1970s. The debate polarised the Muslim community and was a source of minor clashes among various factions within the Muslim community.

It was, however, the *Sharia* controversy during the Constituent Assembly debate in 1977–78 that dragged the issue of politics and the pulpit to centre stage. The constitution drafting committee was earlier inaugurated by General Murtala Ramat Mohammed who came to power through a *coup d'état* which overthrew General Yakubu Gowon. Murtala was assassinated in an attempted coup, organised by some minority elements who also happened to be Christians, mostly from Plateau State. Though Murtala was seen as a national hero, there were attempts at a later stage by some Muslims to see his death as organised by a fanatical Christian group.

In any case, few days after his death, and before the Constituent Assembly was elected and inaugurated, an intellectual, who later became a biographer of General Yakubu Gowon, in an address to the Northern Baptist Convention in Kano, called on Christian organisations in Nigeria to become more politically conscious, thus:

> They should start participating in political activities in order to infuse the Christian ideals of charity into politics... Christians must radicalise their churches for more socially beneficial purposes. The Christian must stand up boldly and speak out against social and political wrongs wherever they are found in the society (Elaigwu, 1977:7).

In terms of the issues, the fears and contentions, the *Sharia* debate of the 1977–78 Constituent Assembly was the same as that of the 1987–88 Constituent Assembly during the Babangida military administration. The Muslims were insistent that *Sharia* is a way of life, it is part of what defines their being as Muslims, and they needed a Federal *Sharia* Court of Appeal to deal with cases brought before it by Muslims. For the Christians, introducing *Sharia* or a Federal *Sharia* Court of Appeal amounts to giving undue preference to the Muslim in a state and Constitution which is secular. In fact, for Rev. Wilson S. Sabiya:

> to entrench the *Sharia* Court in the Constitution is to legalise the inferiority of non-Muslims and the superiority of Muslims... The claim, therefore, that courts cannot be used as instruments of evangelism is totally false. The *Sharia* is Islam and Islam is *Sharia*. *Sharia* is a total way of life, it is evangelism (1979:48).

For the Muslims, the common law is essentially Christian law and even the spirit of the Constitution is Christian in orientation. The Muslims have to struggle to get a well-deserved position in the constitution. Dr. M.T.A. Liman was in fact more practical in advising that "a Muslim vigilante group should be formed at the national level to alert the nation whenever they feel that Islamic interest in any place, at any level is being violated or sacrificed" (Liman, 1977:16). The themes kept on recurring during the 1987–88 Constituent Assembly debates. The debates on *Sharia*, from those that argue for it and those against it, seemed to have provided an umbrella to shelter or define their identity. The draft Constitution was even seen as an Islamic Manifesto by Minchakpu in an article in *Today's Challenge*, a Jos-based Christian magazine. This is because the constitution has maintained an earlier provision which limits *Sharia* Courts of Appeal to states.

There were also "heated polemics" in January 1986 in a debate over Nigerian membership of the Organisation of Islamic Conference (OIC), an organisation in which Nigeria had been an observer for about fifteen years. The Christians' stand was that, by joining the OIC, Nigeria had now become an Islamic state and that this violated its secular nature, which had set the stage for the treatment of Christians as *second-class citizens*, a situation they were determined to resist. President Babangida attempted to justify Nigerian membership of the OIC which he said was just a "forum for cooperation in economic, technical, and cultural matters. The body could help in also easing our economic burden" (*The Guardian*, March 22, 1986). The Jama'atu Nasril Islam issued a statement to assert the rights of Nigerian Muslims and calling on the government to do away with Christian symbols like the cross on public buildings, diaries and the Gregorian calendar and demanded a work-free day on Friday, which among other things is denied Muslims (*New Nigerian*, December 24, 1986). The Christian Council of Nigeria, in its memoranda to the Presidential Advisory Committee set up to look into the application for Nigerian membership in the OIC stated that becoming a member would make Nigeria a Muslim state, thus, adopting the Muslim religion; that Christians in Nigeria "will not agree to wage war against Israel" because they argued that "The Charter... makes it abundantly clearly that the OIC is totally committed to a fight alongside the Arabs, in order to liberate Jerusalem which the conference hopes will ultimately be its headquarters" (*Sunday Tribune*, February 23, 1986). This is, however, wrong because Article 11, Clause 5 of the Charter which they referred to only called for the "support of the struggle of the people of Palestine... to help them regain their rights and liberate their land". But identity politics in Nigeria made even some enlightened people see every Palestinian as necessarily an Arab and a Muslim. Nigeria had to finally withdraw from the OIC.

The theme of the presidential address at the Methodist Church of Nigeria Annual Conference in October 1985 touched on the issue of Christian social responsibility. The president observed that commentaries:

> on the on-going International Monetary Fund (IMF) Loan Debate have thrown into relief some sins of omission in our Christian social virtues in Nigeria... Are Nigerian churches so organised that they can express a responsible opinion, prophetic comment and proposals on a subject matter of this nature? (Adegbola, 1985:61–62).

In an address to the same conference, Chief (Mrs.) Abiola Babatope lamented the situation where Christians in a secular Nigeria had abandoned evangelical drive, become docile and were preaching religious tolerance, leaving the Federal Ministry of Commerce to be disproportionately distributing contracts to the "Muslis business class" who were also busy acquiring titles of *Alhajis* and *Alhajas* "before our very eyes". She went on to say that, with "our non-aggressive posture, we gradually, but steadily lose vantage grounds to those whose faith is in no way superior to ours, but whose heart is grafted in conquest by force" (ibid. 1985: 119–120).

Abubakar Mahmud Gumi, a renowned Islamic scholar, had on several occasions in interviews and in his preaching stated a classical Islamic jurist position that "a Muslim cannot accept or choose a non-Muslim as leader", especially in a situation where there is a contest for leadership between a Muslim and non-Muslim.

It was, however, the 1987 Kaduna State religious crisis that seemed to have set a new tone and tune, if not a new line of battle, in the politics of religion (Ibrahim, 1989). We intend to deal with this in another section.

The Christian Association of Nigeria (Northern Zone), published a book, titled *Leadership in Nigeria* in 1989. This was after the OIC debates in 1986, allegations on Nigeria's acquisition of shares from the Islamic Development Bank (IDB), the Kaduna State religious crisis in 1987 and the removal of some Christian ministers from General Babangida's cabinet. The object of the book was not just to analyse the leadership of Nigeria from independence to the Babangida regime, but was also meant to be a challenge to Christians generally for neglecting their important civic responsibilities. Many Christians have been "privileged to be in position of leadership in Nigeria, and many of them have abused that privilege. Truly, Nigeria is made up of more than 60 per cent Christians... How is it that their presence has not been felt in the affairs of leadership in this country?" (CAN, 1989:5). The association went on to query Christians who, in spite of their control of the Armed Forces Ruling Council (AFRC) in the Babangida era, allowed Muslims to "grab all positions of decision-making", which they used to "smuggle" Nigeria into OIC and IDB, as well as facilitate the imposition of *Sharia*. Why is it that, in spite of even the open acceptance by Gumi that nine out of every ten policemen in the North are Christians, most of the Police Commissioners and Divisional Police Officers (DPOs) are Muslims? There was a further partial autopsy of leadership in Nigeria with a basic message showing a clear disenchantment with the Babangida regime.

The first most detailed response to the CAN booklet was made by M.C.K. Ajuluchukwu in an article entitled "CAN, Christ and Government" (*Democrat Weekly*, August 12, 1989). The article was made into a small pamphlet, no doubt by a Muslim group, and widely circulated. Ajuluchukwu argued that though he shared the same faith with the publishers of the booklet, it seemed in his opinion that they have:

deviated from the divine path of charitable humanity, love, justice and good neighbourliness all of which the Bible imposes upon true Christians... there was nothing in the entire tenure of the First Republic to justify the North zonal CAN's allusion about the nation's ruling class having been dominated by Muslims. Statistically, there were more Christian than Muslim top office-holders during the period under review" (Ajuluchukwu, 1989:3).

Even though the booklet concentrated more on the Babangida regime, the facts statistically showed that there were more Christians in top positions than Muslims. The same argument was buttressed by Bari that during the Babangida regime "there were 204 Christians as against 138 Muslims who have so far participated in the membership of the AFRC, Council of Ministers as well as Council of State" (Bari, 1990:106).

Perhaps, as a response to the early retirement of General Domkat Bali and some other prominent Christian minority elements from the North, CAN came up with another pamphlet not only reiterating the arguments in the above quoted booklet, but also raising other social issues. It was clearly a mobilisational document meant to put "truth in the form of questions". It touched on issues like the administrative restructuring, AFRC and ministerial key positions, university education, corruption, effect of SAP, crime, political manipulation, population, politics of Nigerian petroleum, Nigerian billionaires, multimillionaires and millionaires, social and military expenditure and *Sharia*. The pamphlet stated that:

> Christians in this nation should know some truth about the social injustice, economic inequalities, the growing crime waves, the growing polarisation of the nation along religious lines, the marching forth of the process of Islamization of Nigeria, the institutionalisation of corruption in our social and economic system and many other social vices which are destroying our country Nigeria. Christians, we are called to be the light of the world and salt of the earth (CAN, 1990:1).

Christians in Nigeria, according to the pamphlet, are paying a very heavy price because of their inactivity. They allow themselves to be "deceived, manipulated and ruled by dishonest men".

On Sunday, April 22, 1990 there was the botched coup led by Major Gideon Orkar. The coup announcement was made on behalf of "the patriotic and well-meaning people of the Middle-Belt and Southern parts of Nigeria". Nigerians were informed of the successful ousting of "the dictatorial, corrupt, drug-baronish, inhuman, sadistic, deceitful, homosexually centred, oligarchistic and unpatriotic administration of General Ibrahim Babangida" (*Newbreed* May 14, 1990, 4). The attempted *coup d'état* brought to the forefront the familiar allegations about Hausa-Fulani and Muslim domination of the leadership of Nigeria. The solution of the copyists to the perceived domination of the Hausa-Fulani, as announced, was that the states and *citizen*s identified as Muslim and Hausa-Fulani in Sokoto, Borno, Katsina, Kano, and Bauchi were excised from the Nigerian Federation. The announcement, although quite contradictory, revealed the deep-rooted resentment to the Babangida regime and perception of the solution to the crisis from a group which seemed out of touch with the Nigerian political and economic reality. The coup was crushed within a few hours. It, however, provided an opportunity for the circulation of anonymous documents by the Muslims, especially in the North and West, alleging that CAN was behind the botched coup led by Orkar. This, in their reasoning, was because the majority of the demands of the coup-plotters were similar to those of CAN in their widely circulated documents.

Another issue worth discussing is the statement credited to Chief Francis A. Nzeribe which appeared in a Christian newspaper *The Leader* published in Owe. In an interview which appeared in its May 30, 1987 edition, Nzeribe was quoted as saying:

Christianity and Islam will be the underlying factors in the 1990 elections... time has come for the Christians to be political... Rome and Canterbury cannot afford to fold their hands again because Christians... have realised in a hard way that Islamization of Nigeria is the target of the Muslim world" (*The Leader* May 30, 1987).

Similarly, an elderly Christian activist, Jolly Tank Yusuf called on the Christians "to organise and work with liberal people of other faiths, they must seek to be elected, must fight collectively, must reject their tribe, must forget their differences and denominations and work as a team until we get our rightful place" (*Free Nation*, December 1988). Christians, at least those from organised churches, did answer the call to politics. A special edition of *Today's Challenge* (1992) was devoted to asking the question: Will a Christian rule after Babangida? The question was posed to three presidential contestants, Professor Jerry Gana, Dr. Chris Abashiya, and Engineer Samuel Salifu. Only Salifu was positive in believing that "God will bring a Christian not to retaliate, but to rebuild the nation".

Islamic fundamentalists usually hold very extreme views on participation in politics. The only politics they recognise is Islamic politics, guided by the Qur'an and the Sunnah in an Islamic state. As Falaki argued:

> It is incompatible with Islam, therefore, for a Muslim to pledge support to any political party of a non-Islamic platform or to yield to a non-Islamic government of alien origin and aims. The ruler is not a sovereign over the people. He is a representative employee chosen by the people and derives his authority from his obedience to the law of Allah (Falaki, 1988:22).

Thus, if Islam is taken to be opposed to the post-Renaissance concept of the separation of church and the state, what has become of the biblical call to duty and obligation in rendering unto Caesar what is Caesar's and to God what is God's? We shall attempt to explain below.

Citizenship and Ethno-Religious Violence

Most of the ethno-religious crises experienced in Nigeria during the period under study seemed to be concerned with the issue of the nature and definition of *citizenship* in Nigeria. Citizenship is a "multi-layered concept with its laws combining in different ways". (Bader, 1995:212). It also presumes an inherited status, legal protection, rights and obligations. Citizenship is also an important feature of democracy which also provides a criterion for inclusion and exclusion. It involves active involvement as a means through which one can develop one's capacities into a being, who knows "what it means to participate in and be responsible" for the care and improvement of the common and collective life. Our concern, is with how SAP and its other component, the Babangida transition programme, led to the emergence of a new *citizen*, who is primarily primordial and religiously oriented.

One general feature of the Islamic and Christian fundamentalists' violent ethno-religious clashes is that they seem to either start from higher institutions of learning, or are led by students of higher institutions, or members of the elite class who have attained a higher level of education or place in the society. The Kaduna State crisis in 1987 is a case in point (Ibrahim, 1989). It all started at the Kafanchan College of Education where the "born again Christian students' movement" organised an evangelical week hoisting a banner welcoming students and visitors to "Mission 87 in Jesus Campus". This did not go down well with the Muslim students, especially the activists who interpreted the Christian students' movement banner as one way of "appropriating" the whole "campus for itself".

The crisis started on March 6, 1987 when it was alleged that one of the invited speakers, Reverend Abubakar Bako, had "denigrated the respected personality of the Holy Prophet (SAW) and called him an impostor". He was challenged by a Muslim student activist, Aishatu Garba, and a fracas ensued when other members of the Muslim Students Society (MSS) mobilised and congregated at the scene. The MSS "organised a protest march around Kafanchan town" which has a very large Christian population that resented the Muslim settler "minority" that is controlling the traditional political power. The "indigenous Christian majority of the town" and the environs seized this opportunity and "descended heavily on their Muslim neighbours". Many lives and some property were lost on the side of the Muslim population. With a partisan media, and Muslim migrants from Kafanchan running away from the crisis, the whole state came to be engulfed in Muslim-Christian clashes in almost all the major towns in Kaduna State. Many lives were lost, churches burnt and fear and insecurity gripped the whole state.

The government set up the Donli Commission to investigate the causes of the crisis. Subsequently, a tribunal headed by Justice Karibi Whyte was also set up to try offenders. The tribunal was accused by the Muslims of bias against them and for its inability to force the security forces to produce the principal accused, Reverend Bako. To date, many of the Muslim groups have kept raising the question of the whereabouts of Reverend Abubakar Bako.

The religious crisis in Katsina on March 27, 1991, the Kano uprising of December 26, 1994 leading to the assassination of Gideon Akaluka, and the kidnapping of a Christian preacher by a Muslim group in Kafanchan on September 6, 1996, are similar in many respects. They were all led by the 'Shi'ite' Muslim fundamentalist group under the leadership of Ibrahim El-Zakzaky and they all seemed to revolve around allegations of a Christian attack on the personality of the Prophet of Islam (SAW) or the defilement of the Qur'an.

In Katsina, the immediate cause of the crisis was an article in *Fun Times*, a *Daily Times* publication, of December 1990, which allegedly portrayed Prophet Muhammad in a bad light by alleging that he "had an affair with a woman of easy virtue" whom he later married. This, according to Islam is blasphemous. There were protests in Kano led by the Muslim Students Society of Bayero University. There were also protests in Katsina, led by Mallam Yakubu Yahaya, a staunch member and follower of the El-Zakzaky group. It led to the burning of the Daily Times office in Katsina. The State Governor came out with a threat of death to any person who breached the law. Ibrahim El-Zakzaky addressed his followers and responded to the threat made by the Governor, Col. John Madaki, essentially calling for a *jihad* (i.e. a holy war) and justifying it by saying that paradise awaited any person who died in the course of confrontation with the state. A tribunal, under the chairmanship of Justice Rabiu D. Mohammed, was set up to try those arrested during the riot. Consequently, many of El-Zakzaky's followers were jailed.

In the case of Gideon Akaluka in Kano, he was accused of defiling the Qur'an by using some of its pages as toilet paper. He was arraigned before a court and remanded in prison custody for his personal security because of the *Shi'ite* group's insistence that death is the penalty for such a blasphemous offence in Islamic law. Nevertheless, feeling that the due process of law is a waste of time, some members of the group climbed the thirty-foot wall of Kano Central Prison at night and cut off Akaluka's head. The head was put on a stake and displayed around some places in Kano city. In spite of the group's confession, Akaluka's head was not presented for burial and the Igbo community felt aggrieved and even observed a day of mourning.

Today's Challenge (1996) reported that Muslim *Shi'ites* kidnapped Monday Yakunat, a Christian preacher on September 6, 1996. He was accused by the *Shi'ites* of insulting Prophet Muhammad (SAW). What saved Yakunat from being killed by decapitation was the heated argument among the *Shi'ites* on whether to kill him then or wait for permission from their leader in Zaria. It was while waiting for a reply from Zaria that the Christian community in Kafanchan "mobilised themselves and stormed the enclave of the *Shi'ites*", thereby rescuing Yakunat. In the process of storming the enclave, there was a clash between the *Shi'ites* and the Christians. The casualties included "two persons dead, two vehicles burnt and two motor-cycles also burnt. Three policemen were injured" (*Today's Challenge*, 1996:6).

Any careful observer of Kano's social and political reality will not fail to conclude that things were not likely to go well with Bonnke's proposed visit in October 1991. The level of aggressive ward-to-ward mobilisation carried out by the Christian groups over the German Evangelist Reverend Bonnke's miracle explosion was such that it raised suspicion in the minds of an average Muslim on what their objective was. Complaints were made against the visit by people like Sheikh Nasiru Kabara, the leader of the *Qadiriyya* sect in Africa, to the effect that Bonnke's coming "is a blatant provocation". In fact, Dr. Auwalu Yadudu came out even more forcefully by stating that "Bonnke's crusade was a well-orchestrated plan to provoke Muslims. Somehow, someone is bent upon provoking Muslims and he knows the right buttons to touch" (*Citizen*, October 21–28, 1991:17). The riot that ensued resulted in violent attacks on Christians, churches and their property. Many lives were lost. Many Muslims seemed quite unhappy with the fact that the Nigerian government did not allow South African Muslim preacher, Ahmed Deedat and American Black Muslims leader Louis Farrakhan to preach in Nigeria, but it allowed Bonnke's visit. The riot as Salisu Yakasai, the chairman of the Nigerian Union of Journalist in Kano, stated, was essentially economic, for its main participants and vanguard were the unemployed: "This is not a religious riot at all. Its genesis was purely economic. Even while the Emir was speaking, looting had begun. Religion does not sanction looting" (*Citizen*, October 21–28, 1996:18). As is usual, the government, which was at the centre of the whole crisis and committed all sorts of errors as a result of lack of foresight, set up a commission of inquiry into the crisis. The findings of the report were never released to the public.

A misunderstanding between an Igbo trader and two Hausa boys seemed to have been the immediate cause of the May 30, 1995 riot in Kano. It all started when some women who came to the Sabon-Gari market for some shopping parked their car in front of the shop of an Igbo man. Two boys came, forced the car open and stole a bag from it. When the women came back and discovered their bag missing, the Igbo trader pointed at the two thieves who were arrested by policemen. The missing bag was recovered from the two boys and the police, instead of "charging them to court, released them". The boys then came back to confront "the Igbo man who revealed their identity to the women". A fight which turned into a free-for-all ensued and spread to some parts of the town. A lot of lives were lost, churches and mosques burnt and property looted and destroyed. Unlike in some other riots, the Christians in Sabon-Gari were able to organise and defend their areas and at the same time engaged in counter-violence and destruction of property identified as belonging to Muslims, both Hausa-Fulani and Yoruba. For the first time, also, the predominantly Hausa-Fulani ward of Fagge organised and repelled the attack by Igbos on their shops in Fagge. In their memorandum to the committee set up by the Kano State Government to investigate the civil disturbance, the CAN (Kano Branch) accused the '*Yandaba* group and *Almajirai* (beggars) as the main perpetrators of the violence, arson and looting. They also identified the ineptitude of the Government as contributing to the crisis. They disputed the claim of the Military Administrator that the disturbance was neither "ethnic nor religious", thus:

> .... we wish to humbly disagree with the Administrator by saying that the disturbance was more religious than anything. If it was not religious why were churches the first places to be attacked? Another evidence to buttress the fact that the crisis was partly religious is the harassment and threats of notice to quit to Christians by the Moslem brethren in houses that do not belong to them (Ubah and Oche, 1995:2).

Reverend Samuel Uche and Audu Dirambi made the same observation again, especially about the irresponsibility and helplessness of government (*Today's Challenge*, November 3, 1995). In fact, Uche lamented that:

> there is nothing to show that in Kano State, there's military regime, no! We have a very weak despotic type of leadership, somebody who does not even care. Somebody dull... Kano State needs somebody like Jafaru Isa of Kaduna State" (ibid.:20).

After the completion of the work of the investigation committee, the government set up a tribunal to try those arrested in the course of the riot.

There were so many striking similarities between the Tafawa Balewa-Bauchi ethno-religious crisis of April 22, 1991 and the Zangon Kataf-Kaduna crisis of May 15, 1992. They both revolved around the issues of land, political leadership, or self-determination, market, labelling and of who is an indigene. Tafawa Balewa town was founded by the Fulani just before the jihad. It attracted many migrants, such as Kanuri, Angas, Hausa, and later Sayawa from the surrounding villages. The influx of the Sayawa increased in the 1970s and they were joined by Jarawa and Bununu. They were able to purchase plots of land and settled outside the town. The traditional leadership of the town was in the hands of Kanuri and Angas. For the Sayawa, every Muslim is a settler and any convert from any other ethnic group to Islam will not only be presumed to wear the badge of a settler, but also a Hausa-Fulani. Since they did not want to be under the control of "settlers", they demanded a district of their own and were given Bagoro with one Haruna Yakub as the District Head. But this was not enough for they wanted a Christian as their District Head. The Sayawa were reported as never tired of telling the other ethnic groups, most especially the Muslim and the Hausa-Fulani, that "you settlers (volti-gali) will one day be sent packing back to where your ancestors come from" (*Citizen*, May 13, 1991:21). The crisis started over the use of a slaughter house, which was controlled by the Muslim butchers, by the Sayawa to slaughter pigs and sell pork. The first targets were Sayawa who converted to Islam. Sayawa from the surrounding villages were mobilised to attack the Muslim and Hausa-Fulani population, who claimed that even the police backed the Sayawa in perpetrating the violence. The Muslims gave a list of about ninety-five people (Muslims) killed, nine cars, lorries and many houses burnt.

The Zangon Kataf-Kaduna crisis of May 1992 was a major crisis which polarised the Muslim and Christian population in Nigeria. It was not just because of the level of carnage, but especially because of the politicisation of the crisis, the press distortions and falsifications of events, and the arrest and trial of some prominent Kataf who were alleged to have been the brains behind, and/or active participants in, the crisis. The grievances of the Kataf people against the Muslim Hausa-Fulani were almost the same as those of the Sayawa against the Muslim Hausa-Fulani in Tafawa Balewa-Bauchi State. The Kataf grievances, however, seemed to be more deep-rooted. They were summed up by Dr. Yusuf Turaki, the National Vice-President of CAN in an address at the funeral of Rev. Tacio Doniyo who was killed in the aftermath o the Zangon Kataf riot at Kaduna. Turaki generalised on the causes of ethnic and religious riots in the whole of the Middle-Belt. He mentioned, among other things, the inability of the state governments in the North to:

> create and grant autonomous chiefdoms to ethnic groups, the so called *Kabilu* of the Middle-Belt (and)... southern part of Kaduna State... (and) that the governments in these states give preferential treatment and also grant superior and dominant sociopolitical role and status to settler people against the indigenous peoples (*Today's Challenge*, No. 2, 1992:6–7).

He also alleged the loss of all constitutional rights, social, political, cultural and religious by the minority or the *Kabilu* who are never taken seriously and never listened to by governments of the Northern States. These points were corroborated by the findings of the Cudjoe Commission and by Col. Yohana Madaki, in his interview with *Citizen* in which he, among other things, stated that:

> The problem is the Zaria emirate... I have gone to the Emir (of Zazzau) to talk about this. He won't talk to me. He won't invite me for anything and he is supposed to be my traditional ruler. He doesn't know my language or culture. The issue is one of pride... The chiefs there (in the Southern districts of Zazzau) are the wrong guys (*Citizen*, May 25, 1992:13).

The Kataf also resented the Hausa for referring to them as *Arna* which means pagans. One fact which is not disputed, however, is that the town Zangon Kataf was founded and set up by the Hausa-Fulani and they had been there for about three hundred years. The Kataf, like other ethnic groups live in the surrounding villages. Zangon Kataf, like other areas in the Southern part of Zaria or Kaduna was part of Zazzau Emirate and, thus, appointments of district heads was done by the Emir of Zazzau. One of the major battle-cries against Fulani domination was recorded on June 8, 1953 when "some political activists among the Kaje and Kataf sent a letter of complaint against Fulani rule in Southern Zaria to the newly created Ministry of Local Government in Kaduna" (Turaki, 1993:126). Their complaints against Fulani district heads centred around forced labour, cheating in terms of grain measures in the market, corrupt and oppressive tax assessment, treatment of people with contempt especially by calling them *Arna*, maltreatment of Kaje and Kataf women, segregation and neglect in education. The then Minister for Local Government, Sir Ahmadu Bello, toured the area, confirmed some of the complaints of neglect and misrule and submitted a report to the Resident of Zaria. The recommendation for the creation of a new division was rejected.

The immediate cause of the crisis which started on February 6, 1992 and which later spread to many parts of Kaduna, was the attempt by the Kataf-controlled local council government to move the market from the town to a new place. The Hausa interpreted this as a political vendetta and the beginning of attempts to dispossess them of their shops and means of livelihood. Thus, they resisted and even went to court to get an injunction to prevent the local council from implementing that decision. There was a clash in which 95 people among the Muslim Hausa-Fulani population were killed. The government set up a commission of inquiry led by Justice Rahila Cudjoe to investigate the crisis. Tension was quite high even before the commission could finally finish its job. For example, it was accused of bias by the Kataf when information leaked that they had been indicted. There were also allegations by the Hausa that Kataf men went to their farms and uprooted their crops.

The *Izala* sect in Zangon Kataf, after this incident, sent a letter of distress to the Sultan of Sokoto, seeking his help in solving this problem. But, contrary to allegations levelled against them by *Northern Nigeria in Perspective* (*NNIP* October 1992) and *Today's Challenge* (No. 2, 1992), they did not call for an "Islamic jihad" to start from Zango. In fact, the relevant portion of their letter stated:

> As you are already aware, we, the Nigerian Moslems are full of patience... But if we are confronted beyond the point, Jihad in Nigeria would start in Zango... For fear of being pushed to the wall that might result in our discomfort, distort our peaceful co-existence as Moslems we feel obliged to bring this to the knowledge of the Government and our elders (*NNIP*, October, 1992:46).

On the main day of the attack, armed Kataf youths came to deal with anyone opposed to the relocation of the market. The violence meted out was so organised and systematic that in the end "Zangon Kataf town was destroyed and many people killed... Every space was a graveyard" (*Today's Challenge*, No. 2, 1992:4). The violence later spread to many parts of Kaduna State including Kaduna, Zaria and Ikara towns, with many casualties and property lost by both Muslims and Christians. In a memorandum submitted to the Judicial Commission of Inquiry into the riot, a list of 1, 506 people was tendered as the number of Hausa-Fulani killed at Zangon Kataf. The State Security Service estimated that 424 people died at Zangon Kataf. Property worth 154 million Naira was also alleged to have been destroyed. There was an allegation of police, and even army, complicity in the crisis allegedly resulting in the death of many people from gun-shots. The solicitors to the Hausa community's victims of the riot in Ikara and Zaria claimed in their memorandum that at "both Zaria and Ikara, a total of 18 people were killed", the majority of whom while performing their religious rites. A Northern minority magazine *National Impression* (No. 2 and No. 3, 1992) gave its own statistics of casualties in the crisis, alleging that over three hundred people, the majority of whom were Christians, lost their lives in Kaduna, Zaria, and Ikara towns.

The arrest of some prominent Kataf men who were said to have been involved in the carnage, and their being charged with culpable homicide punishable with death, rioting, and unlawful assembly with arms before the Justice Okadigbo tribunal further polarised the country along religious lines. As is usual, the Muslim and Christian activists had a field day issuing threats and counter-threats. The Kataf people even went to the extent of writing a letter to the Igbo Community Welfare Association (ICWA) in Kaduna "urging them to call their son to order", referring to Justice Okadigbo, chairman of the tribunal, who was an Igbo. The Muslim Hausa-Fulani also threatened that there would not be peace unless those who killed their kinsmen in Zangon Kataf were punished. In spite of protests by the lawyers of the Kataf men arraigned before it, and the later withdrawal of the counsels to the accused, the Tribunal passed a death sentence on the Kataf leader, retired General Zamani Lekwot, and five others. The Evangelical Church of West Africa (ECWA) in a statement, called on the government to understand that the tribunal:

> turned out in the end not to be an instrument of peace, justice and reconciliation, but an instrument of entrenching the will and wishes of the strong and the privileged and also enlarged the human gulf and fanned the embers of violence and hate between the waring communities of Zangon Kataf and is at the moment on the verge of plunging the whole nation unto a serious social, political and religious crisis (*Today's Challenge*, No. 1, 1993:45).

The spokesman of the Kataf, Dr. Harnson Yusuf Bungwan wondered how justice could be said to have been done in a situation where no Hausa person was brought before the tribunal, most of the witnesses were residents of Zango town, and even the police officers conducting the investigation were also Hausa, who "...all have emotional attachments to the victims of the riot from Zango town, being of the same ethnic group or religious persuasion" (ibid: 5). Also, some human rights groups, such as the Committee for the

Defence of Human Rights (CDHR), Universal Defenders of Democracy (UDD), the Constitutional Rights Project (CRP) and even Human Rights Watch based in the United States, appealed for the nullification of the judgement of the tribunal. Archbishop Okogie, the President of CAN warned the government to be prepared to "face the consequences if they confirm the death sentence".

The Muslims and their organisations were quick in dismissing the above claims by, among other things, pointing out that Hausa people were indeed arraigned before the tribunal and that they were tried, discharged and acquitted based on the evidence before the tribunal. Some quipped:

> [Where] were the human rights bodies when 19 Hausa-Fulani men were killed in 1987 in Kafanchan and nobody was tried for their murder? But Hausa-Fulani were later arraigned before the Karibi-Whyte tribunal for destruction of property... where were the human rights groups when the Kataf laid siege on Zangon Kataf town and carried out genocide? What the convicts did to the Zangon Kataf people violated their own human rights (*Citizen*, February 8, 1993:18 and 14).

The Nigerian Muslims in the United Kingdom, in a statement, insisted that the law must take its course:

> The sentence passed on those found guilty of murdering innocent Muslims must be carried out. Justice demands that the rights and interests of the numerous Muslim victims must prevail. The villains must be made to answer for their evil acts (*Citizen*, March 22, 1993:23).

One of the most unfortunate results of the Zangon Kataf crisis was its bringing to the fore-front religion and ethnicity as determining factors of where one may live. The question of who is an indigene, or the 'Katafisation' of people (as one of the columnists of *Citizen* magazine, Bilkisu Yusuf observed), is an incorrect way of dealing with identity or understanding diversity. It is also ironic that self-determination and the liberation of the Kataf people from their emirate oppressors is seen in terms of the creation of a new chiefdom for them.

What came to be labelled as the 'Northern virus', that is religious sectarian violence between Muslims and Christian activists, seemed to have also gripped Oyo State in South-western Nigeria. It particularly centred around the question of representation in the Executive Council in a state where each of the contending religious groups is claiming a majority. Other issues included the opening of morning assemblies with Christian prayers in secondary schools, use of classrooms for church services, teaching of Bible Knowledge in all schools with less than half of the schools teaching Islamic Religious Knowledge (*TSM*, May 8, 1994). The League of Imams and Alfas of Oyo State issued a statement, which appeared in the *Tribune Newspaper* in which they expressed their disappointment with the Military Administrator of the State, Navy Captain Adetoye Sode for what they saw as under-representation of Muslims in his cabinet. They were quoted as saying that "... in a state of over 70 per cent (Muslim) population, only three Muslims were in a cabinet of nine and the two women appointed were Christians. The Second-in-Command to the Administrator... is also a Christian... only one Muslim was appointed a Director-General out of 20 D-Gs" (ibid.:12). The Administrator attempted to tackle the issues by announcing a ban on religious activities in the whole of Oyo State. The Christians, however, continued with their morning devotion, especially in schools they control. The Young Muslim Brothers and Sisters (YOUMBAS) and the more militant National Council of Muslim Youths Organisation (NACOMYO) lost patience with the government's inability to "enforce the ban on organised prayers in schools". The leader of NACOMYO, Ishaq Kunle Sanni and some of his followers took it upon themselves to enforce the ban, through the disruption of early morning assemblies in schools. The Christian leaders complained to the government about Sanni and his activities. He was later arrested, questioned and released. The crisis was averted due to the intervention of another Muslim group, the Progressive Muslim Association of Nigeria, which did not only condemn the action of the youths, but also warned against making Oyo State a religious arena.

Interpretations and Re-interpretations of History

In Nigeria, the turbulence of the religious scene during the period under study fuels the associated agitation in the political arena, especially in the context of growing fears over political domination and religious freedom. Muslim activists express concern and fears over what they consider to be the dominance of Christian culture, westernisation or secularisation in Nigeria. Christian activists are concerned mainly with what they regard as the threat of Islamisation of the country, imposition of *Sharia* on non-Muslims and the use of state resources to subsidise Muslim activities. The battle seemed to centre on perceptions of the imposition of identity on the other or at least maintaining one's ground. This hegemonic contest also involves an interpretation and re-interpretation of events and history in Nigeria. Even the "theological space" is in contest, as seen by the attempt of the Christian and Islamic activist groups to project themselves as the pure and the faithful, unlike the others who are seen as nominal or syncretic.

In Muslim-Christian dialogues, debates or relations, the accusation of Islamisation or Christianisation, as earlier stated, is a recurring theme. For the Christian, any attempt by the state to be involved with anything at any level, so long as it had a tag of Islam, Muslim or Islamic was seen and interpreted as Islamisation. In their defence of or insistence on the assertion of their rights as members of the political community, the Muslims see the attempt of the Christians to raise the banner of the secular nature of the Nigerian state as a red-herring or another way of asserting Christianisation. The Council of Ulama, at one time, called on the Federal Government of

Nigeria to set up a committee to conduct research into secularism (Ujo, 1994:151). Islamisation for Aguwa "is not just making Islamic in quality, traits or way of thinking or acting", but it is the "conversion of willing persons by force" (Aguwa, 1993). But at the conceptual level, Islamisation means the application of the entire belief and value systems of Islam at the level of the state and in the social, cultural and economic realms. It implies the rolling back of the 'secular' status of the state and the establishment of an Islamic state, through the conscious application of the whole tenets of Islam to the life of the nation permeating all aspects of the life of the society (Iqbal, 1984). While the influence of certain Christian beliefs and doctrines in terms of the growth of certain ideas and the development of the western society cannot be disputed, it will be wrong to see Christianity in any modern idea or development. The battle between theocentrism and Christocentrism is deeply rooted in church history. It could be traced to the apolitical bent in Christianity developed by St. Augustine, through his insistence that Christianity did not represent another civil theology, but was meant to "prepare men for the permanent estate of eternity". This was what formed the basis of secularism, which is now challenged by some Christian activists. Although secular society is by no means a "product of the Christian west", one may argue like Munby (1963) that we have to "distinguish between a secular society and state".

Sociologically, secularisation refers to three distinct phenomena—the differentiation between secular and religious spheres, the decline of religious beliefs and practices and the marginalisation of the religious sphere to the private domain. A Christian society could, for example, exist with a secular state which does not express Christian beliefs in any organised way. A secular society is not homogeneous. It is pluralist, tolerant, without official images and does not commit itself as a whole to any particular view of the nature of the universe and the place of human beings in it. Thus, both Islam and Christianity, if we accept this position, could find a place and exist independent of the other in a secular society. Our notion of secularism is thus oriented towards the guaranteeing of religious freedom to all groups; that the state can neither prescribe nor proscribe religion. People may, in fact, need a secular society, especially in a heterogeneous nation to assert their freedom. In an interview with the *Citizen*, Alhaji Ibrahim Dasuki, the then Sultan of Sokoto, dismissed the claims of those who always think of a grand design to Islamise or Christianise Nigeria. His argument was that force can never be used to change one's faith (*Citizen*, October 19–20, 1992).

The major issue today seems to be related to the assertion of religious-cum-cultural identity, which finds expression in the emergence of several books and pamphlets aimed at historical deconstruction or re-interpretation (Umar, 1987; Aguwa, 1993; Bidmos, 1993; Kukah, 1993; Nuhu, 1993; Turaki, 1993; Tyoden, 1993; Basri, 1994; Wali, 1994). The Muslims complain about the media's demonisation of Islam. This is especially so with regards to the press from the South whose portrayal of Islam in a bad light has been consistent since 1880 (Yusuf, 1989). The press does not just distort Islam, by using slanted titles or special semantics in describing anything Islamic, but also often by fabricating stories, expressing subjective opinion showing general unfamiliarity with Islam. According to Bugaje, in his introduction to Basri's book:

> The greater part of this anti-Islamic indoctrination was achieved through Christian Missionary schools ... In the Muslim heartlands, where Christian Missionary schools were not allowed ... the colonial government built public schools where indoctrination against Islam and the inculcation of western tastes and culture were undertaken in a very gradual and subtle manner (Basri, 1994:12).

Bugaje also argued that the colonial government purposely created Sabon-Gari as Christian settlements in Muslim cities to encourage prostitution, drinking of alcohol and gambling, so as to "corrupt the social morality of the Muslim society within the walled city". The conversion of the minority elements in the Middle-Belt into Christianity was done with the purpose of creating hostile neighbours and "fifth columns to weaken the Muslim body politic" and this is what was expressed by their vehement opposition to "*Sharia* during the Constituent Assembly debates of 1978/79 and 1988/89". Umar came down heavily on the "Christian controlled media" which he said, was always ready to insult and humiliate Muslims, and also referred to the history of Nigeria from independence to date as a struggle between those who are anti-God and the Muslims who "accept the commands of Allah". According to him, the "rulers of Nigeria are an integral part of the global system of *Kufr* (unbelief) who dance to the music of the cult of *Kufr*; they cannot represent the interests of the Muslims".

Matthew Hassan Kukah, a Catholic priest from Northern Nigeria, sees the two major media organs, the Kaduna-based New Nigerian Newspapers and the Federal Radio Corporation, as the vital organs of Northern hegemony or Muslim Hausa-Fulani domination. British colonialists established an Anglo-Fulani hegemony in the colonial period, using the already existing caliphate superstructure which came with the Islamic jihad in 1804. The modern democratic system established at independence did not change the equation, but that Anglo-Fulani hegemony is still dominating the Christian and minority groups in Northern Nigeria. Kukah stated that:

> the ascendancy of Hausa-Fulani hegemony has coincided with the alienation and marginalization of the non-Muslims, Christians, and adherents of traditional religions in the region ... since religion has been a major factor of the Muslims, it has become imperative for Christians now to use religion for achieving their sociopolitical and economic goals (1993:x).

Thus, it seems that in order to achieve that objective, there arose the need to re-interpret politics, the *Sharia* question and the Kaduna State ethno-religious crisis of 1987, and the Babangida regime and its politics, so as to clear the ground for more active political involvement.

Turaki's treatment of the role of British colonialism in institutionalising Anglo-Hausa-Fulani rule in Northern Nigeria, employed the categories of Muslim and non-Muslim as his tool for the socio-ethical analysis of the colonial and post-colonial society and politics of Nigeria. The main consequence of colonial policy based on the "colonial racial theories of superiority or inferiority" was "the institutionalisation of ethnic hierarchy and stratified inequality between the Hausa-Fulani and the peoples of Southern Zaria and Middle-Belt in general" (Turaki, 1993:270). He, however, saw the revival of religious and communal sentiments as something quite well in accord with, and conducive to, the political philosophy of the Babangida regime. He repeated the position that the cause of the Zangon Kataf and the Bauchi riots was the demand for chiefdoms by the Kataf and Sayawa:

> These ethnic groups want their chiefs and chiefdoms and not to be placed under Hausa-Fulani rule. The religious riots in Kaduna city, Zaria city and Ikara in Kaduna State in 1987 and 1992 define the resurgence of the colonial religious conflict of the Muslim and the non-Muslim groups in the colonial system. The perpetrators of the riots in Kaduna State and Bauchi State targeted primarily Christians of Northern State origin (Turaki, 1993:226).

It is this issue and others raised above that the "national question" must address.

Conclusion

The late Malam Aminu Kano, a leading politician and social reformer, observed in 1976–77 at a seminar that "Nigeria seems a good fertile ground for religious conflict because of its oil resources, big Muslim population and its Christian elite" (1977:7). A few years after this observation, there was the Maitatsine intra-religious (Muslim) crises in Kano in December 1980, and in Kaduna, Yola and Gombe in 1982, 1984, and 1985, respectively. The major religious conflagration involving Christians and Muslims was the Kafanchan-Kaduna State crisis in 1987. Religiosity in both its Islamic and Christian manifestations, involving the re-evaluation of the role of religion in the society, came to the centre stage.

What seems apparent, however, since the introduction of SAP, is that the growing disparity of wealth and opportunities which came to be tolerated by the government pushed individuals and most especially the youths, with their quest for self-identity but who are now by-passed by the new political economy, into adopting new religious values and orientation. This may be a means of asserting themselves and defining an identity in the absence of other civil modes of identification, especially under an authoritarian military regime. In a situation such as that of the SAP regime and the government's adoption of extremely harsh, contradictory, repressive and conservative policies, combined with a dubious programme of transition to democracy, the youth, elite and even some key political figures identified themselves with religious movements and issues. The level of corruption exacerbated by SAP and the skewing of the spoils of office for only those in the corridors of power made many people retreat back to the mosques and churches as alternative modes of economic survival and political expression of opposition and protest. This, however, was not done in any systematic or organised way.

Most of the religious movements under the leadership of both the Christian and Islamic activists are strongest in cities and urban centres attracting the youths, as well as educated members of the middle-class who were "proletarianised" by SAP. Thus, victims of economic retrenchment whose other multiple modes of livelihood have severely been constrained by SAP became trapped in ethno-religious battles for political, economic and theological survival. The religious movements helped in providing some social welfare services to the followers and have also become a means of accumulation (Kane, 1994).

The response of the state to religious revivals and militancy has been in terms of repression. But religious movements can help to keep the society peaceful, depending upon the agenda of the religious leaders. Religious activism in Nigeria is not likely to be transitory; rather, it is likely to be an enduring phenomenon. Nigerian society is very religious and we cannot but accept that as a given. We can accept a theo-centric society while rejecting a theocratic state. We are reminded by Sanneh (1997) that in the history of religion, secular fundamentalism cannot but beget its nemesis in the form of right-wing religious fundamentalism, so the state and religious activists should always seek the path of moderation and religious freedom for all.

Bibliography

Abdul-Fadl, M., 1987, "Community Justice and Jihad: Elements of the Muslim Historical Consciousness", *The American Journal of Islamic Social Sciences*, Vol. 4, No. 1.

Adegbola, Rev. E. A., 1985, (ed.), *Methodist Church of Nigeria: The Minutes of the 24th Annual Conference*. Yaba.

Adeojo, Chief A.Y., 1989, "Joint Muslim Advisory Council of Oyo State: An Appeal to CAN", *National Concord*, Tuesday, April 15.

African Leadership Forum, 1991, *Religious pluralism and democracy*. Dialogue No. 19, December.

African Leadership Forum, 1994, *Religion and Society*. Dialogue, No. 29, March.

Agbaje, A., 1990, "Travails of the Secular State: Religion, Politics and the Outlook in Nigeria's Third Republic", *Journal of Commonwealth and Comparative Politics*, Vol. XXVII, No. 3.

Aguwa, J.C.U., 1993, *Religious Dichotomy in Nigerian Politics*. Enugu: Fourth Dimension Publishers.

Ahanotu, A., 1992, "Muslims and Christians in Nigeria: A contemporary political discourse", in Ahanotu, A., (ed.), *Religion, state and society in contemporary Nigeria*. New York: Peter Lang.

Ahmed, A., 1988, *Discovering Islam*. London: Routledge.

Ahmed, A. M. K., 1990, *A Comparative Study of Islam and Christianity*. Kano: Triumph Pub. Co.

Ajuluchukwu, M. C. K., 1989, *CAN, Christ and Government*. August. Kaduna: CAN.

Al-Azmal, A., 1993, *Islam and Modernities*. London: Verso.

Al-Faruqi, I. R., 1986, "Meta-Religion: Towards a Critical World Theology", *American Journal of Islamic Social Sciences*, Vol. 3, No. 1.

Anwar, A., 1992, *Tasirin siyasa a addini: Tijjanawa da tirjanawa a Kano, 1937–1991*. Nigeria: Stronghold.

Atanda, J. A., et al. 1989, (ed.), *Nigeria Since Independence. Vol. IX Religion*. Ibadan: Heinemann.

Bader, V., 1995, "Citizenship and Exclusion: Radical Democracy, Community and Justice or What is Wrong with Communitarianism", *Political Theory*, Vol. 23, No. 2, May.

Badone, E., 1987, "Ethnicity, Folklore and Local Identity in Rural Brittany", *Journal of American Folklore*, Vol. 100, No. 336.

Bari, O., 1990, *Leadership in Nigeria: A Rejoinder*. Sokoto: NP.

Basri, G., 1994, *Nigeria and Sharia: Aspirations and Apprehensions*. United Kingdom: Islamic Foundation.

Berger, S., 1982, (ed.), "Religion in West European politics", *Western European Politics*, Vol. 5, No. 2, April.

Bidmos, N. A., 1993, *Inter-Religious Dialogue: The Nigerian Experience*. Lagos: NP.

Brenner, L., 1993, *Muslim Identity and Social Change in Sub-Saharan Africa*. London: Hurst and Company.

Callaway, B. and L. Creevey, 1994, *The Heritage of Islam, Women, Religion, and Politics in West Africa*. London: Lynne Rienner.

CAN, 1989, *Leadership in Nigeria*. Enlightenment Series 1. Kaduna: CAN, Northern Zone.

CAN, 1990, *Do You Know...* Kaduna: CAN, Northern Zone.

Chafe, K. S., 1992, "Religious Movements and Democracy in Nigeria: Islam, Religious Movements in Nigeria in Historical Perspective", conference paper, Zimbabwe.

Dalhat, M. T., 1994, *Makircin rusa Musulumci*. Kaduna: NP.

Dambazau, M. L., 1993, *Politics and Religion in Nigeria*. Kano: NP.

De Hann, M. R., 1972, *Ye Must be Born Again*. Michigan: Discovery House.

Dobbelaere, K., 1981, "Secularization: A Multi-Dimensional Concept", *Current Sociology*, Vol. 29, No. 2, Spring.

Du Preez, P., 1980, *The Politics of Identity*. Oxford: Blackwell.

Elaigwu, J. L., 1977, "Christianity and Nation-Building: The Challenge of Faith in a Modernising Context", lecture at the Northern Baptist Convention.

El-Zakzaky, I., 1992, *Hayyi alal jihad*. NP.

Falaki, A. M., 1988,. "The Islamic Approach", in Sulaiman I., and S. Abdulkarim (eds.) *On the Political Future of Nigeria*. Zaria: Hudada.

Gumbi, A. M. S., 1991, *My Advice to Emirs and Chiefs*. Kaduna: NP.

Gumi, S. A., and S. A. Tsiga, 1992, *Where I Stand*. Ibadan: Spectrum Books.

Harma, L., 1994, "The Prophet and the Proletariat", *International and Socialism*, No. 64.

Ibrahim J. A., 1992, Memorandum by Heirs of Those Killed and Others Injured by the Armed Police and Soldiers on May 20, 1992 at Ikara and Zaria Local Government Area, submitted to Zangon Kataf (Market) Riot and Subsequent Riots Judicial Commission of Inquiry, June 23.

Ibrahim, J., 1989, "Politics and Religion in Nigeria: The Parameters of the 1987 Crisis in Kaduna State", *Review of African Political Economy*, No. 45/46.
Ibrahim, J., 1991, "Religion and political turbulence in Nigeria", *Journal of Modern African Studies*, No. 29(1).
Idris, I. K., et al., 1994, *Kungiyar Al-Zakzaky a mizani: Shia ko Musulunci?* Kano: Umma Computers.
Imam, A., 1971, "Shiga Musulunci", *Gaskiya Tafi Kwabo*, 23 ga Agusta.
Isiyaku, B., 1991, *The Kafanchan Carnage*. Kaduna: NP.
Iqbal, A. M., 1984, "The Islamization Syndrome", *Afkar Inquiry*, Vol. 1, No. 7.
Kane, O., 1994, "Izala: The Rise of Muslim Reformism in Northern Nigeria", in Marty, M., and R. S. Appleby (eds.) *Accounting for Fundamentalism*. Chicago: University of Chicago Press.
Kano, M. A., 1977, "Islamic Schism and Its Role in Muslim Education", International Islamic Seminar on Education, Kano, December 27, 1977-January 2, 1977.
Klapp, O. E., 1973, *Models of Social Order*. Ontario: National Press Book.
Kukah, M. H., 1992, "Zangon Kataf Averting Disaster", *The Guardian*, Thursday, July 2 and Friday July 3.
Kukah, M. H., 1993, "Gumi: An Outsiders View", *Nigerian Tribune*, Monday, February 15.
Kukah, M. H., 1996, *Religion and the Politics of Justice in Nigeria*. Lagos: Constitutional Rights Project.
Lemu, A. B., 1994, *Laxity, Moderation and Extremism in Islam*. Minna: Islamic Education Trust.
Liman, M. T. A., 1977, "Constitution and the Position of Religion in the New Draft", Islamic Foundation National Seminar on the Draft Constitution, Kano.
Madeley, J., 1982, "Politics and the Pulpit: The Case of Protestant Europe", in Sedit, B., "Religion in Western European Politics", *Western European Politics*, Vol. 5, No. 2, April.
Moinuddin, H., 1987, *The Charter of the Islamic Conference: The Legal and Economic Framework*. Oxford: Clarendon.
Munby, D. L., 1963, *The idea of a secular society and its significance for Christians*. Oxford.
Nuhu, H. 1993, "Religious Crisis in Nigeria: An Appraisal, Kano, (mimeo).
Obiayido, A., 1988, *Christ or Devil? The Corrupt Face of Christianity*. Enugu: Delta Publications.
Okeke, C., et al., 1990, "Christian Association of Nigeria (Sokoto State Headquarters Open Letter to the Sokoto State Governor)", *Sunday Tribune*, June 3.
Olukolae, O. A., 1988, *Arise and Build: The Role of Christians in Nation Building*. Lagos: NP.
Olupona, J. K., 1992, *Religion and Peace in Multi-Faith Nigeria*. Ile-Ife: NP.
Qaradawi, Y., 1991, *Islamic Awakening between Rejection and Extremism*. USA: MIT.
Sabiya, W. R., 1979, "The *Sharia* Controversy: Sharia or Jihad", *Journal of Centre of Development Studies*, Vol. 1, December.
Sanneh, L., 1997, "The Separation of Church and State", paper for CODESRIA/Emory University Workshop on Proselytisation in Africa, Dakar.
Sanni, I. K., 1990, "Excerpts from the Press Conference held by the National Council of Muslim Youth Organization (NACOMYO) at NUJ Light House, Victoria Island, Lagos on Monday, May 28. *Weekend Concord*, July 14.
Sulaiman, I. and S. Abdulkarim (eds.), 1988, *On the Political Future of Nigeria*. Zaria: Hudada.
Tela, I. A. H., 1994, *Shianci ba Musulunci ba ne*. Kano: NP.

Turaki, Y., 1993, *The British Colonial Legacy in Northern Nigeria: A Social Ethical Analysis of the Colonial and Post-Colonial Society and Politics in Nigeria*. Jos: Challenge Press.

Tyoden, S. G., 1993, *The Middle Belt in Nigerian Politics*. Jos: AHA Publishing House.

Ubah, A. and S. C. K. Oche, 1995, Memorandum submitted by the Christian Association of Nigeria (Kano State Branch) to the Committee investigating into the civil disturbances of May 30, Kano.

Umar, A. R., 1987, *Our Duty*. NP.

Usman, A. S. and I. K. Sanni, 1992, "The Kaduna State Religious Riot. The Facts Nigerians and the World at Large Must Know: A Rejoinder", *New Nigerian*, July 8.

Usman, Y. B., 1987, *The Manipulation of Religion in Nigeria, 1977–87*. Kaduna: Vanguard Publishers.

Ujo, A., 1994, *Citizenship in Nigerian States*. Kaduna: Passmark.

Wali, N. S., 1994, *Dimukuradiyya Wacce?* Kano: Islamic Foundation.

Yandaki, A. I., 1992, *Matsayin Izala a Nijeriya*. Kaduna: NP.

Yusuf, S., 1989, "The Portrayal of Islam in Some Early Nigerian Newspapers", *American Journal of Islamic Social Sciences*, Vol. 6, No. 2, December.

Newspapers and Magazines

African Concord, Vol. 6, No. 8, June 24, 1991.

African Concord, Vol. 7, No. 6, June 29, 1992.

African Guardian, Vol. 6, No. 15, April 22, 1991.

African Guardian, Vol. 8, No. 23, June 21, 1993.

Al-Madinah, Vol. 1, No. 1, September, 1995.

Citizen, Vol. 2, No. 20, May 13–20, 1991.

Citizen, Vol. 2, No. 19, May 6–13, 1991.

Citizen, Vol. 8, No. 43, October 21–28, 1991.

Citizen, Vol. 3, No. 21, May 25–31, 1992.

Citizen, Vol. 3 No. 22, June 1–7, 1992.

Citizen, No. 3, No. 24, June 15–21, 1992.

Citizen, No. 6, February 9–14, 1993.

Citizen, No. 12, March 23–28, 1993.

Free Nation, No. 2, December 1988.

Newbreed, May 14, 1990.

Newswatch, Vol. 13, No. 18, April 29, 1992.

NNIP, Vol. 1, No. 2, October 1992.

National Impression, Vol. 3, No. 2, 1992.

National Impression, Vol. 3, No. 3, 1993.

TSM, Vol. 5, No. 36, September 6, 1992.

TSM, Vol. 7, No. 18, May 8, 1994.

Today's Challenge, Nos. 2–5, 1992.

Today's Challenge, Nos. 1–4, 1993.

Today's Challenge, Nos. 2 and 3, 1995.

Today's Challenge, No. 2, 1996.

Tell, No. 2, June 1, 1992.

Tell, No. 35, August 26, 1996.

The News, March 8, 1993.
The News, April 4, 1994.
Viva, May 24, 1986.
The Guardian, March 22, 1986.
New Nigerian, December 24, 1986.
Sunday Tribune, February 23, 1986.
Democrat Weekly, August 12, 1989.
The Leader, May 30, 1987.
Fun Times, December, 1990.

Chapter 5

Transformation of Minority Identities in Post-Colonial Nigeria

Abdul Raufu Mustapha

Introduction

This chapter attempts to explore the transformations that have taken place in minority identities in Nigeria in the post-colonial period. A comprehensive effort in this regard would involve the study of many hundred ethnic minorities. What is attempted in this chapter is far less ambitious. A general sociopolitical overview will be followed by illustrations from three of the most problematic areas in the management of minority politics in Nigeria: Zangon Kataf in southern Kaduna State, Ogoni in the Niger Delta, and the Wukari/Takum area of Taraba State. The Kataf and Ogoni cases have received extensive attention elsewhere (cf. Saro-Wiwa, 1995; Naanen, 1995; Human Rights Watch/Africa, 1995; Mustapha, 1996). The issues involved in both cases will therefore be presented only in summary form, more attention being paid to the relatively obscure circumstances in Taraba State. Finally, against the background of developments within minority identities in Nigeria, the chapter will explore the place of identities in the sociopolitical crises of the African state system.

Ethnic Minority Identities: An Overview

Identities are constantly changing, particularly in periods of great socioeconomic flux. Like most other people who came into contact with colonialism, those now referred to as minority ethnic groups in Nigeria crystallised an ethnic consciousness in the early colonial period. It was much later, in the 1950s, that a 'minority' identity emerged, overlapping with their extant ethnic identity. The very notion of ethnic minorities gained currency in Nigerian political discourse from the immediate pre-independence constitutional negotiations of the early 1950s. These negotiations created three regional governments and also expanded the scope for electoral politics and the gradual transfer of powers. There were a number of assumptions that underlay these developments: that the dominant parties represented ethnic interests; that these ethnic interests would be dominant in their respective regions; and that those outside these ethnic blocs, but subject nonetheless to the regional governments, would be at a serious political and economic disadvantage. The smaller ethnic groups in each of the regions tended to see themselves as confronting a situation akin to a majoritarian dictatorship in which majority interests held sway, and the minorities had no say (Willink Commission, 1958). Ethnic minority identity developed, not necessarily as a question of numbers or cultural differences, but as a recognition of their 'powerlessness' in the face of ethnicised electoral politics.

The central deficit in this characterisation was power. As Ekeh (1994) points out, numerical strength and political power did not necessarily coincide in pre-colonial Nigeria. He draws attention to the political domination of the Sokoto Caliphate by the Fulani minority, the exploitation of the more numerous Ibibios of the interior by the Efik of Old Calabar, a similar exploitation of the Igbo of the hinterland by the eastern Ijaw (Izon), and the exploitation of the Urhobo by the Itsekiri. In each of these cases, Ekeh points out that special circumstances arose which placed the minority group in a position to dominate or exploit the majority group, often with disastrous consequences for their colonial and post-colonial relations. However, Ekeh's analysis makes no distinction between the Fulani aristocratic clans in power, and the vast majority of the nomadic and sedentary Fulani, who have no stake in power, and are themselves part of the governed. Secondly, he tends to conflate political domination, as in the sahelian Caliphate, with economic exploitation, as in Old Calabar. These qualifications notwithstanding, his central argument about power and numbers in pre-colonial Nigeria is quite valid.

In the constitutional/political dispensation that unfolded from 1951, numbers corresponded directly to political power. The minority ethnic groups that were so defined in post-1951 Nigeria are, therefore, largely political minorities, because in the unfolding electoral and regional politics, small numbers in one's constituency translated into powerlessness. In most, but not all cases, issues of culture, history or sociopolitical development played no part in the characterisation.

The response of the minorities to their situation in the period 1951–1983 was basically three-pronged, each impacting on the elaboration of minority identities. In the first place, some minority groups ganged up to demand a regional government of their own. One such grouping was the COR (Calabar, Ogoja and Rivers) movement, which sought to extricate the minority groups in those provinces from the perceived clutches of the Igbo-dominated Eastern Regional government. Recognition of a common circumstance had forced a unity of purpose among some of the groups. Particularist identities now overlapped with the newly constructed identity of being minorities in a similar boat. An identity that was constructed and imposed by circumstances beyond their control was now appropriated in their response to the emerging political situation.

Secondly, failing to get new regions of their own, the ethnic minorities sought to limit the powers of regional governments over their affairs. They sought to do this by arguing for a stronger central government which would ameliorate regional excesses. In particular, the minorities agitated for a centralised police force (Willink Commission, 1958). To a large extent, minority groups have tended to develop a more abiding faith in the Nigerian nation-state, relative to their compatriots from the majority groups of Igbo, Hausa and Yoruba. In the centrifugal crises of 1966–67, minority groups virtually stood alone in consistently defending the integrity of the Nigerian nation-state. And the concentration of power at the centre after 1970 had the active support of many bureaucrats from minority backgrounds.

The third response of the minorities was to form political alliances with dominant political parties in other regions, in order to secure a modicum of protection from their 'own' regional governments and governing parties. Minority parties such as the Bornu Youth Movement, the Benin Delta People's Party, the Niger Delta Congress and Middle Belt People's Party emerged in this context (Okpu, 1977). This strategy was to implicate the minorities in the struggle over power-sharing and ascendancy at the centre between the three dominant groups and their political parties. In many instances, minority politics, governed as it was by the search for access, became mere extensions of the politics of the majority parties to which particular minorities were allied. Amongst the political class in the minority areas, there emerged the odd admixture of both oppositional and clientalistic strands.

Of course, the above tendencies were not the only ones at work in the development of minority identities in this period. The creation of states from 1967, ostensibly to meet minority demands, altered minority attitudes in two ways. Firstly, some minority groups now found themselves in control of new states, often with some other minorities subjected to the control of such state governments. This led to the emergence of statism or state consciousness in some cases, and in others, to the development of political squabbles between what are now 'majority minorities' on the one hand, and 'minority minorities' on the other. Some of the solidarity built up under such organisations as the COR State Movement and the Middle Belt Congress started to collapse.

The second way in which the creation of states affected minority consciousness was that it became apparent that state creation, very much like the constitutional provisions guaranteeing fundamental human rights in the 1951–1966 period, could not safeguard minority interests. Minority agitators for state creation had assumed that states would be created for minorities alone, given the fact that the majorities already had political control of some governments. In the event, states were created for both majorities and minorities, with majority interests still dominant in most states. And these states were created in an era of increased political and economic concentration of powers at the centre. The minorities realised that they had acquired access to and even control of state governments precisely when power had shifted elsewhere. The problems surrounding state creation not only split minority solidarity in many cases, they also introduced a heightened consciousness of the federal centre, intensified struggle for access to that centre, and an increasingly acrimonious relationship between that centre and some minority groups, particularly those from the oil-producing areas of the Niger Delta.

Fiscal centralisation meant federal control of revenue from oil, a resource found largely in southern minority areas. In pre-centralisation years, regions had fiscal control over their agrarian and mineral resources. The multiplication of demands for state creation arose partly because political entrepreneurs from both majority and minority groups saw the creation of a state under their control as the surest way to plug directly into the centralised national purse. Contractors, civil servants and local politicians collude to dredge up real or perceived differences in order to justify particular claims to new states and central patronage. Minority groups in the north continue to play along with this distributive logic. On the other hand, the southern minorities have become increasingly resentful, claiming that their God-given resources have been commandeered by others.

Another development which affected minority identities was the process of class formation. The political elite which spearheaded agitation in minority areas from the 1930s and against minority status from the 1950s was made up largely of priests, teachers and clerks. Education and familiarity with western modes of thought were the determinant factors in elite status. By the 1980s, the elite in many minority areas had greatly expanded and now included young professionals such as lawyers, doctors, and a sprinkling of businessmen. Increasingly, elite status is determined not just by education, but also by wealth and life-style. These younger elements of the minority elite did not have the political connections of the older elite and were more prone to suffer the impact of competition for jobs, contracts and other resources at the national level. They were, therefore, less likely to be clientalist in their orientation; indeed, many became increasingly confrontational in their quest for a 'fairer' share of political and economic resources. Even by the mid-1960s, restive young men from the minority ethnic groups were beginning to side-step their political associations and embark on 'direct action' to agitate for their interests (Okpu, 1977:136).

On the whole, economic and political change, including economic crisis and the military centralisation of power, have tended to alter the parameters of political and economic advantages. In turn, these changes have redefined perceptions of minority interests and identity, leading to the frantic reformulation of that identity and the repositioning of various groups in the political terrain to take advantage of particular shifts, or to shield themselves from potentially negative consequences. I argue that the result is hardly the realisation of legitimate minority claims, but the fragmentation and destabilisation of the entire political process.

Illustrations of Changing Identities: Zangon Kataf, Ogoni and Taraba

Some of the general points made in the preceding section can be further elaborated in the illustrative cases discussed here. The central objective is not just to pin-point changes in minority identities, but to seek to explain such transformations. These explanations are presented against the background of the enormous transformations of the Nigerian state and economy since 1970. While these latter changes are not directly addressed, relevant developments are occasionally referred to.

Zangon Kataf: The Historicity and Continuity in Minority Identity

Zangon Kataf falls within a region in central Nigeria which has become prone to inter-communal clashes over land and other agricultural resources. There were the Kasuwan Magani riots in 1980/1, the Gure/Kahugu riots in Saminaka Local Government Area in 1984, the Lere riots in 1986, and the Kafanchan riots in 1987. The dynamic of communal blood-letting in this region has come to be epitomised in the national consciousness by the very bloody confrontations in Zangon Kataf in February and May 1992. The central problem here is not just the 'pure' expression of the proverbial majority/minority divide, but the manner in which notions of history, citizenship and justice are fiercely contested by neighbouring communities to a point where there is little common ground left for conciliation and compromise (Mustapha, 1994).

Zangon Kataf is a Hausa settlement (*zango*) within a territory occupied by the Kataf, a minority ethnic group in north-central Nigeria. The original town was established as a trading post for Hausa merchants en route to the Niger Basin in the early part of the 16th century. While the Hausa of Zangon Kataf and the Kataf tribal polity established economic and commercial relations, they had little in the way of social relations, Zangon Kataf being a wholly Hausa settlement. The Hausa settlement was also politically autonomous. By the end of the 18th century, the settlement became subordinated to Kauru, a larger Hausa settlement within the territory of another ethnic minority in the same region, the Ruruma. Early in the 19th century, Kauru itself became subordinated to Zaria, one of the major Hausa states that constituted the Sokoto Caliphate.

For much of the 19th century, the minority ethnic groups south of Zaria, the Kataf included, were raided for slaves to supply the domestic needs of the Sokoto Caliphate, and for export on both the trans-Saharan and the trans-Atlantic slave routes. From the Kataf point of view, the Hausa community of Zangon Kataf were seen as distinct from the Hausa slave raiders from Zaria. With the imposition of British colonial rule at the turn of the 20th century, however, the Kataf polity was subordinated to the Emir of Zaria, under Lugard's policy of Indirect Rule. Kataf territory became Katuka District of Zaria Emirate. In 1902, 1904, 1905 and 1907 the Kataf attacked Zangon Kataf, allegedly for colluding with the British and the Hausa Emirate of Zaria in their designs to subjugate the Kataf. The colonial army was called in to suppress the attacks. Subsequently, Zangon Kataf town was moved to its present location around 1915. For much of the 20th century, especially between 1920 and 1950, there has been a steady influx of Hausa people to Zangon Kataf, primarily from the Emirates of Zaria, Kano, Katsina and Bauchi.

The Zangon Kataf crises started over the construction of a new market by the Local Government Authority. Disagreement between some members of both Kataf and Hausa communities over the issue led to clashes early in February 1992, resulting in a number of fatalities. From the 15 to 17 May 1992, fresh rioting erupted in Zangon Kataf. The immediate unfolding of the May riot has become the subject of intense controversy as each community tries to justify its conduct. There are divergent positions as to who started the killings. There is no doubt, however, that most of the victims were the Hausa of Zangon Kataf. There is evidence to suggest that at least 1,536 Hausas were killed in Zangon Kataf. Most of the houses in the town were razed to the ground and Hausa household property valued at N29,173,850 destroyed. It has also been estimated that about 71 motor vehicles and 25 motor cycles and bicycles were also destroyed. These events precipitated rioting in other parts of Kaduna State; large-scale rioting broke out in Kaduna, Zaria, Ikara, and Kauru. Kaduna is the state capital, while Zaria and Ikara constitute the Hausa heartland of the State. In Kaduna and Zaria, hundreds of lives were lost, either in the rioting, or in police/military actions that followed. Seven people were reportedly shot dead by the police in Ikara (Mustapha, 1994).

In the arguments which the Kataf put forward to justify their conduct during the crises, we begin to see elements of continuity and transformation in their identity. They argue that the Kataf have historically welcomed strangers into their midst. These strangers were given clan/communal lands to cultivate but there was no alienation of the land from the original household, lineage or clan, as the case may be. Individual ownership was not part of the tribal land tenure. Strangers were often absorbed into Kataf society, especially the *Netzit* (Our People) who are the other minority ethnic groups of the region, particularly from southern Kaduna State and parts of Plateau

State. The Kataf argument goes on to suggest that when the Hausa merchants came to the Kataf polity in the 16th century, they were given land to build their settlement but the rights of ownership over the land remained with the Kataf clans. A mark of this continued ownership, consistent with their traditional tenure system, was their abiding right to harvest the tree crops on the land which they had given to strangers to cultivate. Since most of the Hausa immigrants were traders or craftsmen, they rarely had need of farmland.

Though both communities remained politically and culturally distinct, there was little conflict between them, even when slave raiders from Zaria Emirate launched attacks on the Kataf. The problem started, the Kataf claim, from the imposition of British colonial rule in the early 20th century. While the Emir of Zaria, for regional geo-political reasons succumbed to colonial imposition without a fight, the Kataf forcefully resisted colonial domination. Against this background, the Kataf were regarded by the British as 'ungovernable'. Given their lack of a centralised state structure and their traditional religion, they were regarded as 'uncivilised pagans' who were incapable of self-governance. Furthermore, racist colonial anthropology characterized the Kataf as inferior to the lighter-skinned Fulani elite of the Emirates, who were not only monotheists but had also built up a large empire, the Sokoto Caliphate. The Kataf claim that the British were therefore favourably disposed to accept the Zaria claim that the Kataf polity had been 'conquered' by Zaria in pre-colonial times. As far as they were concerned, Zaria, through Kauru, might lay claim to the political allegiance of the Hausa community of Zangon Kataf but that had nothing to do with the political autonomy of the Kataf or their ownership of the land on which the town stood.

With the loss of their traditional political system based on clans and their subjugation to an 'alien' authority, the Kataf claim that they became victims of a series of injustices. They were excluded from the district administration, which became a wholly Hausa affair, right down to the messengers. They were also subjected to various indignities by the 'alien' local administration: cultural denigration by being derogatorily referred to as *arna* (non-Muslims or pagans) and *kabila* (non-Hausa), tyrannical excesses by the Emir's Native Police (*dogarai*), and subjugation to the unsympathetic arbitrariness of the Emir's Alkali courts, which dispensed a form of law based on Islamic principles which were alien to the Kataf. They also complained of excessive taxation, confiscation of their goods for failure to pay, and exclusion from the markets built with Kataf forced labour. They claimed that the ordeal of forced labour was not extended to the Hausas of Zangon Kataf.

Above all else, the Kataf complained that the colonial and local administrations encouraged the influx of Hausa settlers to the area, leading to the forcible transfer of Kataf farmlands to new Hausa immigrants. The emergence of large-scale farming in the 1970s intensified this process through the agency of various state administrations. At the same time, the intensification of development projects in the country from the 1970s, fuelled by oil-boom petro-dollars also increased contestation over land rights, as individuals and groups sought to receive the compensation paid by the state for land acquired.

The Kataf claim that they protested their situation through numerous petitions to the colonial administration, often with the assistance of Christian missionaries who had gained a foothold in the area. After a riot by the Kataf in 1933, and again in 1946, they agitated for the formation of an Independent Tribal Council composed of 'indigenous'—that is Kataf— representatives. These demands were not met, even though they had the support of some colonial administrators. After another episode of rioting in 1953, the principle of including some Kataf in the District Council was accepted but it was made clear that the district still remained under the Emir. As a result, a few Kataf got into the administration, especially at the Village Head level. The agitation for an Independent Tribal Council continued. Kataf agitation for an 'indigenous' District Head subsequently led, in 1967, to the transfer of the *Sarkin Yakin Zazzau* from the District and his replacement by the first 'indigenous' (Kataf) District Head, Bala Dauke Gora. He was also conferred with the traditional Zaria title of *Kuyambannan Zazzau*. Considering that the emirate officials from Zaria defined 'indigenousness' in the districts of southern Kaduna to include the Hausa and Fulani communities of the area and continued to appoint the same as 'indigenous' officials, the Kataf, along with other minority ethnic groups in the area, reverted to their old demand for their own independent, 'traditional', chiefdoms in 1974.

The 1976 Local Government Reform created the possibility for the minority ethnic groups of southern Kaduna State, who nevertheless constituted a huge majority over the Hausa-Fulani communities in the area, to vote in their own people as chairmen of the local government councils. However, in their view, this development did not address their problem as the elected local government chairmen were incorporated into the Zaria Emirate Council as subordinates of the Emir. Furthermore, all District and Village Heads, though employees of, and paid by, the local government, continued to be appointed by, and reported directly to, the Emir of Zaria. Though Kataf men were now both Local Government Chairman and District Head, Kataf disaffection continued to simmer, fuelled by what they regard as their continued subordination to Zaria, and the alleged nepotistic appointment of the minority, but now 'allegedly indigenous', Hausa-Fulani elements from the southern Kaduna area to political and other offices in the state and federal governments as 'representatives' of the people of the area. They formed the view that elements of the local Hausa-Fulani communities were using their wider connections within the Nigerian state system and the society in general to continue their effective domination of the southern Kaduna minority groups. A Kataf Chiefdom was created in 1996. However, tensions rose again in late 1996, when some Kataf Christians protested the building of a mosque by the Hausa community.

This Kataf version of events is hotly disputed by the Hausa community of Zangon Kataf (Mustapha, 1994). Nevertheless, it illustrates how exclusivity in inter-group relations during the pre-colonial era can be carried on into the post-colonial period. Though identities are constantly changing, some elements of that can actually remain constant over a long period of time. Secondly, the colonial impact was to turn exclusivity into open hostility. Thirdly, the series of crises in southern Kaduna State from about 1980 reflect, not just the history of animosity between these minority communities and their guest Hausa communities, but also socio-economic pressures deriving from land alienation and the extension of 'development'. At the cross-roads of these historical and contemporary tensions lies a bitter conflict over notions of citizenship, group and individual rights, and justice (Mustapha, 1994).

For the Kataf, citizenship is defined by autochthony, not only to emphasise Kataf 'traditional' qualities such as membership of clans but also to exclude the Hausa-Fulani immigrants. On their part, the Hausa of Zangon Kataf emphasise residency as a criteria for citizenship. This is not just a matter of expediency, for it also conforms to Hausa values and historical practices. Similarly, Kataf notions of rights emphasise the group rights of the land-holding lineages, to the total exclusion of the individual rights of the immigrants. On the other hand, and consistent with their land tenure practices, the Hausa tend to emphasise individual rights. Justice for the Kataf is the correction of *historical* injustices; for the Hausa it is *criminal* justice, aimed at punishing those who have broken the laws during the riots. It is not clear to what extent these issues are fought over *within* the Kataf community but, on the whole, Kataf identity has evolved largely as a negative reaction to the continued presence of the Hausa community in its midst.

But the evolution of Kataf identity is not entirely negative. As noted earlier, there is the concept of *Netzit* (Our People), through which the Kataf seek to make common cause with other groups in southern Kaduna and Plateau States. These groups have very similar historical, cultural, political and demographic characteristics but the concept of 'our people' is almost certainly a development of the colonial era and expresses not just the similarities in the circumstances of these peoples but also their common opposition to being subjugated to the Hausa-Fulani Emirates. The evolution of Kataf identity expresses not just long-standing animosities, but also fits neatly into the regionally based 'majority/minority' divide that emerged in the terminal colonial period. Despite later transformations in Kataf identity such as the increasing identification with Christianity, the basic elements of Kataf identity suggest that the late colonial construction of majority/minority is of continuing relevance.

Ogoni: Changing State/Minority Relations

With the imposition of formal colonial rule, the economic exploitation of the Igbo in the hinterland by the eastern Ijaw and the Efik of Old Calabar came to an end. This exploitation had been based on an advantageous position on the trade routes, and better access to firearms. With formal colonisation, ethnic identities crystallised. With the constitutional and electoral developments of the 1950s, the smaller ethnic groups were transformed into 'minorities'; a point dramatically made by the replacement of Eyo Ita, of Efik 'minority' background, by Nnamdi Azikiwe, an Igbo, as head of the regional government. Thenceforth, the eastern minorities protested real or imagined domination (Willink Commission, 1958) and sought to protect themselves through alliance with the ruling parties of the other regions. During the Civil War, 1967–1970, the eastern minorities were firmly on the federal side. The favourable disposition of many eastern minorities towards the central government persisted till the mid-1980s.

The causes of the collapse in confidence are traceable not to direct state/minority relations *per se* but to the wider dynamics of Nigerian politics and economy which gradually, but radically, altered state/minority relations, particularly in the Niger Delta. First, state creation, a crucial panacea in minority eyes right up to 1967, did not solve the problem of minority marginalisation. The 'majority' three groups continued to control more states and to benefit enormously from the distributional logic of federal governance. The more the minorities agitated for state creation, the more the status quo was maintained by the creation of states in both majority and minority areas. Consequently, minority groups started making radical demands for the restructuring of the entire federation along confederate ethnic lines.

Second, minority groups, particularly from the Niger Delta agitated against the revenue allocation formula which lay at the heart of distributional politics. Prior to the creation of states, the principal criterion for revenue allocation was the principle of derivation. In the process of concentrating economic powers on the centre, the principle of derivation was dropped. This change occurred precisely at the point when oil, found largely in southern minority areas, became the mainstay of the national economy. The minorities complained that they got only 3 per cent of the wealth from their area, the bulk going to the political constituencies of the majority groups. Minority agitation led to the increase of their share to 13 per cent, but this is a far cry from the 50 per cent many minority organisations were agitating for. Minority demands have therefore been widening to include demands for 'self-determination' so that they could control their land and resources. Coupled to this particular demand was the minority complaint that while their resources were being used to develop other parts of the country, their own areas were left without basic social amenities and subjected to environmental pollution.

Third, the minorities clamoured for power sharing, complaining that political and administrative offices were monopolised by the majority groups, particularly the Hausa-Fulani and the Yoruba. Many minority organisations, such as the Ika Group, the Akwa Ibom Emancipation Group, the Ijaw Ethnic Nationality Rights Protection Organisation, the Movement for the Survival of Ogoni People (MOSOP), and the Ukwani Forum agitated for the rotation of political offices between ethnically defined zones, and a radical restructuring of the central government and army along confederate lines (Okwuosa, *et al.*, 1994).

The central government which had been seen as an ally up to the early 1980s was now seen as the major blockage of the realisation of minority interests. The numerous anti-Hausa agitations of the northern minorities in the Middle Belt, pointed out in the Zangon Kataf case, were matched, amongst the southern minorities, by a broad anti-central government agitation. Also attacked were multinational oil companies like Shell, and the elites of the majority groups, particularly the Hausa-Fulani and, to a lesser extent, the Yoruba. We can see therefore that minority agitation increased amongst both the northern and southern minorities in the 1980s, but their respective targets and demands were different.

By the early 1990s, many southern minority groups were thoroughly disaffected, with the consequent radicalisation of their organisations. Separatist confederate demands, coupled with direct action against the multinational companies became more pronounced. The first major confrontation took place in Umuechem in October 1990, and involved a confrontation between the youth of the community and staff of Shell. The Nigerian army was called in on Shell's behalf, leading to the sacking of the Umuechem community with many fatalities, including the community leader. A seething resentment against the federal government gradually broke into the open. Also in October 1990, MOSOP was formed, and adopted the Ogoni Bill of Rights which called for a halt to environmental degradation and the control of Ogoni resources by the Ogoni. When the government did not respond to the Bill of Rights, the Ogoni internationalised their struggle through the Unrepresented Nations and People's Organisation (UNPO), and made direct demands on the oil companies for compensation. In 1993, mass demonstrations were carried out and a section of the MOSOP leadership demanded that the Ogoni boycott the 1993 presidential elections. This amounted to a repudiation of the legitimacy of the centre (Mustapha, 1996).

At this point, differences within the MOSOP leadership emerged around the structure and strategies of the organisation. The conservative faction, representing an older generation used to bargaining for political offices at the centre 'on behalf of their people', disagreed with the proposition that MOSOP should be an umbrella organisation for other Ogoni organisations: National Youth Council of Ogoni People (NYCOP), Federation of Ogoni Women Association (FOWA), Council of Ogoni Traditional Rulers (COTRA),

Ogoni Teachers Union (OTU), and Council of Ogoni Churches (COC). The logic behind this organisational restructuring was the claim that the conservative faction of MOSOP leadership often took decisions without follow-up action aimed at implementation (Saro-Wiwa, 1995). This re-organisation was, therefore, aimed at challenging ineffective leadership by instilling 'organisational discipline'. As far as the conservative faction was concerned, the suggested reorganisation was a ploy to strengthen the hand of the radical faction under the leadership led by Ken Saro-Wiwa.

They accused Saro-Wiwa of seeking to gain total control of the organisation and of instigating his youthful supporters to undertake 'militant action' against those members of the MOSOP leadership and the entire Ogoni elite who posed a challenge to his ambitions. The division came to a head over the question of boycotting the 1993 elections and the conservative faction withdrew from MOSOP. In subsequent developments, four Ogoni chiefs were murdered, allegedly by NYCOP militants instigated by Saro-Wiwa. Saro-Wiwa and eight others were subsequently 'tried' and executed under questionable circumstances (Mustapha, forthcoming). Despite state repression, the situation in Ogoni is far from resolved. About 50,000 Ogoni were estimated to have fled continued repression in Nigeria through the neighbouring Benin Republic. In mid-1997, the refugee camp still had 2,500 persons.

In the Ogoni case, we can discern a number of strands in the evolution of southern minority identity. Unlike in the case of the northern minorities, where agitation was largely directed against a majority group, the Hausa-Fulani, the southern minorities directed their agitation against a central government that was once seen as an ally. Secondly, while northern minorities tended to make demands for 'traditional' issues, such as the restoration or creation of their own autonomous chiefdoms, southern minorities tended to call the very foundation of the centralised military state into question by demanding a confederation and the rotation of state offices. Southern minority identity was being shaped, not so much by the demand for cultural autonomy as is the case with the northern minorities, but by the demand for political, economic and administrative autonomy. They were not so much asserting their distinctness, but demanding political recognition and expression of that distinctness. Their demands therefore related directly to what it meant to be a 'Nigerian'. By changing the current definition of what it meant to be a Nigerian, loaded as that definition is with inequalities and iniquities, they hoped to eradicate their 'minority' status. The subsequent confrontation with the centralised state is producing a radicalised, separatist identity amongst the southern minorities. The ideal, far from realised, of a common citizenship is increasingly called into question and challenged.

At stake is not just the notion of 'Nigerianness', but also that of 'Ogoniness'. In the course of the agitation for Ogoni rights the MOSOP leadership was divided over three crucial issues. The first conflict was over the Ogoni strategy within national politics. While the conservative faction was indeed committed to the cause, many of its members were evidently wedded to the clientalist politics of the Nigerian state. On the other hand, the radical faction adopted a stance of non-cooperation, bordering on confrontation, with the state. The second conflict, closely related to the first, was the question of who would lead the movement and in what direction? Here, ideological and political disagreements were mingled with personal ambitions and personality conflicts (Mustapha, forthcoming). Thirdly, generational rivalries and differential experiences tended to pit the clientalists against the younger professionals. These conflicts became reflected in the construction of Ogoni identity as the clientalists were dubbed 'vultures' parasitizing on the Ogoni plight, while the radicals were in turn attacked as 'violence-prone thugs' intent on promoting their political careers even if it meant the physical elimination of their opponents. A leading conservative likened Saro-Wiwa to "Stalin who eliminated all his colleagues as soon as he took over" (FGN, n.d). Each side presented itself as the 'authentic' voice of the Ogoni and the rival faction as 'illegitimate'. The conservatives were accused of opportunism in their relations with the central government. On the other hand, Saro-Wiwa was portrayed as being in a diabolical alliance with international financiers intent on using the Ogoni case as a pretext for destabilising Nigeria. These conflicting perspectives and definitions were often fought out in newspaper advertisements and press releases.

The federal government has become to the Ogoni, what Europe is to the contemporary Tory Party in Britain. Consequently, Ogoni identity became bifurcated and contested, creating a fertile ground for state intervention. Interestingly, the Ogoni have about four dialects or languages and five kingdoms—Babbe, Gokana, Tai, Nyo-Khana and Ken-Khana. But the overtly politicised nature of contemporary 'Ogoniness' dictated that these linguistic and historical political divergences within the Ogoni had little relevance to the struggle between the warring factions. Nevertheless, the Ogoni struggle had the impact of emphasizing their distinctiveness, making it possible for the state to stir up anti-Ogoni sentiments within other neighbouring minority groups.

Taraba: Minority against Minority

In the 1950s, after the minority groups woke up to the potential and real consequences of their minority status, there was a sense of common purpose amongst the minority groups of each region, expressed in romanticised notions of the Middle Belt movement in the north, the COR movement in the east, and the Midwest State movement in the west. Opinions were not always united across the board, but sufficient numbers of minority groups were committed to these movements to give them credibility. In the late 1970s, these pan-minority sentiments continued to find expression in Club

19, a political grouping formed with the purpose of bringing a 'majority of minorities' into power at the federal level. Even as late as 1993, a pro-Babangida group was formed, calling itself the Fourth Force, and claiming to represent the minorities across the country. It claimed that the minorities put together were more than the three majority groups and therefore had a duty to unite and dictate the political fortunes of the country. However, much of the common ground built around a shared minority identity has been destroyed over the years, partly by the creation of states and the emergence of statism and also by minority competition in some states. General political and economic developments in the country have tended to exacerbate these divisive trends. As a result, divisive issues have gained prominence, pitting minority group against minority group. We must therefore add the minority/minority divide to the prior majority/minority divide. The ways in which these developments evolved in the transformation of identities is examined in the bloody three-cornered fight in Taraba State between the Jukun, the Tiv, the Kuteb and the Chamba.

In 1991, what amounted to a civil war broke out in the Wukari/Takum areas of Taraba State. For clarity, these conflicts should be disaggregated into the Wukari crisis which raged between 1991–92, and the Takum crisis which took place between 1992–93. At the root of both crises were pre-colonial and colonial animosities tightly linked to contemporary conflicts over political and administrative offices and agricultural resources. The Zangon Kataf case can be seen to represent the continued resilience of historical animosities, shrouded in competing contemporary claims to political, commercial and agricultural resources. And the Ogoni case can be seen as a reaction to centralizing and monopolistic developments within the nation-state. The Taraba case represents a mixture of both tendencies. The 'Hausa factor' was also present in Taraba.

The Wukari Crisis

Between 1991 and 1992, large-scale fighting involving the use of sophisticated weapons took place around the Jukun paramount town of Wukari. The principal protagonists were the Jukun and the Tiv. Others such as the Kuteb, Chamba and 'Hausa' were subsequently dragged in to a lesser degree. The 'Hausa' of Wukari deserve a brief comment: their lingua franca is Hausa though a large number of them actually come from non-Hausa areas such as Borno. Unconfirmed, but realistic, estimates suggest that about 5,000 Jukun and 15,000 Tiv lost their lives in the course of the crisis. In all, about 53 villages with an estimated population of 250,000 inhabitants were razed to the ground and the population dispersed. Farm stock and farms were burnt.

The historical setting for the crisis started in the 1910s, when the colonial administration allowed or encouraged the Tiv to migrate in large numbers into areas that are regarded as Jukun territory. Colonial policy, reflecting the idiosyncratic attitudes of various officials on the ground, had quite contradictory effects. Right at the beginning of Indirect Rule, Palmer formed the opinion that the Tiv, who did not have a centralised state system, should be brought under the *Aku Uka* of Wukari, the paramount head of the Jukun. He argued that Jukun influence extended into Tiv territory under the Kwararafa Empire which was noted for its military exploits. The Tiv were clearly cast as an 'inferior' group to the Jukun. Consequently, Tiv areas such as Katsina Ala, Zaki Biam and parts of Kwande were administered under Wukari Division. It was only in 1926 that a Tiv Division was created bringing most of the Tiv areas under a common administration. Even then, some areas remained under Wukari. These colonial boundary adjustments have continued to create confusion as to who belongs or belonged to where and the nature of their rights in such areas.

A second strand in colonial policy was to encourage the Tiv to migrate into Wukari Division itself. The Tiv were not only a large group, their population also expanded much faster than those of their neighbours. In some areas in Tiv territory, particularly in Kwande and Vandekya to the south, population pressure was acute, rising around 1937 to 190 persons per square mile. By 1952, some areas in Shangev were reported to have over 600 persons per square mile (NAK/Makprof, 4545). This pressure on the land was accentuated by the Tiv farming system of slash and burn and shifting cultivation. The combination of population pressure and farming system led the Tiv to expand into the territory of their neighbours in search of fresh, fertile land. Moves to introduce more sustainable farming methods failed and by 1948, some colonial officials were claiming that:

Tiv expansion is not due to land hunger or to the results of uneconomic methods of farming but to a 'traditional code demanding expansive advance in a predetermined direction'. Such a demand for 'lebensraum' and the population movements in which it results are difficult to control... (NAK/Makprof, 4545).

The expansion of the Tiv into Idoma territory to the south-west and Ogoja territory to the south was particularly resisted, leading the colonial administration to encourage Tiv migration "in the Northerly and Easterly directions" (NAK/SNP, 17/9). Indeed by 1914, a 'Munshi Wall' (Munshi was the colonial name for the Tiv) had been erected to the south and west. The decision to encourage Tiv migration into Jukun territory reflected a reversal of colonial perceptions of both groups. The 'superior' Jukun, with their history of a centralised state, were not expanding, economically and demographically, as the 'inferior' Tiv. Since this had a direct bearing on the capacity of the colonial state to raise tax revenue, official perceptions of both groups changed. Wukari was now described as having a 'decaying population', while the Tiv were:

superior in every way to all the peoples by which it is surrounded—totals now about 500,000 souls—and has a percentage of about 40 children per 100 of the population. The food producing capacity of the tribe is perhaps the greatest per head of population of any tribe in Nigeria—but it is clear that unless provision is made for their expansion, the land available for them now will not continue to support them... (NAK/Makprof, 2403).

The 'hard-working' Tiv were therefore encouraged to move into the territory of the 'lazy' Jukun and the other groups to the east and north. Tiv settlements were established in such areas as Wukari, Muri, Shendam, Lafia and Wamba Divisions. By the 1990s, the Tiv formed an absolute majority of the entire population of Wukari Local Government. Not only were the 'strangers' more wealthy than their 'hosts', they now had the population base, in a one-person-one-vote ethnicised electoral setting, to gain political ascendancy.

The conflict over Tiv expansionism and over agricultural resources simmered for many decades, reaching a new level in 1979, when Tiv candidates started winning elections in the area. In that year, Tiv candidates from Wukari Local Government were voted into the Gongola State House of Assembly; Dr. Agbide, a Tiv, even became a Commissioner in the Gongola State government. With the creation of Taraba State from Gongola and the consequent narrowing of the electoral base, the political stakes were raised. The first skirmish occurred in 1987 when the Babangida administration initiated local government elections on a non-party basis. Danladi Yakubu, a Hausa 'stranger' was elected chairman of Wukari Local Government to the chagrin of the Jukun who were clearly in an electoral minority, albeit in what they regarded as 'their' home territory. The Jukun blamed the Tiv for supporting the Hausa candidate. The whole affair was put down to a Tiv/Hausa conspiracy against the Jukun. The Jukun and the Hausa had been political allies in the First Republic (in the NPC) and the Second Republic (in the NPN). But the fragmentation of established political networks since the military intervention of 1983 saw the collapse of the Jukun/Hausa alliance and the emergence of a Tiv/Hausa alliance.

With the approach of gubernatorial elections in the newly created Taraba State in 1991, matters came to a head. Fearing a Tiv 'take-over' of the new state, the Jukun resorted to 'ethnic cleansing'. The Jukun elite was however careful to state its case in more 'civilized' terms. They accused the Tiv of lawlessness in occupying Jukun lands and establishing bogus chieftaincies over the same. Secondly, they accused the Tiv of 'disloyalty' to a place where many of them had lived for generations. They claimed that the Tiv preferred to pay their tax in the predominantly Tiv Benue State, whilst living in Taraba. Tiv attachments to their natal home base—for burials and weddings etc.—were held up as justifying the assertion that they were not really 'Tarabans'. On their part, the Tiv denied that they were recent migrants, claiming that they had been in Muri Province since the early colonial period.

They asserted their rights to the land, both as early members of the previous administrative unit, and as 'Nigerians'.

It is clear, however, that Tiv nationalism had a hand in the whole affair, particularly after the Tiv elite in Benue mobilised men and materials to come to the aid of their brethren in Taraba. It is suggested in some quarters that the Tiv elite wanted to present their group as the 'largest minority group in Nigeria', with political presence—and clout—in Benue, Taraba, Nasarawa, Plateau, Kogi and Cross River States. As for the 'Hausa', they accused the Jukun of belligerence towards 'outsiders' as witnessed in the attack on the Igbos in Wukari in the 1980s. Some 'Hausa' were also killed in 1991.

Though the Wukari crisis was presented as a clash over land resources, the real stakes—hardly commented upon in the open—were political. At issue was the question of who was 'indigenous' to the area and therefore had prior political rights in the new Taraba State. New political and administrative changes gave new meaning to demographic trends, forcing the issue of identity high on the political agenda. This was an issue which pit minority against minority. This did not mean, however, that minority/ majority issues were absent even in Taraba. Federal government response to the mayhem in Taraba was so slow in coming, suggesting that the area being a 'minority' area, no real stakes were involved. Secondly, in Zangon Kataf where Hausa interests were directly involved, government resources were poured in to rehabilitate the area and prison sentences were handed out to alleged instigators and perpetrators of the killings, mostly Kataf. In Wukari and Takum, however, no trials were held despite virtually three years of carnage. And no government resources were made available for reconstruction. The minorities may be fighting for political supremacy in circumscribed political spaces, but they have yet to dent the suffocating dominance of majority interests. When the federal government finally stepped in, it sent in troops to restore law and order, and brokered a deal requiring the Tiv to register their land interests with the local government authority. The underlying demographic and political issues remain unresolved.

The Takum Crisis

In the Takum crisis, there is the total fragmentation of minority identity for reasons related to the Wukari crisis. This crisis resulted in killings and the destruction of property in 1992 and 1993, but the scale and casualties were much less compared to the Wukari crisis. In 1992, a Chamba/Jukun group opened fire with automatic rifles on the Kuteb annual cultural festival, the *kuchicheb*, killing about six people. In the rash of fighting that took place afterwards, two Kuteb and five Chamba villages were destroyed with the loss of many lives. In the 1993 version of the same ceremony, more killings took place, but these were largely restricted to outlying rural areas. During the mayhem, the crisis was presented as an extension of the Wukari crisis.

The Kuteb were seen as allies of the Tiv/Hausa, while the Jukun were seen as allies of the Chamba. No doubt, there was some element of justification for these perceptions, but the reality was more complex. The main fight was between the Chamba and the Kuteb, with passive or active alliances being struck with other groups; the Kuteb refused to support the Jukun attack on the Tiv, forcing the Jukun to sympathise with the Chamba. Meanwhile, Kuteb/Tiv relations remained cool, with potential for open conflict over Tiv expansion onto Kuteb land.

The issue at stake was also political, instigated by the fragmentation of Jukun identity and the emergence of conflicting political claims arising therefrom. Here, pre-colonial animosities mingled with identity constructions in the colonial and post-colonial period to produce tensions in intergroup relations. The tensions were then fought out in the political realm.

In the course of colonial occupation at the turn of the century, the British first made contact with the Jukun at Ibi on the Benue. This gave the Jukun an early start in the acquisition of western education and advancement in the colonial and post-colonial bureaucracies. Furthermore, colonial officials tended to favour the Jukun over all other groups in the region because of their centralised state system and pre-colonial history in the Kwararafa Empire. The other ethnic groups were included in Wukari Division on the understanding that they had been part of the pre-colonial Jukun empire. This privileging of Jukun identity around Wukari/Takum forced many members of the other ethnic groups in the area to adopt Jukun identity.

Closely allied to the Jukun are the Chamba, who had migrated into the area from the region of present-day Cameroun Republic. A group of the Chamba settled in Ganye, while another group moved on to Donga and Takum. The Chamba were able to impose their domination over the majority Ichen in Donga. Even though the Ichen have the larger population, Donga district remains a Chamba preserve. They also raided the Kuteb for slaves, and moved into the Takum area. With the privileging of Jukun identity in the colonial period, the Chamba of the Wukari/Takum region, but excluding those of Ganye, adopted Jukun language and identity. Most of the other ethnic groups also assumed Jukun identity to varying degrees. Being 'Jukun' then meant a 'core' Jukun group plus a host of other associated ethnic groups, the most important of which were the Chamba, the Kuteb and the Ichen.

This broader 'Jukun' identity started to collapse in the 1950s, with the looming prospect of electoral politics. Secondly, increased educational opportunities had heightened awareness of ethnic differences and generated a pool of ideologues and political entrepreneurs eager to 'rediscover' their 'true' identity. This process of self-assertion was particularly noticeable amongst groups like the Kuteb who retained some cultural/linguistic distinction from the Jukun. In the face of this challenge, the ruling *Aku Uka* of Wukari, Atoshi Agbumanu, embarked on a forceful campaign to consolidate

'Jukun' identity around the 'core' Jukun by promoting the formation of the Kwararafa Congress in the 1950s. In response, the Kuteb formed the *Kuteb Yatso*, a cultural self-help movement. Kuteb grievance was basically economic. They claimed that of the three districts that made up Wukari Division—Wukari, Takum and Donga—most of the taxes came from Takum but the Kuteb who formed the vast majority of that district got the least in terms of social amenities, scholarships and bureaucratic appointments. On the other hand, Wukari district was said to have contributed the least, but monopolised all resources in Wukari. The Kuteb had not only began a process of self-assertion, they had also started a conflictual relationship with the Jukun.

The strained relationship worsened as the electoral system got under way in 1954. It is claimed that in that year, a tripartite understanding was reached to share political offices in the area between the three major groups —Jukun, Chamba and Kuteb—under the banner of the dominant regional party, the NPC. Ibrahim Sangari, a Wukari Jukun was voted into the Federal House of Representatives in Lagos and Jolly Tanko Yusuf, a Takum Chamba, was sent to the regional House of Assembly in Kaduna. When new elections were called in 1959, the Kuteb felt it was now their turn to nominate a candidate to the regional assembly. The accord collapsed, leading to the defection of the Kuteb to the Tiv-led UMBC. Though Tanko Yusuf retained his seat, Sangari was defeated by a UMBC candidate.

By the 1990s, this process of the fragmentation of a broader 'Jukun' identity had accelerated as the Kuteb challenged what they saw as a Jukun/Chamba hegemony. Furthermore, the Chamba, even though they remain Jukun-speaking, became more assertive of a separate identity of their own. This assertiveness was evident in the invitation to the Chief of Ganye to present the staff of office to the current *Gara* of Donga. From a common 'Jukun' identity in the early colonial period, there was the development of three identity conglomerations built around the Jukun, Chamba and Kuteb. Indeed, the process of fragmentation continues even within the conglomerations. The Jukun conglomeration is facing increasing self-assertion from its sub-groups, the Tigun, Ndoro, Nama, Jibu, Ichen and Kpanzun. Meanwhile, the Ayikuben, Mamu, Ohomeghi and the Bete are increasingly asserting their separate identity of the Kuteb conglomerate. The Chamba conglomeration faces similar pressures from the Tikari, Lufum, Daka Jidu and Paati. But the Chamba conglomerate seems to be more homogenous and coherent than the other two.

It was within this process of the fragmentation of 'Jukun' identity that each of the three major groups started staking out its territorial and political space. And this process ultimately brought the Chamba and the Kuteb into conflict over the chieftainship of Takum. The Kuteb claim that under the colonial system, the chieftainship of Takum—chief and kingmakers—was an all-Kuteb affair. Then under the first post-colonial regional government, the law was changed in 1963. Kuteb kingmakers were reduced from five to four, and three non-Kuteb members were brought in; the leaders or clan heads of the Jukun, Chamba and 'Hausa' in Takum. The Kuteb claim that this change was instigated by Jolly Tanko Yusuf, over whose candidacy, the tripartite electoral pact had broken down. In 1975, the Benue-Plateau State Government made further changes to the law. Kuteb kingmakers were reduced from four to two, Chamba representation was increased from one to two, and 'Hausa' representation was abolished. The Jukun clan head was made chairman of the committee of kingmakers and deputy to the chief. Effectively, a Chamba/Jukun alliance on the committee would most likely lead to a three-against-two majority in favour of a non-Kuteb chief. The Kuteb claim that the 1975 changes were instigated by Ibrahim Sangari who lost his Lagos seat in 1959, but in 1975 was a Commissioner in the Benue-Plateau government.

On their part, the Takum Chamba argue that the federal government recently divided Takum Local Government Area into two, Ussa and Takum, with all the Kuteb in Ussa and the Jukun and Chamba in Takum. There is the hint that the Kuteb should 'move over' to their own local government area. The argument goes further that Takum was originally Jukun, the Jukun name for Takum being *Yoka* or 'inside the walls'. The argument continues that Takum had previously had both Jukun and Chamba chiefs, and that it was only in the 1930s that Kuteb chiefs were appointed. Since then, the Kuteb are said to have had four chiefs, but under no circumstances would they be allowed to monopolise the chieftainship to the exclusion of both Chamba and Jukun. The Kuteb counter by arguing that since the Jukun have the *Aku Uka* of Wukari, and the Chamba have the *Gara* of Donga, the Kuteb must retain the *Ukwe* of Takum.

It was the tension deriving from this political contestation which fed into the Wukari Crisis, leading to the killings of 1992 and 1993. Here again, the central issues remain unresolved. The *Ukwe* stool is now vacant, and it is possible that jockeying for it may lead to further crisis.

Conclusion: Identity Issues and the African Crisis

Much work has been done since the early 1980s on identity issues in Africa. There is however a clear difference in the orientation of studies emanating from academics in the West and those from academics in Africa. In the West, the central focus is on the cultural impact of colonialism, particularly on the 'invention' or 'imagination' of African ethnicity and 'tradition' (Ranger, 1994, 1995). These studies have deepened our understanding of the precise nature of the colonial impact and the resulting transformations in identity. Unfortunately, much of this scholarship from the West is historical in nature, lacking any obvious connection to the contemporary crisis in Africa. The main debates between 'social constructionists' who emphasise the imagined and invented nature of ethnicity, and 'primordialists' who emphasise age-old primordial qualities, often come across as quibbling over interpretative nuances, completely unconnected with the urgency of contemporary African life. On the other hand, scholars in Africa have tended to pay only limited attention to the historical dimensions of identity in Africa, concentrating instead on its structural manifestations in the African crisis.

For example, Mamdani (1996) has explained the genesis of the recent Rwandese civil war and genocide in terms of the changing notions of citizenship and identity in Uganda. He argues that the shift from citizenship based on blood-line and ethnicity to one based on residency made it possible for the Rwandese refugees in Uganda to enlist in the Museveni-led NRA. With the end of the war, there was a reverse shift in the definition of citizenship, with ethnicity and indigenity returning to prominence. He argues that it was this shifting identity of the Rwandese refugees/citizens in Uganda which precipitated the RPF armed return to Rwanda. In another context, Mamdani examines the conflicting ways long-term migrants from Mali and Burkina Faso in the Ivory Coast are regarded as migrants and citizens by the opposition and the government respectively. These conflicting perceptions had consequences for the electoral politics of the transition from one-party rule in Ivory Coast.

Another example is Mafeje's (1991) study of agricultural production in Sub-Saharan Africa. He argues that in most of these societies, land is held by lineages. Women continue to belong to their natal lineages even after they get married and re-locate to their husbands' lineage. In their lineage of residence, women are responsible for the reproduction of the lineage and also for agricultural production. Yet their access to land is constrained and mediated in these lineages of residence precisely because they are considered to be members of their natal lineages. He poses a challenge to African jurisprudence to address this gendered disjuncture between residence/identity/resources.

Both the Western and the African strands in the study of identity issues have enriched our understanding of African society and politics. However, it would seem that much could be gained by linking the study of identities to the crisis in Africa. From this perspective, we can begin to highlight some central connections between the tendencies within minority identity transformation and the crisis of the Nigerian state. To begin with, it must be restated that even under 'normal' circumstances, identities are in constant transformation. They would have still been transformed, with or without the crisis in the state. Indeed as I have tried to show, many of the transformations, both positive and negative, started almost as soon as 'minority' identity emerged in the 1950s. The unique thing about the crisis of the state is that it generates the institutions, personalities, processes and dynamics which condition and give meaning and context to the transformations in identity. It accelerates some tendencies while discouraging others; often, it imbues 'neutral' developments with added meanings.

In the Nigerian context, two related crises are of particular relevance; the rise of a centralised military authoritarian state, and the economic crisis. By the time the military took over power in December 1983, the Nigerian state was already highly centralised and the democratic ideal was highly contested at different levels of the state and the society. With the return of military rule, a militaristic authoritarianism was grafted onto the centralised structures of the state. Though this military authoritarianism started as a collective leadership under the Buhari/Idiagbon regime, it soon degenerated into a one-man autocratic rule under Babangida and Abacha. Related to this political development is the economic crisis which became pronounced from about 1982, leading to the adoption of a Structural Adjustment Programme in 1986. Structural adjustment has since become just another aspect of this economic crisis, deepening the crisis of a common social citizenship (Olukoshi, 1996). Combined together, economic crisis and military authoritarianism created an atmosphere of diminishing resources, and a personalised and idiosyncratic distribution of the little that was left.

The stage was therefore set for political entrepreneurs to seek to maximise access to economic and political resources by mobilizing particularistic identities and hitching these constituencies to the political agenda of the military autocrats. As a community magazine in south-western Nigeria put it:

> The reality of today's Nigeria is that any tribe, state, community or interest group that does not want to be lost in the crowd, should devise means of consistently putting its interests, needs and problems across to the Government... (Idanre Community Magazine, Sept. 1996).

More often than not, the 'devices' employed rely heavily on advancing particularist and exclusionary claims. As a consequence, there is a heightened sense of ethnic consciousness and conflict (Osaghae, 1995). The transformation of minority identities since 1985 is best understood against the background of this wider dynamic. While some minority groups joined the frenzy of advancing particularist goals and interests—as in Taraba State—others saw themselves as 'victims' and resorted to the same particularism as a means of defence—Ogoni and Zangon Kataf. The combination of economic crisis, structural adjustment and political engineering under autocratic tutelage was bound to destabilize existing consensus, leading to the politics of difference and the splintering of common identities. As Bangura (1995:7) succinctly puts it:

> Recession and economic restructuring have reduced the resources available to the state sector, and thus the incentives for disadvantaged groups or individuals to remain loyal to previous social and political arrangements offered by the state. In addition, ethnic affiliations and forms of mobilization have become important as the scope for plural forms of organisation has widened. I would like to stress the point that it is impossible to liberalise ethnically plural societies under conditions of economic decline without ethnicity becoming a major feature of political organisation. The demand for forms of politics that are devoid of ethnicity is actually a pipe dream!

Bibliography

Bangura, Y., 1995, "Reflections on Recent Patterns of Political Development in Africa", a talk delivered at the Graduate Institute of International Studies Seminar on "International Security", Geneva.

Ekeh, P., 1994, "Political Minorities and Historically-Dominant Minorities in Nigerian History and Politics", State University of New York, Buffalo.

FGN, Federal Government of Nigeria, n.d., *Ogoni Crisis: The Untold Story*.

Human Rights Watch/Africa, 1995, "The Ogoni Crisis: A Case-Study of Military Repression in South-western Nigeria".

Mafeje, A., 1991, "African Households and Prospects for Agricultural Revival in Sub-Saharan Africa", *CODESRIA Working Paper* No. 2/91, Dakar.

Mamdani, M., 1996, "From Conquest to Consent As the Basis of State Formation: Reflections on Rwanda", *New Left Review*, No. 216.

Mustapha, A. R., 1994, "Ethnicity and Democratization in Nigeria: A Case Study of Zangon Kataf". mimeo.

Mustapha, A. R., 1996, "Civil Rights and Pro-Democracy Groups in and outside Nigeria", International Workshop on the Nigerian Democratization Process, CEAN, Bordeaux, France.

Mustapha, A. R., (forthcoming), "Dissent and Confrontation in the Niger Delta: Isaac Boro and Saro-Wiwa Compared".

Naanen, B., 1995, "Oil-Producing Minorities and the Restructuring of Nigerian Federalism: The Case of the Ogoni People", *Journal of Commonwealth and Comparative Politics*, 33(1).

NAK (National Archives Kaduna), Makprof 2403 – Migration from Tiv Division.

NAK, Makprof 4545 – Land Use and Migration: Tiv Tribe.

Okpu, U., 1977, *Ethnic Minority Problems in Nigerian Politics: 1960–1965*. Uppsala: Acta Universitatis Upsaliensis.

Okwuosa, A. C., I. K. Ogbonnaya and O. Magbadelo, 1994, "Minority Rights and the Constitutional Question in Nigeria", *Nigerian Journal of Democracy*, Abuja: CDS.

Olukoshi, A., 1996, "Constitutionalism and Citizenship in Africa: A Select Overview of Theoretical and Empirical Issues", conference on "Constitutionalism and Citizenship in Contemporary Africa", Naivasha, organized by the Nordic Africa Institute.

Osaghae, E., 1995, *Structural Adjustment and Ethnicity in Nigeria*. Uppsala: Nordiska Afrikainstitutet.

Ranger, T. 1994, "The Invention of Tradition Revisited", in Kaarsholm, P. and J. Hultin, (eds.) *Inventions and Boundaries: Historical and Anthropological Approaches to the Study of Ethnicity and Nationalism*. Roskilde: IDS.

Ranger, T., 1995, "The Nature of Ethnicity: Lessons from Africa", Warwick Debates. Warwick University.

Saro-Wiwa, K., 1995, *A Month and a Day: A Detention Dairy*. London: Penguin.

Willink Commission, 1958, *Nigeria: Report of the Commission Appointed to Enquire into the Fears of Minorities and the Means of Allaying Them*. London: HMSO.

Newspapers and Magazines

Idanre Community Magazine, Sept. 1996.

Chapter 6

National Council of Women's Societies and the State, 1985–1993: The Use of Discourses of Womanhood by the NCWS

Charmaine Pereira

Introduction

The military regime of Ibrahim Babangida seized power in 1985 through a palace coup ousting the previous Buhari regime. The new administration promised to build a new social order resting on solid economic and political arrangements. On the economic front, immediately after assuming power, the government declared a 30-month economic emergency programme and a Structural Adjustment Programme (SAP) was formally introduced in September 1986, including elements such as devaluation, privatisation, the removal of subsidies on social services and the retrenchment of workers.

The effects of the economic crisis and of SAP, whilst debilitating for the majority of the population, women as well as men, have been more punitive for most groups of women than for men, given the multiple demands and responsibilities facing women (Commonwealth Expert Group on Women and Structural Adjustment, 1990). Women are more likely to be retrenched by employers than men. The resulting loss of wages and the inability to buy essential commodities for the household means that women have to exercise considerable ingenuity in the attempt to make ends meet. Women's time is increasingly used to take care of the sick since illnesses previously on the decline in the 1980s, such as bilharzia, guinea worm and diarrhoea, have re-emerged. Cutbacks in education support by the state leave those women who are responsible for children's school fees, text books and clothing, in a very difficult situation. New levies and taxes on the informal sector affect more women since they predominate in that subsector. With the marked deterioration of the formal sector, men who formerly dominated this sector have moved to the informal sector. Rising prices of commodities have also made it extremely difficult for women with little operating capital to survive in the informal sector (Shettima, 1995).

On the political front, the process of 'transition' to a Third Republic began with the inauguration of a Political Bureau in 1986. The Bureau was set up for the purposes of mobilising Nigerians to debate and to collate their views on the future political and socio-economic structure following a return to civilian rule. Guidelines included for discussion included the roles of women, youth and labour; the system and forms of government as well as forms of representation. Two women were included in the Political Bureau, one of whom was Mrs. Hilda Adefarasin, the President of the National Council of Women's Societies. Mrs. Adefarasin's appointment can be interpreted as reflecting the government's agenda of using structures for women and women's organisations to disseminate government policies and objectives to 'grassroots' women. Such actions were motivated more by the desire to expand the regime's own constituency, than by any concern for the eradication of the various forms of oppression endured by women.

Women in Nigeria (WIN), a radical organisation committed to the elimination of gender and class inequalities in Nigerian society, called for a future constitution in which social justice, self-reliance and popular democracy would be guaranteed along with the elimination of all forms of exploitation, oppression, discrimination and subordination of women. It asked for the removal of all restrictions on women's right to own land; the right of women to confer privileges, rights and duties on spouses and children as men do; and the recognition of child bearing and rearing as socially productive and economic work (Women in Nigeria, 1986).

Most of these recommendations were either trivialised, neglected or displaced by both the Political Bureau and the Babangida government. Those which were accepted were token gestures. The Bureau recommended the allocation of a mere 5 percent of the legislative seats to women in all the three tiers of government (Directorate for Social Mobilisation, 1989), in contrast to the fifty percent called for by WIN (Women in Nigeria, *op. cit.*) and the thirty percent recommended by the National Council of Women's Societies (NCWS), (Chizea, 1990). The government's reaction to the Political Bureau's recommendation was, "... government does not accept the implications of reverse discrimination ... Government believes in equality of sexes, individuals and groups" (Federal Government of Nigeria, 1987:24).

The populist, human rights posture adopted by the Babangida regime was blatantly contradicted by its actions in a number of arenas. The consequences of economic stabilisation policies and SAP have generally been to worsen living conditions with the result that the regime imposing such policies increasingly loses popular support. This was true for the Babangida regime—in order to stay in power and continue to enforce SAP, the tendency has been to use suppression rather than persuasion (Beckman, 1992). The so called 'transition' to civilian rule turned out to be highly authoritarian and repressive. Journalists were harassed and intimidated, and newspaper houses were closed. Several trade unions were banned. People classified as extremists were prohibited from contesting for power. The judiciary was seriously undermined through the establishment of military tribunals, disregard for court orders and through ouster clauses in several decrees promulgated by the government (Ibrahim, 1993; Civil Liberties Organisation, 1992, 1993).

The imposition of structural adjustment by the state and the narrowing of political space have not gone without protest and resistance. Students, market women, trade unionists and others have demonstrated several times against SAP. The Nigeria Bar Association has criticised the regime and reiterated its commitment to the rule of law. The Association of Democratic Lawyers was formed in 1985 to defend those harassed or detained by the state. Since 1987, human rights violations have been monitored and publicised by the Civil Liberties Organisation (CLO). Alliances such as the Campaign for Democracy (CD) have been formed among groups with similar objectives, including groups such as WIN.

The extreme marginalisation of women in the Nigerian state and national politics under both military and civilian regimes preceding the Babangida government (Mba, 1989; Mama, 1995a), continued in somewhat modified vein under his tenure. There were no women on the new Armed Forces Ruling Council, or at ministerial level, although the practice of appointing women as commissioners continued. There were no female state governors. A proclamation at the local level, however, stated that one in four local government councillors should be women. 1987 saw only two out of 301 women being elected as chairs of local government, an actual decline on previous local government elections.

It is against the background so far documented that the proliferation of state structures for women, established during Babangida's tenure, should be viewed. The Better Life Programme and the National Commission for Women were set up at federal and state levels, and women and development units were created in the state ministries of culture and social welfare. The establishment of such structures suggests, on the face of it, a concern with improving the conditions and status of women. There is a clear contradiction, however, in the fact that state structures for women are associated with the high visibility of select groups of women at the same time as other women's autonomous demands and struggles are the target of state neglect or repression.

The rationale underlying the so called commitment to improving women's status and participation seems to be rooted, at least partly, in an attempt to increase the legitimacy of the regime, both internationally and with regard to the populist agenda at home. In an international context where economic aid and professed sympathy for the rights of women are increasingly linked, the championing of 'women development' (read Women in Development) should be recognised for the opportunism that it represents. Furthermore, the Women in Development (WID) paradigm has been severely criticised by feminist scholars on the grounds that it assumes that women have not been contributing to development. In the process, women's work is ignored and the multiple ways in which development strategies themselves have contributed to women's marginalisation and oppression have been denied (DAWN, 1988).

Research on women and the state in Africa has tended to focus on the effects of the colonial and post-colonial state on women, pointing out ways in which both have strengthened the power of men over women, and how the state has been primarily a vehicle of male elite interests (Parpart and Staudt, 1989). Women's struggles to defend and promote their individual and collective interests under the changing conditions of colonialism and the post-colonial order have also been highlighted (e.g. Amadiume, 1987; Mba, 1989; Tsikata, 1989). More recently, attention has turned to analysing why the state affects women in the ways specified.

Whilst there is considerable agreement that post-independent African states can be characterised as patriarchal, the reasons for this vary. Some attribute it to the fact that the colonial regimes which post-colonial states are derived from excluded women, others point to the nature of pre-colonial African cultures and yet others to the actual processes of state formation. Chazan (1989) takes the position that women have neither been significantly involved in modern state creation nor have they been able to establish regular channels of access to decision-makers. The varying degrees of discrimination and coercion exhibited by state policies towards women are the consequence. Mama (1995a) suggests that the picture is more complicated than this. Instead of limiting ourselves to a consideration of the impact on and exclusion of women, she points out that a more useful approach might be to examine the ways in which state formation and state practices are all gendered, and to analyse the involvement of women in these processes and practices.

In many African countries, 'official' non-governmental umbrella women's organisations bear a particular relationship to the state, which is grounded in a specific social and political history. The organisational structures and practices that emerge tend to constrain the nature and scope of the activism of the women concerned. Such activism is usually legitimated by recourse to particular constructions of what it means to be a woman—what a woman's 'identity' is or should be—and therefore, what kinds of actions are appropriate as well as inappropriate for women to be seen to be engaged in.

This study focuses on the Nigerian version of this phenomenon, the National Council of Women's Societies (NCWS). The multi-faceted changes arising from the impact of structural adjustment on Nigerian society and the politics of transition form the crucible within which particular constructions of womanhood are transformed as well as preserved. The focus here is on how the hegemonic discourses of womanhood drawn on by the NCWS have been shaped, to varying extents, by the history and politics of the organisation and its relations with the state, and by ideological struggles that have a bearing on the capacity for women to engage in democratisation.

'Identity' and Women's Activism

1985, the year that ushered Ibrahim Badamasi Babangida into power, was also the year that marked the end of the UN Decade for Women (1976–85). A deeper understanding of the convergence of issues affecting women's lives led many groups of women to question some of the fundamental concepts and approaches of their societies. The editors of the Indian women's journal *Manushi* wrote:

> Today we no longer say: 'give us more jobs, more rights, consider us your 'equals' or even allow us to compete with you better'. But rather: Let us re-examine the whole question, all the questions. Let us take nothing for granted. *Let us not only redefine ourselves, our role, our image—but also the kind of society we want to live in* (Kishwar and Vanita, 1984:244–45, emphasis mine).

This redefinition of women and of self, of image—what is often referred to as 'identity'—is explicitly linked above to the question of social change and of struggle. This may not always be the case. In the international women's movement, questions of identity have often been linked to questions of politics, though the specific ways in which such linkages have been manifested varies. For our purposes, it is useful to highlight some of the connections between concepts of identity, politics and women's activism.

Feminists from the Third World have pointed out that women's identities within and across nations have been shaped by a complex amalgam of national, racial, religious, ethnic, class and sexual identities (e.g. Basu, 1995). The relationship between identity and activism is difficult to establish. Moreover, identity itself is neither uniform nor monolithic. Often, women's experiences of their identities as gendered subjects may not assume a feminist form. Chinese women, since the 1980s, have challenged the androgynous ideals of the past by emphasising their femininity. In the U.S., the growing consciousness that identities are multiple rather than singular has often led women to emphasise race, ethnicity and sexual orientation as much as gender. Consequently, identity politics flourishes at the same time that a unified women's movement has become more dispersed (Basu, op. cit.).

Imam (1993) points out that politics in Nigeria has often been that of ruling groups mobilising identity politics—the identity of groups defined by specific ascriptive characteristics such as ethnicity, religion, regionalism—in order to create power bases. Increased identification with others defined as members of the same community runs alongside the intensification of boundaries against those defined as being outside that community. The dynamic nature of identity is highlighted in her exposition: identity politics is prominent during specific historical periods when the mobilisation of particular collectivities is tied to struggles over state power.

Basu's (1995) account of women's movements has emphasised their local origins, character and concerns. This is in sharp contrast to the notion that 'sisterhood is global' (e.g. Morgan, 1984; Bunch, 1985; Peterson and Runyan, 1993). Basu points out that feminists from the industrialised Western world have been apt to make sweeping generalisations about commonalities among women across the globe. Such generalisations aggravate tensions not only along north-south lines but also along other lines of cleavage, including class, race and sexual orientation.

Whilst the multiplicity of 'identity' is expressed in Basu's conceptualisation above, the retention of the term is associated with a number of problems. Rowbotham (1994) captures succinctly the usage and limitations of 'identity' in the international women's movement:

> In the modern movement, the word 'identity' has been used as a means of ensuring that particular groups of women's needs and views are not overruled by others in positions of greater privilege. Identity has been a means of staking out a distinct territory, opening up space for many diverse experiences, instead of presenting a limited interpretation of what women might want, based on a narrow elite. However, the problem with the concept of identity is that it tends to become rigid, fixing individuals artificially into a single aspect of their lived experience (Rowbotham, 1994:14).

The term 'identity' not only embodies a tendency to reify single aspects of people's lived experience, hence not addressing the multiple and contradictory aspects of human thought and action. It also assumes a dualism between internal, psychological spheres and external, social spheres. Instead of 'identity', post-structuralist theory uses the term 'subjectivity' to refer to 'individuality and self-awareness—the condition of being a subject', emphasising that human beings are constituted *by* the social domain (for example, discourses, language, culture) rather than the other way round (Henriques et al., 1984). 'Subjectivity':

> marks a crucial break with humanist conceptions of the individual which are still central to western philosophy and political and social organisation. ... post-structuralism proposes a subjectivity which is ... in process, constantly being constituted in discourse each time we think or speak (Weedon, 1987:32–33).

Discourses, which carry the content of subjectivity, are constituted by the collective knowledges and beliefs of social groups (Mama, 1995b). Discourses of womanhood are historically constructed notions of what it means to be a woman. They exist within networks of power, such that hegemonic discourses include normative content concerning what it is 'appropriate' for (all) women to do and what not to do. Discourses thus not only include the content of subjectivity but also construct the boundaries of women's 'appropriate' behaviour and action in society, including political action. Hegemonic discourses appear to be universal in their depiction of women, regardless of actual differences among groups of women.

Political discourses have tended to be organised around essentialist views of political subjects, in this case, the unitary category 'Woman'. A movement organised around such a category effectively privileges certain voices and marginalises others. Paradoxically, the very attempt to universalise 'Woman' makes the category more exclusionary. Political subjects are not fixed and the contexts within which they are mobilised are diverse. In the context of gender, de Lauretis suggests an understanding of a "subject engendered in the experiencing of race and class, as well as sexual relations; a subject therefore not unified but rather multiple, and not so much divided as contradicted" (de Lauretis, 1987: 2).

A non-essentialist account of political subjects is one which accords a central place to diversity and heterogeneity. Westwood and Radcliffe (1993) point out that there are no simple dichotomies between public and private, practical and strategic interests in this conception. Instead, such dichotomies are recast in relation to the multiplicity of sites in which women are engaged in power struggles, from the domestic sphere and the world of the household to the streets. Such an approach is linked to an alternative way of understanding politics, not one that defines the political in terms of what spheres and arenas of life can or should be ones penetrated by the state (e.g. Halvorsen, 1991). Given the emphasis on plurality, it becomes necessary to understand the complexities of diverse struggles and the implications for the kinds of terrain that have been carved out for the political.

In Africa, women's movements have been intertwined with movements of national liberation and state consolidation (Urdang, 1979, 1989; Mba, 1982; Likimani, 1985; Badran, 1988; McClintock, 1991). Given the key role that women played in many of the region's liberation movements, Mama raises the question of why their absence was so conspicuous subsequently: "did all the women and women's organisations active in the independence struggles simply opt out of public life once independence was achieved, or were they disenfranchised?" (Mama, 1995a:39). In many post-colonial societies, a 'modernist' position on women and gender relations has been adopted, with attendant perils (Kandiyoti, 1991). Whilst Kandiyoti's examples are drawn primarily from the Middle East and South Asia, it is instructive to note the parallels with nationalist projects in Africa, to highlight the nature of the 'modernist' position on women and its associated problems.

Nationalism in Africa, as in the Middle East and South Asia, appealed primarily to a narrow stratum of the bourgeoisie and bureaucracy who, despite their political credentials as anti-imperialists, could nevertheless be accused of falling prey to Western cultural hegemony (Ibrahim and Pereira, 1994). For the achievement of progress to proceed without undue dilution of national identity, the central symbols of this identity had to be preserved and protected from contaminating foreign influences. Tensions between modernist and anti-modernist strands in nationalism found a focus around the place and conduct of women. Nationalists were keen to establish the indigenous and patriotic credentials of their modernising projects. Women participating in nationalist movements similarly tended to justify their departure from narrowly prescribed roles in the name of patriotism and self-sacrifice for the nation. Their activities, whether they were civic, charitable or political, could most easily be legitimated as natural extensions of their womanly nature and as a duty rather than a right (Kandiyoti, 1991).

In the contemporary Nigerian context, the National Council of Women's Societies epitomises this approach to women's activities in public life. The NCWS has expressed attachment towards a particular conception of what it means to be a woman—effectively reifying women as wives and mothers within the existing social order. The emphasis in this study is on the use of specific discourses of womanhood by the NCWS, in the context of their organising and activism, with particular reference to the period of the Babangida regime. It is not my intention to suggest that the NCWS's discourses of womanhood are definitive of women's actual subjectivities—their individuality and experiences. Rather, the emphasis on discourses is intended to highlight the ways in which specific configurations of understandings and beliefs about "what women are or should be like" and therefore, "what women can be seen to do", are historically specific and historically influential ideals constructed by social groups. I will begin by considering what kinds of politics and activism have been associated with the NCWS, and what forms of organisational structures and practices have emerged in the process.

NCWS and Organisational Politics

The NCWS was formally set up in 1959 (Mba, 1982) but its origins can be found in the Ibadan-based Women's Movement, established in 1952. The aims of the movement were: universal suffrage; admission of women to the native authority councils; nomination of women from the movement to the Western House of Assembly; more secondary schools for girls; lowering of the bride price; and controls over Syrian and Lebanese trading monopolies. The manifesto of the movement included the aim of educating and organising Nigerian women to 'accept the leadership of the movement on all matters political, economic and educational' (Mba, 1982:182). The Women's Movement was affiliated to the International Council of Women, membership of which was restricted to non-communist countries.

In 1953, the Women's Movement participated in the formation of the Federation of Nigerian Women's Societies (FNWS), an organisation with a radically different ideological orientation. The aims of the FNWS were to encourage Nigerian women to take part in the political, social, cultural and economic life of Nigeria; to create facilities for female education; and generally to raise the status of women to win equal opportunities with men (Mba, 1982). The FNWS was affiliated to the Women's International Democratic Federation, which was socialist in outlook and included Communist countries. When the leader of the Women's Movement, Elizabeth Adeyemi Adekogbe, failed to win a significant enough position in the leadership of the FNWS, she subsequently pulled out and attempted to build up her own movement instead.

In 1954, the Women's Movement changed its name to the Nigerian Council of Women (NCW). There were more changes than just the name. From then on until 1958, the movement ceased its political propaganda on behalf of women, it did not criticise any actions of government, and it did not hold a general assembly. In 1959, the NCW combined with the Women's Improvement Society, another Ibadan-based organisation, to form the National Council of Women's Societies (NCWS). The Women's Improvement Society had been formed in 1948 and was concerned with social welfare work, such as improving conditions in the markets and building hostels for girls (Mba, 1982).

The NCWS's own, somewhat less detailed account of its origins is different (NCWS, 1993). Primacy is given to the role, in 1957, of the Minister of Community and Social Development of Western Nigeria, the late Oba C.D. Akran whose ministry was responsible for voluntary organisation. According to this account, the Oba got leaders of women's societies in his region together, following the attendance of three (unnamed) women leaders at an international conference at which there was no formal Nigerian delegation. He advised them to form one central body which government would recognise and which would speak for women in Nigeria and abroad. The founding of the organisation is dated from 1958, when 'the nucleus organisation which later grew into the national body known as the National Council of Women's Societies, Nigeria has (sic) taken root' (NCWS, 1993:10). Whilst there is admittedly scant detail in this account, one may well ask why it is the role of the male governmental official that is highlighted here and whether the unnamed female leaders did not initiate any autonomous action in this direction either prior to or following the Oba's intervention.

During the colonial era, class differences among women began to acquire increasing importance in women's politics. Mba (1982) has documented both the changing character of women's demands and the increasing divisions among them as they were differentially incorporated into the state. Women's organisations such as the precursors of the NCWS articulated goals compatible with state-drawn boundaries, including more political representation for women and more secondary schools for girls. Class differences among women were partly reflected in the different battles fought by different groups of women for different rewards: poor women had less to gain from marriage and were therefore more interested in autonomy, unlike elite women for whom marriage was more rewarding materially.

From its beginnings, the NCWS defined itself as a non-political body. Its aims were to promote the welfare and progress of women, especially in education, and to ensure that women were given every opportunity to play an important part in social and community affairs. Unlike the FNWS, the NCWS received a government subvention annually and was regarded by government as the organisation representing women. Internationally, the NCWS was affiliated to the International Council of Women.

Membership was initially organised on a regional basis and included some class differentiation. In 1960/61, the NCWS established branches in Lagos and in the Eastern Region (at Enugu) and the Northern Region (at Kaduna). Each regional branch contacted all the women's organisations in the region and invited them to join the national council. Women could join the council as individuals or as members of other organisations. The Lagos branch of the NCWS combined both elite and market women. The membership in other branches was composed largely of elite, well-educated and prosperous women who felt concerned both for their own interests and for those of their 'less fortunate sisters' (Mba, 1982:189).

In general, the NCWS was far less active both in articulating women's interests and in attempting to influence government than the FNWS or the Women's Movement (in its early days). As a co-ordinating national body which included women from all over Nigeria, it lacked the communal base of support that Abeokuta and Ibadan had provided for the FNWS and the Women's Movement. Moreover, the group leadership was not as effective and did not have the same mass appeal as the dynamic leadership of Funmilayo Ransome-Kuti and Elizabeth Adekogbe.

More recently, the NCWS has supported policies which are antagonistic to women's gender interests, such as their successful mobilisation for the defeat of the 1981 Abortion Bill. Similarly, NCWS has regularly supported policies contrary to the interests of the working class and peasantry, such as calls for belt-tightening in the face of Austerity Programmes and the subsequent Structural Adjustment Programme. Moreover, the organisation approved the knocking down of kiosks and the ban on street trading, which many poor urban women rely on for their earnings, in support of Buhari's War against Indiscipline programme (Imam, 1997).

Alongside the activities of women organised under the auspices of NCWS there is the continued viability of a more traditional form of political action. This is the mass mobilisation of communal and market women's associations in defence of their interests. These associations of women as daughters, wives and traders continue to provide the basis for the mobilisation of the masses of women in the political system of the militarised state today as they did in the precolonial and colonial periods of Nigeria's history. During the precolonial period, however, the power of such organisations was considerably greater than is the case today. The Igbo daughters' and wives' associations had powers to adjudicate not only among women but on some issues, also among women and men, at the village level and individually (Okonjo, 1976). In the colonial era, Igbo women's associations protested against colonial taxation in the 1929 Women's War and succeeded in postponing taxation for some years and dismantling parts of the Warrant Chief system (van Allen, 1976). Subsequently, a number of processes combined to erode the strength of precolonial indigenous women's organisations, including the chauvinism of British Victorian gender ideology and incorporation into the world economic system.

Since independence, mass action by women in the informal sector has continued but it has been sporadic, un-coordinated and has not been sustained. Women's collective action is far more localised and materialistic, and has not produced long-term leadership. The women have generally reacted to measures by government, both civil and military, that threaten their economic interests (Mba, 1989).

Today, a wide gap exists between urban and rural women, between the elite on the one hand, and the working class and peasantry on the other. Those women who have the national leadership potential—the urban educated middle-class women—lack the mass support needed for effective political action. Most of these women, moreover, insist on the depoliticisation of 'women's issues' and operate within the framework of voluntary associations that cannot enforce sanctions on their members. Urban market women and rural women have the potential for mass mobilisation and can enforce effective sanctions, but they lack the national leadership and political objectives (Mba, op. cit.).

Relations with the State

As was the case in the early days, the NCWS is still recognised by the federal government as the only umbrella non-governmental organisation (NGO) representing women's interests. All women's organisations in Nigeria are required to affiliate with the NCWS if they are to be recognised by the state. Given its history of non-confrontational relations with government, its recognition as the 'formal' women's NGO is no surprise. One of the consequences of the long-term association between NCWS and the state has been to narrow the space for potentially competing women's organisations forming their own relations with the state (Hassan, 1996).

Relations between NCWS and the state can be characterised as state-supportive and state-supported, although the exchange is by no means on an equal basis. Essentially, the relations take the form of patron-client ties. The NCWS continues to receive an official government subvention, currently amounting to fifty thousand naira annually (Sambo, 1996). Recognition within official structures and access to state resources is provided in exchange for support for government policies and the use of NCWS's networks and organisational machinery by the state in the mobilisation of women for state-determined purposes. The interdependence that is implicit in such relations is not symmetrical, however, since coercion, on the part of the state, is involved as well as co-operation. In addition, there are ideological features such that the institutions themselves are viewed in gendered terms, the state signifying a masculine sphere and the NCWS, a feminine one.

The gender ideology espoused by NCWS is the hegemonic one in which men and women are said to have complementary roles, that is they occupy equal but different spheres of activity and influence. Numerous newspaper articles express this view but one example from the NCWS will suffice to illustrate the point. Mrs. Hilda Adefarasin, one of the past National Presidents of the NCWS, has been reported as stating that "women are not seeking opportunities to overthrow men in the scheme of things ... women were rather seeking 'recognition and support as partners in progress with the menfolk'" (see *Triumph*, 1988:1). This line of thinking is likely to be partially rooted in the specific histories of female autonomy for some groups of Nigerian women and in gender segregation for others. The emphasis on complementarity, however, denies relations of subordination in which even the most influential women occupy positions lower in the hierarchy than men of equivalent social standing. In addition to complementarity, a significant element is that of support. Women are expected to support men, not to be seen to be confronting them or demanding equality and thereby fostering hostility and antagonism:

> There is no need ... for a woman to be liberated from a man. ... The men own the government. There is a need for women to fully participate in government but we need some level of understanding. We (the NCWS) are not there to take away what they have but we are there to assist them in doing whatever they do better (Dogonyaro, 1996).

Since "men own the government", the sphere in which they carry out the activities associated with government, the state, is by extension also gendered male. And women's support of men translates into NCWS's support of the state, a position commonly referred to as AGIP, the support of "any government in power", regardless of its ideological perspective. One press report put it this way:

Mrs. Adefarasin (then-national President of NCWS) stated that it was their duty as mothers to co-operate with any government in power to ensure that government aims and aspirations are well spread out especially to women in the rural areas (*Daily Times*, 1986:32).

The relations between the NCWS and the state can be conceptualised in terms of the relations of exchange between the two, an extension of Palmer's (n.d.) explanation of the process of change in gender relationships in developing societies. According to Palmer, changing gender relationships are viewed as being connected to the relative access of each gender to material and other assets, such as wages or political influence. The 'generating core' of the connection is constituted by the relations of exchange between women and men: exchange of economic powers, of familial powers, of other institutional and culturally determined powers, and of political powers. Each set of exchange relations governs the genders' access to and use of resources in the society and economy. In a similar way, relations between NCWS and the state can be viewed as being conditioned by the relations of exchange between the two, which will depend on the relative access of each to material and other assets. The forms and patterns of controlling, accessing and managing resources reflect varied social and economic conditions. Such arrangements have been articulated in diverse cultural idioms and are rooted in specific histories of accumulation and struggle.

The dynamic character of patron-client ties has been highlighted by Newbury (1988). She points out that the degree of reciprocity in the relationship may increase or decrease with time and exchanges between the partners may vary from rather fixed and defined duties to diffuse and ad hoc demands. In the Nigerian context, changes in NCWS's patron-client ties during the Babangida regime are related to a growth in state power, expressed through political centralisation and attempts to increase state penetration at the local level. The latter is particularly evident in the form of the Better Life Programme, instituted by the First Lady. This has given rise to a female patron-client network, overlapping and in itself dependent upon, the official malestreamed state relations of patronage.

Female Patronage

The constitution of the NCWS requires that:

> the wife of the Head of the State or the spouse of the President of the Federal Republic of Nigeria shall be the patron of the Council and in the case of the State Branches, the wife of the state Governor, in the case of the local government branch, the wife of the chairman (*sic*) (Article XVII, 19).

Female patronage of the NCWS has taken on a distinctive character under the Babangida regime. One of its salient features is its embeddedness in the development of a highly visible femocracy.

The central feature of a femocracy is that it is "a feminine autocracy running in parallel to the patriarchal oligarchy upon which it relies for its authority, and which it supports completely" (Mama, 1995a:41). The femocracy under consideration here is the female power structure created by the wife of the Head of State, Maryam Babangida, under the auspices of the Better Life for Rural Women Programme (BLP) which she launched in 1987. Initially under the umbrella of the Directorate for Food, Roads and Rural

Infrastructure (DFRRI), BLP was launched at a workshop on rural women held on September 13–16, 1987, in Abuja.

The idea of focusing on rural women was not new. Essentially, BLP signified the co-option of radical discourse (Mama, *op. cit.*). Long before BLP, Women in Nigeria (WIN) had emphasised the importance of rural women, describing them as the backbone of the nation's food production and the most exploited section of Nigerian society (WIN, 1985). On the international scene, the conditions facing rural women had attracted the support of an international women's movement seeking to include and articulate the concerns of the most exploited groups of women from the Third World (e.g. DAWN, 1988). In addition, donor organisations were sympathetic to and prepared to fund initiatives targeted at rural women.

The Better Life Programme soon evolved beyond DFRRI. Following the Abuja seminar, attended by the wife of the Chief of General Staff, Mrs. Rebecca Aikhomu, the wives of all the military state governors were called upon to set up Better Life committees in each state. They were instructed to familiarise themselves with rural women's problems and link them with the appropriate government agencies, and to initiate and monitor programmes. Governors' wives were to encourage rural women to "become more active and useful to themselves, their families and their environment at large"; the method of doing this involved training and income generation (Mama, 1995a:49). Considerable skepticism has been expressed over the view that national programmes such as the BLP are capable of bringing about strategic change in rural women's positions, including pragmatic change in their economic endeavours (Mama, 1995a; Vereecke, 1993; Udegbe, 1995). The reality is that they merely serve the interests of elite and reinforce class distinctions among women.

The premium placed on the ranks of husbands as a prerequisite for women's leadership, prominent in the operations of the BLP, has its precursors elsewhere. Given the domination of Nigeria by military regimes, the emergence of the Nigerian Army Officers Wives Association (NAOWA) is a reflection of the general body politic. Organisational characteristics associated with the military, such as the emphasis on rank and hierarchy leading to rigid stratification, and centralised authority, permeate the ways in which military wives associate, whether it is in NAOWA (Motojehi, 1989) or the BLP.

The femocracy of the BLP—military governors' wives who automatically became the chairpersons of the state level BLP committees, headed by the First Lady—constituted the multi-tiered system of female patrons of the NCWS, with the First Lady as overall patron of the organisation. Such a system of patronage has rested on highly unequal relationships with wealthy and influential women whose visibility and influence were dependent on their relationships with senior men in the military state, not on their own competence or ideas. This has had the effect of entrenching male authority over women in the context of relationships of dependence and mitigating against the development of women's autonomy, whether in the NCWS, among rural women or even among the high-flying patrons themselves.

Discourses of Womanhood

The sense in which the state signifies a masculine sphere was alluded to earlier. By extension, national politics is also gendered male. The contemporary political sphere in Nigeria appears to be gendered in such a way that the arena in which formal institutional politics is practised is viewed as the legitimate province of elite men. Women's activism, on the other hand, is considered to be most appropriate when it is 'non-political' and therefore located in either informal or non-governmental sites. Political activity by women, which brings women into closer contact with men, challenges a number of notions about "a woman's place". Views such as the following are expressed by women and men alike:

> Two women went into politics ... from Katsina and Kaduna states. These women were disowned by their communities, because any woman who's exposed to men must have a very low moral value. Politics is a dirty game. Exposure to men, unless she's very strong, will lead her to do what she's not supposed to do. It's only for women who are loose, or of low virtue (Tambaia, 1996).

Since women's presence in politics is interpreted as their incursion into a domain from which they should be excluded, it follows that for many women, a considerable amount of energy goes into legitimating what is perceived as an illegitimate intrusion. One way of dealing with the potential loss of status that activity in the malestream political sphere entails for women is undoubtedly the excessive reiteration of the virtues of 'traditional' womanhood and acceptance of male authority (Geisler, 1995). Fending off criticisms of the NCWS's plans to establish a women voters league in 1990, when the ban on partisan politics would be lifted, Hilda Adefarasin, the National President asserted that "... it was wrong to say that women wanted to take over political power from men, since they had not forgotten their traditional roles as mothers and wives"(see Onyegeri, 1987).

There is no doubt that women do legitimate their entry into the political sphere as wives and mothers, and there are reasons for doing so. Women's status in society is derived to a large extent from their reproductive role and it is as mothers that women are recognised as adults. By utilising this image, women can strengthen and legitimate their political involvement in the eyes of the state, as well as those of men and other women in the society at large.

Whilst motherhood is used to legitimate women's entry into the malestream political domain, it also has the effect of naturalising the demands of the discourse. In so doing, it clouds the process of invention that is an inherent part of the formation of any discourse, even one that is on the face of it, as 'natural' as motherhood. Naturalising the discourse also has the effect of obscuring the extent to which different groups of mothers have different experiences and preoccupations, face differing problems and have different interests. Until recently, most social and political analysts have tended to accept as a given, the social and self-definition of certain groups of women as mothers. Essentially, this is the view that motherhood lies at the core of women's identity, shaping their political choices. Indeed, motherhood has often been used to explain or dismiss women's behaviour as opposed to being treated as a phenomenon that itself needed explaining.

The content of motherhood is both flexible and contradictory. In the context of women's activism and the political choices they make, motherhood is capable of being recruited for progressive as well as reactionary ends. Women have positioned themselves as mothers in opposition to authoritarian and repressive military regimes in South America (e.g. Chuchryk, 1989) as well as in the service of right-wing nationalisms (e.g. Sarkar, 1995). And whilst women can bolster their political involvement through the use of the discourse of motherhood, conversely, the state can also exploit the cultural identity of women as mothers to secure their political support (Corcoran-Nantes, 1993). In short, there is nothing automatic about either women's political use of motherhood or its relationship to the state.

In the last two decades, feminist theory has succeeded in problematising 'motherhood'. The international debate has exposed shortcomings in common-sense views of motherhood as 'naturally' the role of women, but there is no consensus on how to conceptualise this now controversial institution. Western feminists have shifted along a spectrum that is located between attacks on motherhood as a patriarchal construct and affirmations of it as a valuable identity and responsibility that must be defended against male control and masculinist values. Third World feminists have sharply criticised what they regard as the ethnocentrism of much of this debate while most recently, post-modern social theory has provided tools for the radical deconstruction of the unitary concept of motherhood (Walker, 1995).

In what follows, I will explore the specific construction of motherhood evident in NCWS pronouncements and the use made of this discourse. Motherhood, and the concomitant responsibility for family affairs and child rearing, is generally viewed in these pronouncements as the ultimate destiny of all women. What seems at first to be an enunciation of a traditionalist discourse on motherhood is, however, articulated as a set of statements derived from a developmentalist and statist discourse. For women, being mothers and looking after the family lies at the core of their involvement in national life, and of the reproduction of values required as prerequisites for the development of the nation-state. Assisting "women in towns and villages in their important role as home-makers and nation builders" (e.g.

NCWS, 1993:10) has been described as an essential activity of the organisation.

Moreover, women's performance in the public sphere is not to be viewed as an impediment to motherhood; rather, it should be fundamentally an extension of women's familial responsibilities. Education and work must be encouraged but should be subordinated to the supreme goal of motherhood. The political choices available to women as mothers are derived from their responsibilities and activities in raising children as 'good' citizens and thereby contributing to the goal of national development.

This construction reflects the confluence of two rather different currents that underlie NCWS's ideology and organisation. One current was that present in Christian missionary proselytisation, in which Victorian ideologies of domesticity were imported to Nigeria during the colonial period and propagated through schools (Denzer, 1992), medical centres and churches. Such ideologies embodied the European ideal of women being restricted to the domestic sphere in the role of wife-and-mother and were based on the institution of the nuclear family. In her role as mother, the woman was viewed as the ultimate line of defence against the disruptive, destabilising forces of modernity (Pereira, forthcoming).

> The continuing influence of this ideological strand in NCWS's activities is evident in its justification for and provision of 'skills centres'—centres that basically provide domestic training for young women. The rationale for the provision of one such centre, offering training in fashion designing, pattern drafting and dressmaking, is described thus:

The purpose of the centre is the development of the nation. Its aims are "to improve the status of women by providing continuing education; to encourage productivity and self-reliance by improving skill in various fields beneficial to the nation..." (Ayoola, 1988:7).

Another current, also shaped under the peculiar circumstances of colonialism, was the developmentalist legacy inherited from the nationalist period and the onset of Nigeria's flag independence. The emergent nationalism split the social world into a public, 'modern', state-centred domain where the colonial power (the West) reigned supreme, and a domestic, 'traditional' domain where the indigenous cultural tradition was superior. The state-centred world, which became the domain of men, was one of modernisation/westernisation, essentially one of change and disruption. The domestic world, the home, the family, was exclusively African and feminine, essentially traditional. But the 'new Woman' of the nationalist era was also educated and enlightened, serving both her husband and the nation. Women's involvement in the public sphere, however, was to take place on terms that threatened neither male authority nor male defined 'tradition'.

From my analysis of the pronouncements of NCWS, it is my contention that, in the post-colonial era, these two inspirations—the family as a bulwark against modernity and the construction of a modern, nationalist womanhood—have become synthesised in the discourse of *civic motherhood*. Here, civic motherhood is defined as a discourse in which motherhood is constructed in such a way as to legitimate women's incursion into the political arena, by claiming a special relationship with the nation-state. It is not that motherhood becomes devoid of its customary emotional and affective load. On the contrary, women's whole being is still viewed as tied up with motherhood: to be a woman is to be first and foremost a mother. To be a good mother, to nurture the family, raise the children and serve the husband is the supreme destiny of any woman. What is distinctive about the discourse of civic motherhood is that the emotional and affective strands of its construction have become overlaid with a specifically civic depiction of motherhood. This depiction is one in which women's involvement in child rearing is central to the development of a properly disciplined citizenry, fit to meet its duties and obligations vis-à-vis the nation-state. Such activity is also an integral aspect of women's contribution to the development of the nation. The following statements illustrate this point:

> The convention advised parents especially mothers to spare time for the homes, check their children's involvement in social vices as their contribution towards the building up of a morally disciplined nation (NCWS Newsletter, 1991).

> If we believe that if you educate a woman, you educate a nation, we all know that we are saying that the general development of a country still lies in the hands of the women, because it is the women who ... give the children the orientation and the upbringing. Because in most cases, the men are not really there (Audu, 1996).

The legitimisation of women's entry and participation in the malestream political sphere is read through the discourse of civic motherhood as essentially an extension of their duties and responsibilities as mothers. Such legitimisation is provided not only by members of NCWS but by officials of the state as well. A representative of Rivers State Governor, Col. Yombe, contended that:

> with the changing role of women, emphasis should shift from the confines of the homes to a wider perspective. He urged women to combine their natural role as wives, mothers and home makers with their chosen careers to ensure a truly civilised nation (*Daily Times*, 1989:3).

Whilst the occupation of a civic space might, on the face of it, allow greater opportunity to at least address the necessary redistribution of power between men and women, this is done in a way that is highly ambivalent. The emphasis on the complementarity of male and female 'roles' does not address the question of the gender division of labour and ultimately does not pose a challenge to existing power relations. Implicit in the notion of complementarity is the view of women as domestic helpmates, entrenched in the bourgeois Victorian ideology of domesticity. Mission schools taught girls to become "civilised helpmates", "purer wives and better mothers".

That the discourse of motherhood outlined above is hegemonic can be illustrated by the use made by it of various state governors. A one-time governor of Kaduna State, Major Umar, noted that:

> women by virtue of their position and role as mothers and housewives, have always occupied a special place in society ... their task of bringing up children and moulding their character for future leadership could not be over-emphasised (Modibbo, 1985:16).

Four years later, the new governor of the same state, did likewise:

> Colonel Mukhtar urged them (women) to live up to their roles as mothers and lead exemplary lives worthy of emulation by their children and that they should be proud of their identity and use it to achieve high ideals (Modibbo, 1989:21).

The discourse of civic motherhood was clearly used by both NCWS and the state in the support of government policies, both in relation to the so called political transition programme and the Structural Adjustment Programme. Babangida's deployment of motherhood during the transition programme is telling:

> Women, as wives and mothers, cannot afford to sit on the fence or act as observers in the political transition. They have a tremendous stake in the future of this country (Babangida, 1990:10).

In similar vein, Chizea, Chairperson of the NCWS Task Force on the Political Transition Programme, appealed to "every Nigerian woman to please endeavour to take up the challenges for women for the transition to the Third Republic by playing their full roles as mothers of this great nation" (1991:13).

The NCWS has consistently supported Babangida's Structural Adjustment Programme by appealing to Nigerian women to "plan their family expenditure prudently", as their own contribution to making the national budget work. In their 1986 New Year message, the NCWS had this to say:

> ... we have a responsibility to make the 1986 budget work at all cost (sic) so far as it concerns us as women and housewives. [The new year] will undoubtedly be a 'test' for us all because the economic urgency which confronts our nation will require of us a belt-tightening far greater than others ... (*New Nigerian*, 1986:22).

Whilst motherhood is the dominant discourse of womanhood utilised by the NCWS, within the organisation other discourses have recently come to the fore. This was evident in the run-up to the 1993 elections, when for the first time in the history of the organisation, the post of National President was held by a Northerner (Hajiya Leila Dogonyaro). Questions of regional identification, as opposed to the 'universal' experience of motherhood, became an alternative base for solidarity. This took place in the context of Northern women expressing a protest against marginalisation and the domination of the leadership of NCWS by women from the South (Yusuf, et al., 1996). This contest has to be set against the fears in the general body politic of a North/South split, following Babangida's imposition of a two-party system for the proposed return to civil rule. The fear of being in whichever group does not gain central state power in the Third Republic, and of therefore being deprived of access to a relatively huge oil revenue, has fuelled identity politics in the population at large, and within NCWS.

Implications for Democratisation

The above discussion illustrates some of the ways in which the NCWS and the state have drawn on the discourse of motherhood so as to contribute to the legitimisation of social and political power. This has had the effect of narrowing the ideological space available for progressive forces to utilise subaltern discourses of womanhood to affect either the accepted beliefs and understandings of 'a woman's place' in Nigerian society, or to use such discourses to critically challenge the policies and practices of the state. The narrowing of such space is especially significant given that existing mainstream political discourses are resoundingly silent on the issue of fundamental social change in general, and on the question of what kind of society promises an improved life for women excluded from access to power.

The view that women have not been able to establish regular channels of access to decision-makers (Chazan, 1989), is not upheld by the example of the NCWS. Whilst it is true that the vast majority of women in post-colonial African societies are denied such access, Chazan's position does not take into account the point that different groups of women have radically differential access to the state and the question of what kind of access is open to which groups of women needs to be addressed. For groups such as the NCWS, 'official' non-governmental umbrella women's organisations, access to state resources has been institutionalised on the basis of particular relations of exchange which have been established historically. It is clear that such access and the relations associated with it are highly undemocratic.

The exploration of patron-client relations, in particular the female network of patronage, has drawn attention to changing relations of dependence and autonomy for women. The implications of these are evident in a number of interconnected areas. The first concerns the existence and deployment of a highly conservative gender politics embodied in anti-feminist discourses of womanhood—notions of 'the way women ought to be' (see Mama, 1995a). These have reinforced the status quo rather than challenging it. Among the elite, the social importance attributed to 'wifehood' has been enhanced, at the expense of valorising women's autonomy.

Secondly, the style of patronage engaged in by the NCWS has consolidated its linkages with the military state, reinforcing the incorporation of a select group of women into the state as clients. The consolidation of linkages with the military state arises out of the multiple and overlapping, but differentiated, character of female as well as male patron-client relations. State mediation in gendered class formation is underpinned by the NCWS acting as a vehicle of class interests (see Lovett, 1989). In a comparative study of the then-Soviet Union, China, Cuba and Tanzania, Croll (1986) showed how women's organisations under governmental auspices 'have so far been more effective in soliciting women's support for official policies than in getting policies changed to meet women's needs' (Croll, 1986:251). The common interests of all women members are rarely served by organisations such as the NCWS, whose dependency on state patronage for respectability and access to resources mitigates against such a role. Instead, NCWS serves the specific interests of sub-groups of women, belonging in many cases to different socio-economic strata. In this context, the growth and consolidation of the NCWS contributes to the process of socio-economic differentiation in Nigeria (see Sorensen, 1992; Woodford-Berger, 1993). At the same time, the existence of the NCWS, whilst deriving from a history of women's autonomous organising, has implications for state formation. We have already referred to the history of marginalisation and exclusion of women from the state and national politics, instituted through colonialism and deepened in the post-colonial era. Paradoxically, the existence of the NCWS affects the state by contributing to the protection of male, mainstream arenas of decision-making, since what are construed as 'women's issues' are bracketed off under the non-governmental umbrella of the NCWS. In this way, women's exclusion from state arenas is legitimated and perpetuated. What this process highlights is the centrality of relations between women and men in understanding the recursive relationship that exists between gendered state and class formation. Whilst the Babangida regime has experienced a number of protests and challenges to the state, it has also witnessed increased attempts by groups such as the NCWS to deliberately align themselves with the state. Such processes are manifestations of accommodation to the regime, rather than resistance. The much vaunted `revitalisation' of civil society assumed as one of the beneficial processes of socio-economic change accompanying Structural Adjustment Programmes, is hardly merited. Instead of 'revitalisation', cleavages within society have been accentuated and certain sections of civil society are exhibiting deepening dependency on the state. The social relations underlying this process have shaped, in part, the use of conservative discourses of womanhood. Whilst the state under the Babangida regime has empowered some groups of women, this has occurred in the context of relationships and processes that are disempowering to the vast majority of women, since they are embedded in structures and systems of gender discrimination and subordination.

Bibliography

Amadiume, I. 1987, *Male Daughters, Female Husbands*. London: Zed Books.

Ayoola, O., 1988, "Women Upliftment, NCWS Starts Skills Centre", *Daily Times*, March 8.

Babangida, I. B., 1990, Goodwill Message from the President, Commander-in-Chief of the Armed Forces, on the occasion of "The One-Day Political Seminar for Women under the Auspices of the National Council of Women's Societies", on Saturday, October 6.

Badran, M. 1988, "Dual Liberation: Feminism and Nationalism in Egypt, 1970–1985", *Feminist Issues*, 8(1), 15–34.

Basu, A. 1995, "Introduction", in Basu, A., (ed.) *The Challenge of Local Feminisms*. Boulder: Westview Press, 1–20.

Beckman, B., 1992, "Empowerment or Repression? The World Bank and the Politics of African Adjustment", in Gibbon, P., Y. Bangura and A. Ostad, (eds.) *Authoritarianism, Democracy and Adjustment: The Politics of Economic Reform in Africa*. Uppsala: The Scandinavian Institute of African Studies.

Bunch, C. 1985, *Feminism in the 80s: Bringing the Global Home*. Denver: Antelope.

Chazan, N., 1989, "Gender Perspectives on African States", in Parpart, J. and K. Staudt, (eds.) *Women and the State in Africa*. Boulder/London: Lynne Rienner. 185–201.

Chizea, D., 1990, *Report of the Chairman of the NCWS Task Force on Political Transition Programme*, November.

Chizea, D., 1991, "Transition to the Third Republic: The Challenges of Women", in Chizea, D. and J. Njoku, (eds.) *Nigerian Women and the Challenges of Our Time*. Lagos: Malthouse Press. pp. 10–14

Chuchryk, P., 1989, "Subversive Mothers: The Women's Opposition to the Military Regime in Chile", in Charlton, S., J. Everett and K. Staudt, (eds.) *Women, the State and Development*. New York: State University of New York Press. pp. 130–151.

Civil Liberties Organisation, 1992, *A Harvest of Violations: Annual Report on Human Rights in Nigeria, 1991*. Lagos: Civil Liberties Organisation.

Civil Liberties Organisation, 1993, *Human Rights in Retreat*. Lagos: Civil Liberties Organisation.

Commonwealth Expert Group on Women and Structural Adjustment, 1990, *Engendering Adjustment for the 1990s*. London: Commonwealth Secretariat.

Corcoran-Nantes, Y., 1993, "Female Consciousness or Feminist Consciousness? Women's Consciousness Raising in Community-Based Struggles in Brazil", in Radcliffe, S. and S. Westwood, (eds.) *'Viva': Women and Popular Protest in Latin America*, pp. 136–155. London: Routledge.

Croll, E., 1986, "Rural Production and Reproduction: Socialist Development Experiences", in Leacock, E. and H. Safa (eds.) *Women's Work: Development and the Division of Labour by Gender*. South Hadley, Mass.: Bergin and Garvey.

de Lauretis, T., 1987, *Technologies of Gender*. London: Macmillan.

Denzer, L. 1992, "Domestic Science Training in Colonial Yorubaland, Nigeria", in Hansen, K. (ed.) *African Encounters with Domesticity*. New Brunswick: Rutgers University Press, pp. 116–139.

Development Alternatives with Women for a New Era (DAWN), 1988, *Development, Crises and Alternative Visions: Third World Women's Perspectives*. London: Earthscan.

Directorate for Social Mobilisation, 1989, *Report of the Political Bureau 1987*. Abuja: MAMSER.
Federal Government of Nigeria, 1987, *Government Views and Comments on the Findings and Recommendations of the Political Bureau 1987*. Lagos: Federal Government Printer.
Geisler, G., 1995, "Troubled Sisterhood: Women and Politics in Southern Africa", *African Affairs*, 94, pp. 545–578.
Halvorsen, K., 1991, *The Gendered State: A Review of Some Recent Studies on Women and the State*, working paper D 1991:1. Bergen: CHR. Michelsen Institute.
Henriques, J., W. Hollway, C. Urwin, C. Venn, and V. Walkerdine, 1984, *Changing the Subject: Psychology, Social Regulation and Subjectivity*. London: Methuen.
Ibrahim, J., 1993, "The Transition to Civil Rule: Sapping Democracy", in Olukoshi, A. (ed.) *The Politics of Structural Adjustment in Nigeria*. London: James Currey. pp. 129–139.
Ibrahim, J. and C. Pereira, 1994, "On Dividing and Uniting: Ethnicity, Racism and Nationalism in Africa", paper prepared for International Development Information Network (IDIN), CLACSO, Buenos Aires, November 1994.
Imam, A., 1993, "Politics, Islam and Women in Kano, Northern Nigeria", in Moghadam, V. (ed.) *Identity Politics and Women: Cultural Reassertions and Feminisms in International Perspective*. Boulder: Westview Press. pp. 123–144.
Imam, A., 1997, "The Dynamics of WINning: An Analysis of Women in Nigeria (WIN)", in Alexander, M., and C. Mohanty (eds.) *Feminist Genealogies, Colonial Legacies, Democratic Futures*. New York: Routledge. pp. 280–307.
Kandiyoti, D., 1991, "Identity and Its Discontents: Women and the Nation", *Journal of International Studies*, 20(3), pp. 429–443.
Kishwar, M., and R. Vanita (eds.), 1984, *In Search of Answers: Indian Women's Voices from Manushi*. London: Zed Books.
Likimani, M., 1985, *Passbook Number F.47927—Women and Mau Mau in Kenya*. London: Macmillan.
Lovett, M., 1989, "Gender Relations, Class Formation and the Colonial State in Africa", in Parpart, J., and K. Staudt, (eds.) *Women and the State in Africa*. Boulder/London: Lynne Rienner. pp. 23–26.
Mama, A., 1995a, "Feminism or Femocracy? State Feminism and Democratisation in Nigeria", *Africa Development*, XX(1), 37–58.
Mama, A., 1995b, *Beyond the Masks: Race, Gender and Subjectivity*. London: Routledge.
Mba, N., 1982, *Nigerian Women Mobilized: Women's Political Activity in Southern Nigeria, 1900–1965*. Berkeley: Institute of International Studies.
Mba, N., 1989, "Kaba and Khaki: Women and the Militarized State in Nigeria", in Parpart, J., and K. Staudt, (eds.) *Women and the State in Africa*, pp. 69–90. Boulder: Lynne Rienner.
McClintock, A., 1991, "'No Longer in a Future Heaven': Women and Nationalism in South Africa", *Transition*, 51.
Modibbo, A., 1985, "Umar Takes Women to Task", *New Nigerian*, December 13.
Modibbo, A., 1989, "Governor Mukhtar Commends NCWS", *New Nigerian*, March 20.
Morgan, R., 1984, *Sisterhood Is Global: The International Women's Movement Anthology*. Garden City, New York: Anchor Books.
Motojehi, D., 1989, "NN Editor Bares Her Mind about NAOWA", *New Nigerian*, 22 March 1989, p. 2.
NCWS Newsletter, 1991, The 13th Biennial Convention Enugu 1990. *NCWS Newsletter* 10, 5.

NCWS, 1993, "The 14th Biennial Convention of the National Council of Women's Societies, Nigeria", at the U.K. Bello Complex, Minna, Tuesday 30th March – Friday 2nd April 1993.

Newbury, C., 1988, *The Cohesion of Oppression*. New York: Columbia University Press.

Okonjo, K., 1976, "The Dual-Sex Political System in Operation: Igbo Women and Community Politics in Midwestern Nigeria", in Hafkin, N., and E. Bay, (eds.) *Women in Africa: Studies in Social and Economic Change*. Stanford Calif.: Stanford University Press. , pp. 45–58.

Onyegiri, E., 1987, "Women (sic) Society Plans Voters League in 1990", *The Guardian* 4, (3,482), 1, Friday July 24.

Palmer, I. n.d., "Monitoring Women's Conditions", unpublished draft for UNRISD. Cited in Rogers, B., 1980, *The Domestication of Women: Discrimination in Developing Societies*. London: Tavistock.

Parpart, J. and K. Staudt (eds.), 1989, *Women and the State in Africa*. Boulder/London: Lynne Rienner.

Pereira, C., forthcoming, "'No Seamless Narrative': A Gender Analysis of Psychology in Africa", in Imam, A., F. Sow and A. Mama (eds.) *Gender and the Social Sciences in Africa*. Dakar: CODESRIA.

Peterson, V. and A. Runyan, 1993, *Global Gender Issues*. Boulder: Westview Press.

Rowbotham, S., 1994, *Women in Movement: Feminism and Social Action*. New York: Routledge.

Sarkar, T., 1995, "Heroic Women, Mother Goddesses: Family and Organisation in Hindutva Politics", in Sarkar, T. and U. Butalia (eds.) *Women and Right-Wing Movements*. London: Zed Books. pp. 181–215.

Shettima, K., 1995, "Engendering Nigeria's Third Republic", *African Studies Review*, 38(3), pp. 61–98.

Sorensen, A., 1992, "Women's Organisations Among the Kipsigis: Change, Variety and Different Participation", *Africa*, 62(4), pp. 547–566.

Tsikata, E., 1989, "Women's Political Organisations 1951–1987", in Hansen, K., and K. Ninsin, (eds.) *The State, Development and Politics in Ghana*. Dakar: CODESRIA. pp. 73–93.

Udegbe, B., 1995, "Better Life for Rural Women Programme: An Agenda for Positive Change?", *Africa Development*, XX (4), pp. 69–84.

Urdang, S., 1979, *Fighting Two Colonialisms: Women in Guinea Bissau*. New York: Monthly Review Press.

Urdang, S., 1989, *And Still They Dance: Women, War and the Struggle for Change in Mozambique*. London: Earthscan.

van Allen, J., 1976, "'Aba Riots' or Igbo 'Women's War'? Ideology, Stratification and the Invisibility of Women", in Hafkin, N., and E. Bay, (eds.) *Women in Africa: Studies in Social and Economic Change*. Stanford Calif.: Stanford University Press. pp. 59–85.

Vereecke, C., 1993, "Better Life for Women in Nigeria: Problems, Prospects and Politics of a New National Women's Program", *African Study Monographs*, 14 (2), pp. 79–95.

Walker, C., 1995, "Conceptualising Motherhood in Twentieth Century South Africa", *Journal of Southern African Studies*, 21(3), pp. 417–437.

Weedon, C., 1987, *Feminist Practice and Post-Sructuralist Theory*. Oxford: Blackwell.

Westwood, S. and S. Radcliffe, 1993, "Gender, Racism and the Politics of Identities in Latin America", in Radcliffe, S., and S. Westwood, (eds.) *'Viva': Women and Popular Protest in Latin America*. pp. 1–29. London: Routledge.

Women in Nigeria, 1985, *The WIN Document: Conditions of Women in Nigeria and Policy Recommendations to 2000 A.D.* Zaria: WIN.

Women in Nigeria, 1986, *Proceedings of Conferences, Symposia and Workshops on Women and Nigerian Political Development, Awareness and Mobilisation*. Zaria: WIN.

Woodford-Berger, P., 1993, "Associating Women: Female Linkages, Collective Identities and Political Ideology in Ghana", paper presented at "Colloque du transformation des identités féminines: formes d'organisation feminines en Afrique de l'Ouest", 26–28 Mars 1993, Ngaoundéré, Cameroun, organized by the Nordic Africa Institute.

Newspapers and Magazines

Daily Times, 1986, "Focus on Women's Roles", July 21.
Daily Times, 1989, "Assist Government Promote Peaceful Co-Existence", February 28.
New Nigerian, 1986, "NCWS Appeals for Prudent Family Spending", January 1.
Triumph, 1988, "Women not Planning to Overthrow Men", January 25.

Interviews

Audu, Esther, (President of NCWS Federal Capital Territory), Interview granted to me on July 19, 1996, in Abuja.

Dogonyaro, L. (National President of NCWS, 1993–1995), Interview granted to me on June 21, 1996, in Kaduna.

Hassan, Abbas, (Journalist), Interview granted to me on July 25, 1996 in Abuja.

Sambo, Amina, (National President of NCWS, 1995–1997), Interview granted to me on July 25, 1996, at the NCWS Secretariat, Abuja.

Tambaia, Lata, (State President NCWS Kaduna State), Interview granted me on July 11, 1996 in Kaduna.

Yusuf, B., (Journalist), L. Dogonyaro (past National President, NCWS), Husamot Ajala (past National Secretary, NCWS), Nimi Thom-Manuel (past National Publicity Secretary, NCWS), 1996, Interviews granted to me on March 18, in Kaduna.

Chapter 7

Adjustment and the Transformation of Labour Identity: What's New and Does it Matter?

Jimi O. Adesina

Introduction

There is a lot we know today about the impact of over fifteen years of trying to 'reform' Africa's economies. We know that the heady predictions made by supply-side economists, in the early 1980s are at best naïve. A dosage of stabilisation shock, it was confidently stated, is good for stemming the rot in public finance and liberalisation is good for restoring growth. At worst, the predictions result from an exercise in mass vivisectomy, with the scientists themselves groping in the dark (Adesina, 1994:viii). As Adesina (1994) argued, much of the World Bank's prognosis of the development crisis in Africa was misplaced. More recently Garba has demonstrated that the Bank's *adjustment with growth* programme in Nigeria "did not target any of the internal, external or the fiscal balancing problems revealed by Nigeria's initial conditions between 1981–1985 and in 1985" (1996:55). The economies of most African countries remain regressive—the manufacturing base is weakened and the prospect of growth based on the real sector's performance is at best weak. We know, also, that poverty has deepened in Sub-Saharan Africa in the decade and a half of adjustment (cf. Rodgers and van der Hoeven, 1995; World Bank, 1994). Of the regions of the world, Africa is the only one where poverty is expected to grow into the next century. Today, we talk of the 'africanisation of poverty' (Tabatabai, 1995; Jamal, 1995; World Bank, 1990) in the same breath as we talk of the 'feminisation of poverty' (Rodgers and van der Hoeven, 1995).

When it comes to the specific impact of adjustment on the labour movement, especially organised labour, we know enough about some of the linkages. The politics of adjustment has received some attention regarding its impact on organised labour in Nigeria. While we know enough about these aspects of adjustment, the micro-level impact, regarding changing forms of identity, remains an enigma. It is not just the problems that the conceptual crisis of post-modernist discourse throws up that makes talking of labour identity rather than identities difficult. Even in the post-structuralist discourse, there are considerable ontological problems in grappling with identity much less its transformation. Trying to read off identities from social action has its own conceptual problems, since the language of politics is also about the politics of language. Reading-off identity from the phenomenological account of the social actor (in the language of structuralism) also creates its problems: the social actor is an interrogating agent. The interviewer is as much an issue in the response as is the question being asked. I will be addressing some of the conceptual and methodological issues in the very concept of identity in section 2 of this chapter. My attempt is to deal with the problematic of identity in the specific context of bearers of labour-power.

Between the post-modernist 'deconstructionist' attack on the unity of meaning and the structuralist reading of the agency's identity from the 'social structure', we must try to glean the changing terrain of labour identity in Nigeria. In section 4, we will attempt to glean such shifts from what has been happening at the macro-level. For this reason, we will examine two issues. First is what we know about the adjustment of the politics of (organised) labour, especially since 1988. Second, we will examine the changes at the labour market and household levels that affect the individual worker. In tying the shifting terrain of identity to the Structural Adjustment Programme, we may, I suspect, be imputing to the adjustment programme issues that co-occurred with it, rather than being causally connected to adjustment. The politics of the annulment of the 1993 presidential elections, more than the adjustment programme, for instance, has significantly impacted on the identity terrain in Nigeria. This is a thesis that I will be developing in section 5 of this chapter and this immediately ties with the issue of transformation.

Again, paradoxes rather than definitive claims may be what are more important. Are we experiencing transformation in labour identity or are we dealing with something more mundane or profound? Is the domain of politics bringing into dominance, identities that would have laid dormant were the reality of national political life to be different? The human agency is a bearer of multiple identities. The dominance of a given identity may be a function of the dominant language of politics of the 'significant other' with which workers and organised labour have to contend. In this respect, rather than a 'transformation' of labour identity, we may be dealing with shifting language of public discourse. An assumption of 'transformation' of labour identity with a pessimistic conclusion may replace the heroic myth-making of the 1960s and the 1970s, in several analyses of the labour with its inversion: our own 'end of ideology' thesis. It is in this sense that my subtitle for this chapter is: What is new and does it matter? Indeed, is anything new?

Again, paradox. In the same period that the organised labour movement—within the framework of the Nigeria Labour Congress—caved in under the boots of the military regime, the various indices of labour militancy went up, and sometimes, it was a steep climb. Are we dealing with labour politics where it really matters or something ephemeral? If basic socio-economic indicators show worsening material conditions for workers and an increasingly tight labour market, will that portend transformation of labour identity or the persistence of identity?

Conceptual Issues in Labour Identity

A discussion of identity, especially labour identity brings us into the terrain of ontological discussions of being and consciousness. The idea of labour raises questions of production activities and relations. As I argued elsewhere—and that discussion will loom large here—there are important conceptual issues that need straightening out (Adesina, 1993). First is what I consider the need for an awareness of analysis of different levels of abstraction. Much of the crisis in ontological discussion of workers, I argued "results from the location of that analysis on the wrong level of abstraction... Often the analytical movement from categories of high levels of abstraction... to specific manifestation in real life is undertaken as if this movement is unproblematic" (Adesina, 1993:121).

> As an analysis moves from higher to lower levels of abstraction, (and it embraces the increasingly complex nature of issues being investigated) we develop 'increasingly more complex concepts... until the complexity of the world of appearance is reproduced in thought or on the page' (Fine and Harris, 1979:7).

The categories (concepts) employed in this process of reflecting the increasing complexity of everyday life will reveal this sensitivity to the complexity; at least it ought to. Sometimes some analysts of so called orthodox Marxian bent proceed as if the category of class in the analysis of capitalism-in-general is the same as when they are analysing concrete manifestation of class. 'Even the most abstract categories', are 'in the specific character of this abstraction, themselves... (products) of historical relations, and possess their full validity only for or within these relations' (Marx, 1973:3105). Here one comes to the issue of what I called the "territoriality of class":

> Class, as a category of low levels of abstraction, must re-immerse itself in real social contexts. Class is, for instance, cultural; or put differently class has culture. The culture of class is fundamentally specific and grounded in a given context of time and space (Adesina, 1993:128).

In the territoriality of class, class identity co-exists with other forms of identity: ethnic, gender, racial, religious, etc. This is where the interaction of class and non-class identities (or what I called primordial identities) comes in giving specificity to a given class category. As a category of the highest level of abstraction, the class identity of workers, in the context of commodity relations, is defined by two factors: non-ownership of means of production and dependence on the exchange value of labour-power for subsistence. Such specification suffices as long as our objective is the analysis of capitalism-in-general. Concrete expressions of the same class category, when dealing at much lower levels of abstraction show the interaction between class and primordial identities.

Nowhere is this more clearly so than when gender-discourse shattered the 'temple of our familiar', forcing our attention to the depth to which the labour process is fundamentally gender-structured. The same applies to race. As I noted, "studies on the experience of work in the United States of America, colonial Africa, and South Africa point to the significance of race in the structuring of the labour process" (Adesina, 1993:128). Similarly:

> Where the primordial is at the heart of class structuration, *it is part of class*. In other words, the pattern of privilege and subordination has primordial resonance, and is necessary for sketching the boundaries of class itself... We can hardly make sense of class without acknowledging the immediacy of the primordial (Adesina, 1993:129).

However, there are three more levels to go in this conceptual understanding of this analysis of labour identity. First, that the resonance of primordial identities in labour identity will depend on "the primacy of primordial identities in the larger society... in terms of institutionalised privileges and subordination" (Adesina, 1993:129). Second, is the constitutive power of language of class or race for instance, of the dominating subject. Therborn (1980:28) referred to this as the 'alter-ideology of the dominating subject'. This 'alter-ideology' "attempts to constitute the dominated subject in subordinate roles, and to strip away the bases of group and individual self-assertion that may enhance resistance to the dominating subject" (Adesina, 1993:130). Frequently, the privileging of one segment of the dominated subject (here workers) co-exists with the constitution of the dominated subject in these subordinate roles:

> The power of mediation [i.e. by the alter-ideology of the dominating subject] of the worker's subjectivity is not only in structuring the experiences of the worker, but in the ways that they subvert the confidence of the worker in what his or her intuition suggests (*ibid.*, p. 131).

It is not only in undermining class resistance that this manifests itself, it may do so in the context of the construction of common identity between fractions of the dominated and the dominating subjects, based on shared non-class identities.

Finally, while the constitutive power of language is available to the dominating subject, the dominated subject also grapples with and rescues his/her own subjectivity in an array of counter-culture, or more appropriately their (workers') culture. In primordially segmented class of subordinate subjects, however, such counter-culture or revolt faces another factor:

> In so far as revolt is itself discursively constructed, the impact of the primordial experience will depend on how the primordially subordinate faction of the working class sees the primordially privileged faction ... Of course, the constitutive language of the primordially dominated segments of the working class will militantly assert their particular experience of commodity relations (ibid, p. 133).

The constitutive languages that seek to construct identities or mobilise must be understood "in relation to the political languages with which they are in conflict" (Stedman Jones, 1983:22). In the construction or mobilisation of identities (class or non-class), language, as a:

> 'part of social being'... must be seen, like other parts of social being, as multilayered, complex, fractured, composed of incoherences and silences, as well as the smooth flow of would-be authoritative public discourses (Gray, 1986:367).

Our discourse above will be central to my attempt to grapple with issues of labour identity under the Structural Adjustment Programme. In other words, I am just as interested in the dominating subjects' discursive mobilisation of non-class identities at specific points, the alter-ideology that is deployed, and labour's own production of interest, and mobilisation of its interest.

The domain of consciousness and identity is, of course, a favourite terrain of the post-modernist attack on unity of representation, reason, or epistemology, and a word is useful at this stage regarding it implications for our analysis. I am unconvinced, though, that beyond the *narco-intellectualism* of Foucault (a kind of intellectual hippiedom), post-modernism, despite its seduction, is more than an intellectual variant of the 'post-trauma syndrome' so common with Vietnam veterans; in this case a *post-discursive trauma syndrome*. While the attack on teleological orientation of much of 'modernist' discourse is valid, the dissembling of all epistemological unity or the phenomenological unity of representation hardly addressed the more profound dimensions of lived experience. A narcotic-induced 'experience' with its disembodied imageries can hardly be the basis for genuine ontological discourses. The paradox of post-modernism is that, in its attack on modernist discourse (or meta-narratives), post-modernism is replacing one 'master discourse' with another, since to be viable, it aspires to being a distinct epistemology, hence a meta-narrative of a kind! I agree with Paul Thompson (1993) that what we are dealing with is essentially a "fatal distraction".

The discussion thus far might be forgiven for suggesting that the issues of identity construction or mobilisation and the language of class, gender, race or ethno-regional identities take place, belong in sedate environments. As history tells us (and we will see this below) the forging, mobilisation, transformation, and dissolution of given identities are consummate social phenomena defined by violence, physical and emotional. Sometimes, the violence that is involved is organised around the state, and at other times within the civil society.

Beyond the conceptual issues are those that are methodological in nature. To conceptually construct identities and their interaction is one thing. Empirically demonstrating this in the context of field-research is another.

Methodological Issues in Changing Identity of Labour

An investigation of changing labour identity raises some methodological issues. When we talk of the changes or transformation of identity the problem of knowing arises. The competing explanations of identity—from structuralist perspective to post-modernist discourse—offer contrasting ways of knowing. If people are no more than bearers of social roles (or predominantly so, at least), how we approach a specification of their identity, and when it is changing or transforming, will differ from in situation where the human agency is privileged. The privileging of structure means we can read off the agency from the prescribed social roles and patterned relations. The phenomenological sociologist will insist, via methodological individualism, on the primacy of the agency's phenomenological rendering of his/her situation and therefore the meaningfulness of his/her action.

The post-modern discourse with its concern for 'knowledge of localised understanding and acceptance of a plurality of diverse language forms' asserts 'the fragmentation of grand narratives and the discrediting of all meta-narratives (Hassard, 1993:9). In pushing methodological individualism to its extreme, the post-modern discourse becomes a negation of unifying functions of theory. The method of knowing makes one narrative as valid as any other, and our method of enquiry must remain trenchantly ethno-methodological (in the extreme, one must say).

Attempting to simply read off the nature of identity from the social institutions or structure and identity transformation will fail to grasp language of class or gender as a constitutive process of the human agency. On the other hand, an approach which relies on the agency for the meaningfulness of his/her action (hence a privileging of interview or ethno-methodological approach) will fail to understand, at least two difficulties. One, that the research subject in the interview setting is also interrogating the interviewer. Two, that the meaningfulness of the agency's action is not a once and for all thing. It is a constitutive process, actively interacting with the posture and perception of other agencies, and the historicity of the event or moment that is being phenomenologically rendered.

Beyond what may sound like methodological pessimism, I believe that we can approach the issue of identity construct and identity transformation using multiple techniques of social research. Since the present chapter is not derived from any *new* field research into the changing nature of labour identity in the context of the Structural Adjustment Programme, I will draw my reading of labour identity from several methodological sources. First, is an attempt to make sense of what conclusions we can draw from secondary sources including official statistics. Second, also deriving from desk-work is reported research findings. Third, are my earlier works that, though not directly concerned with the transformation of labour identity, have implications for labour identity. Last, is a reflection on my personal ('participant observer') involvement in the Nigerian labour movement. This involves direct interaction with the key actors in the events of the past decade in the Nigerian labour movement. Added to this is my personal involvement with union organisation and activism, especially since 1992. This chapter benefits from a reflection on some of the insights gained so far. If the first two sources provide what, Mahmood Mamdani calls a 'hawk's-eye' view, then the 'participant observer's' experience will provide a 'frog-eye' view.

Before going on to examine the issue of labour identity and its transformation, if any, it is useful to briefly look at the labour specific dimension of the Structural Adjustment Programme.

Structurally Adjusting Labour

Much of the discussion on the emergence of Structural Adjustment Programmes, as the new economic orthodoxy in Sub-Saharan Africa, has identified the link with the debt crisis of the early 1980s; and that need not delay us here. The translation of the crisis of debt-ridden economies to the virtual stranglehold of the World Bank and the International Monetary Fund on national annual budgets; hence even short-run economic planning requires a more studied look. For instance, annual budgets are subject to the approval of the Bretton Woods institutions, and the critique of annual estimates, as statements of economic intents have become routine. Yet two decades ago, governments would have been scandalised if World Bank officials concerned themselves with something so far outside the Bank's mandate. Further still, and for our immediate concern in this chapter, is how these affect labour; not as innocent bystanders in the cross-fire of resource allocation but as primary targets of the new economic orthodoxy.

Williams (1994) approached the starting point for the fundamental changes in the mandate of the Bretton Woods institutions from two ends. First is the crisis that major private banks in the West, that had lent moneys to governments in developing countries, faced in recovering the debt. Second is the report of the Brandt Commission, which had pushed the debate about a New International Economic Order into previously uncharted waters. It suggested the setting up of the World Development Fund (WDF): "a kind of internationalisation of the welfare state" where progressive taxation of all countries provides the finance for resource transfer from the North to the South that will be needed for "a world system of public expenditure" (Elson, 1982:112). Where the Bank and the IMF were clubs excluding several countries, and with internal power structures that were skewed to the major advanced capitalist countries with the United States as the prime comptroller, the World Development Fund will operate as a co-operative, equally sharing power between countries of the North and South.

Between the hard-nosed demand for debt retrieval of the Western bankers and the "do-gooder" orientation of the Brandt Commission, stood the ideological ground shift of the neo-Right in United States and Britain. For the Reagan Administration and the Thatcher government, the Brandt Commission was the spectre of neo-Keynesian thinking that had become the mortal political enemy to be vanquished. In addition, behind the Reaganite and Thatcherite politics was the fierce resurgence of marginalist (supply-side) Economics that insists on a return to market-based public policy. The spectre of a world run around the idea of the WDF provided the impetus within the Bank and the Fund for substantial changes in their mandate, while the groundswell of the neo-right economic counter-revolution provided the intellectual basis for a total re-working of development planning. The amended mandate of the Bank and the Fund provided the basis for the two institutions becoming the lightning-rod of neo-right economic thinking, and acquiring the superintending roles over detailed economic decision making process of most sub-Sahara African countries.

Structural Adjustment and Labour: New Rules of Engagement

The linkage with concerns over labour matters, as I argued elsewhere, is to be found in the "urban bias" thesis and the idea of "rent-seeking". Urban-based interest groups are responsible for skewing development investment in their direction to the detriment of rural-based groups (Adesina, 1992; 1994). The thesis has greatly affected the dominant paradigm and policy orientation within the Bank and the Fund. Lipton, for instance, tied the bits and pieces of neo-classical disillusionment with the 'Third World' "together and created a polemic against the 'urban coalition'" (Toye, 1990:2). In Africa, the argument runs, the urban coalition has interest in rent-seeking activities. As Toye noted:

> Instead of a series of isolated "policy mistakes", developing countries were seen to be in the grip of a syndrome in which dirigisme and rent-seeking were mutually reinforcing, and the perpetrators and the beneficiaries were the urban coalition (1990:2).

The content given the idea of *interest groups*, as I noted, is important in analytical and policy terms:

> In traditional pluralist paradigm, interest (pressure) groups through their competing pockets of allegiance, power and mobilisation of the citizenry prevent the development of autocracy in the polity and state. Interest groups guarantee the survival of the democratic polity. For conventional sociology, interest groups are vital for an organised solidaristic society, and mitigate anomic tendencies. By contrast interest groups in the UBT bear "an unambiguously negative connotation. They were divisive and parasitic; if successful they caused social rigidities or were otherwise socially destructive (1992:19).

The urban bias thesis was central to the distributional and timing components of the rationale for and the politics of adjustment; what Toye (1990:5) calls "the politics of the knife edge." Authoritarian regimes were needed "to ride roughshod over the newly-created special interest groups" (Lal, 1983:33). This means the need for authoritarian (or "strong" government) regimes to suppress entrenched special interest groups that will attempt to undermine adjustment programming. This notion of authoritarian regimes facilitating adjustment implementation was recently reaffirmed in an official World Bank publication. Faruqee (1994) credited what he defined as the initial 'impressive beginning' of adjustment programming to the military character of the Babangida regime. "The military government could initiate the reforms without worrying about how they might hurt some groups (Faruqee, 1994:238).

Urban-based organised labour are central to the World Bank's definitions of groups that must be severely restrained. And this ideological position was often presented as the 'primitives' of the new normative economics. For instance, concerning Nigeria, he Bank asserted that "the expansion of Government changed the structure of relative prices and wages. Rising wages and an appreciating currency squeezed the profitability of non-oil exports and undermined their competitive position internationally, while cheap food imports competed for domestic food production" (1993:vii). Earlier, the productivity of African labour was the central point of attack (cf. World Bank, 1981:93). The extent of the falsity of such proclamations is the subject of my *Labour in the Explanation of an African Crisis* (1994), the arguments need no repeating here. Garba (1996) has further demonstrated that the policy instruments of adjustment deployed with the formal adoption of SAP in 1986 did not in fact address the constraints facing Nigeria at the time. Rather than a situation of persistent decline in the lead-up to 1986, important economic indicators showed that "1985 marked a resumption of positive growth and sectoral GDP" (Garba, 1996:59).

The rendering of labour as culprit in rent seeking (involving the conspiracy of urban-dwellers against sound economic policy-making and the rural poor), provided the basis for imposing the set of macro-economic policy instruments grouped under "Structural Adjustment Programme". Exchange rate devaluation, fiscal restraint, domestic credit cuts, and higher interest rates (Garba, 1996) translated into the demand for more flexibility in the labour market: numerically and in the wage rate. In the mirror of marginalist economics, organised labour is a cartel interfering with the normal functioning of the market, forcing employers to pay wage rates above what the market can clear. Dismantling organised labour opposition did not only make political sense for international bureaucrats cut in the mould of the Nazis but economic sense, as well. It is in this sense that the fundamental changes in the landscape of organised labour in Nigeria, and, therefore, changes in the constitution of identities, make sense. However, as we have argued elsewhere (Adewum and, 1999), we must separate the *politics of adjustment* qua *adjustment* from the personal hegemonic project of Ibrahim Babangida. I will argue further that, we need to separate whatever political and economic justifications for repression against the labour movement we can find in adjustment programming from the nascent neo-fascist agenda currently being played out in Nigeria. The latter agenda involves a total reconstitution of the political geography of Nigeria through the mobilisation of regionalist and religious identities, at the behest of the dominant faction of the Nigerian power elite. To correct the potential one-sidedness that our earlier work may give, I should stress here that, the politics of adjustment provided the enabling environment that translated the nascent neo-fascism of the Babangida and Abacha regimes into economically justifiable projects. In altering the terms of social discourse, so profoundly, adjustment facilitated the repression of trade unions and the impoverishment of the mass of wage-dependent households. The diplomatic support that the Babangida regime received from the West, because of its conformity with the economic programme of adjustment, eliminated the external diplomatic or economic constraints that might have forced it to respect the basic rights of unions.

It is in the light of the above-mentioned that we begin to make sense of the major transformation in the landscape of the Nigerian labour movement and at the same time the persistence of affirmation of a labour identity. In the next section, I will look at contrasting images of labour identity in Nigeria.

A 'Hawk's-Eye' View of Labour Identity in Transition

The organised labour in Nigeria had since the 1940s developed a reputation for militant defence of workers' rights and policy advocacy in issues that concern the working people—even if fractiously so. The issue of identity of labour, at a collective and organised level, was bound by the trenchant advocacy of the central labour organisations of organised labour. The strategic position of organised labour within the economy informed this position, and there were also the antecedents of the labour movement's participation in past political struggles, especially during the colonial period. The labour movement's political advocacy was prominent in the period before the civil war, and in the 1970s and the 1980s (Adesina, 1994). With the 1978 reorganisation of trade unions, the Nigeria Labour Congress (NLC) replaced the previous four labour centres: the mantle, as it were, fell on the NLC.

Since 1979, the advocacy of the NLC (under the leadership of Hassan Sumonu) focused as much on the issues of sovereignty as it did on the defence of popular rights and the workers' welfare needs. The 1981 "Workers' Charter" of the NLC focused as much on the wage level as it did on the issues of popular assess to education, health care, and so on. The NLC was a major source of the critique of the excesses of the political class between 1979 and 1983. In 1981, a general strike was called by the NLC with the affiliate trade unions. The strike pressed for a revised minimum wage and general improvement in the conditions of employment of workers. As Otobo (1981, 1992a) shows, while the civilian environment of governance provided a more tolerant atmosphere for trade unions to operate, unions came under new types of attack by the state. The critical disengagement of the NLC from partisan party politics did not diminish its advocacy for improved minimum wage and pensions, and protests over arrears of salary owed to public sector workers in several states (Otobo, 1992b, Adesina 1990). In the protection of the occupational interests of members of its affiliated unions, the NLC became the single largest opposition to the rule of politicians. Otobo (1981) has documented various efforts to break the NLC and influence the election of its leadership at the first triennial conference in 1981. The objective was not only to promote a more accommodating leadership in the NLC but also to weaken the Congress.

The effort to weaken the Congress did not stop with the 1981 triennial delegates' conference. Historical ideological (often contrived) and personal ambition of unionists combined with the state hostility to NLC's populist and trade union advocacy to provide the enabling environment for its destabilisation. With the 'progressive' wing of the trade union movement retaining control at the 1984 Enugu triennial delegates' conference, "the oppositional efforts for the 'democrats' continued. Most of the unions under their influence refusing to pay affiliation dues, while those that paid only paid token amounts in a desultory fashion" (Otobo 1992a:97). The NLC's oppositional stand to the increasingly vicious military dictatorship of the Buhari regime guaranteed that the unionists waging oppositional campaigns against the NLC found a ready audience with the regime.

Organised Labour and the Politics of Adjustment

A more systematic campaign of destabilisation against the NLC however, came under the Babangida regime. In section 3, above, I have shown the immanent hostility of the conceptual framework that underpinned adjustment to unionism (or labour in general).

The advocacy of the NLC was against the "conditionalities" of the IMF during the so called 1986 national 'debate'. The critique of government policy by the NLC was, however, more comprehensive: it hinged on the impact of the policies on the livelihood of the members of its affiliate unions and national sovereignty.

In October 1985 the Babangida regime declared a state of national economic emergency that was to last for fifteen months. A general pay cut of between two and 20 percent was announced. The amount derived from this pay cut was to be paid into the National Economic Recovery Fund. This decision was made unilaterally and without consultation of any sort with the NLC or any other union within the trade union movement. Over the next three years the general impact of adjustment fell severely on the working people. The defence of the occupational and pecuniary interest of its members brought the Congress into ever more open confrontation with the regime.

In 1987, NLC made a robust response to the Babangida regime's argument for the removal of the 'oil subsidy' with a comparative study of minimum wage and real income of workers in some oil producing countries.

As Otobo noted, "the build-up to the (third triennial delegates' conference at Benin) was largely influenced by developments within the economy, notably the impact of the Structural Adjustment [Programme] SAP on wage earners and citizenry in general, and the reaction of the NLC to these" (1992b:97). As in 1981 and 1984, the state embarked on a concerted programme of destabilisation of the NLC to secure a leadership that was amenable to it. There is little doubt that the Babangida regime felt a need to remove NLC as an opposition to the regime's planned removal of the oil 'subsidy' for April 1988. The removal of subsidies was one of the conditionalities of the creditor community under the adjustment programme. As Otobo pointed out:

> NLC expressed contrary views to those of government on practically all issues: arbitrary arrests and detention of people under the Buhari regime; unilateral deductions from salaries of public servants in 1987; cost of living indices; the official claims of the 'gains' of the structural adjustment policy; the exchange rates of the naira; removal of petroleum subsidies; educational policies; human rights record; to political appointments. To say that [Ali] Ciroma's executive was unpopular with the Babangida administration would be a gross understatement (1992b:97).

As in the previous cases, the regime had ready allies within the labour movement itself, and the 1988 delegates' conference provided the basis for neutralising the NLC. In the elections held at the conference, the prime government ally suffered a crushing defeat winning four votes to Ali Ciroma's two hundred and eighty votes (Otobo, 1992b). The same pattern emerged in the election of other officers of the NLC.

The sealing of the NLC secretariat by armed state security personnel on Monday 29 February, marked a new shift in the government's overt effort to rein-in the NLC. This was followed with the Babangida regime evoking the National Economic Emergency Powers decree of 1985, and dissolving the leadership of the NLC. A sole administrator was appointed to run the affairs of the Congress.

Military Dictatorship and the Adjustment of Labour Politics

The appointment of the Sole Administrator (to run the Congress), I believe, was a major departure for the constitutive identity of organised labour (at the NLC level) and in the adjustment of labour politics. The regime secured an NLC it wanted on the basis of this take-over of the Congress. In the elections held in December 1988 an NLC president was chosen primarily because key unionists felt he would be acceptable to the Babangida regime. From then on, the independent advocacy of NLC would suffer great reversals. On 30 December 1988, Paschal Bafyau and others were sworn in as elected leaders of the NLC.

In spite of the dissolution of the NLC leadership in February 1988, labour protests on deterioration in living standard and against the impact of adjustment policy instruments did not abate. Indeed, the wildcat protest of shopfloor workers and students against increases in fuel prices, in March/April of 1988, forced the government to negotiate with the same union leadership it disbanded less than six weeks earlier. While the NLC leadership under Bafyau took a collaborative position with the regime, the restiveness of shopfloor workers and some unions did not abate. Indeed by 1992, the country exploded in a rash of industrial unrest that followed the successful strike by ASUU between July and September—but that is an issue for the next section of this chapter.

The annulment of the 1993 presidential election created a new groundswell of opposition and heightened the stakes in the struggle for democracy. Nonetheless, the NLC under Bafyau vacillated even here. Although the official position of the National Executive Council (NEC) of the Congress was that the "government should rescind the annulment, releasing the results, and the winner declared immediately" (NLC, 1993), the NLC president issued a contrary statement. In the statement, the NLC president called for the President of the Senate to take over power in the interim. Later when the increase in fuel prices became a rallying point for the labour movement, the Bafyau-led executive would call off a national strike without securing a reversal of the price increases. It led to acrimonious division within NLC's Central Working Committee. A year later the renewed struggle for democracy focused on the release of the winner of the June 12 presidential elections and his being sworn in. Here again, vacillation became the hallmark of the NLC: it reluctantly called a national strike but called it off barely twenty-fours into the strike; even before many of its state organs could join the strike. The petroleum and natural gas workers went ahead with an eight-week strike and the senior staff union from the oil industry pressed for the rational management of the oil industry and the restoration of democracy.

When eventually the leadership of the oil workers' union was dissolved, and the union high-jacked by the Abacha regime, the same fate befell the NLC.

Since 1994, the NLC has remained under a government-appointed sole administrator. As several union leaders are finding out, the issue for the Abacha regime is not whether the leadership is pliant but that centralised unionism represents a source of opposition to the neo-fascist agenda of the Abacha regime. Much of 1995 was spent with the union leaders and the minister of labour closeted together deciding on the re-structuring of the trade unions from 41 to 29, and who would become the next democratically-elected president of the NLC. When in early 1996, the decree on this restructuring was released, the same unionists (general-secretaries) were barred by the law from even contesting the presidency of the NLC.

It is instructive that at a workshop in Lagos (in April 1996) looking at the implications of the decree, the union leaders present were more concerned with their being barred from the NLC presidency than numerous clauses in the decree that violate trade unions' freedom of association and encourage state interference. In spite of the repeated assurances given to the ILO, by Nigeria, that by June 1996 a democratically elected NLC leadership would represent labour on the Nigerian delegation, those promises remain unfulfilled. NLC remains under a government appointee, as sole administrator, and there is no indication that the regime of Sani Abacha intends allowing any election of any sort. Indeed, in early October 1996, the government, in an apparent effort to test the waters, suggested that no national level unionism will be permitted: all union activities are to be restricted to company or enterprise level.

If we are to properly understand identity, we must look not only at the micro-level but at the meso- and macro-levels, as well. The identity of labour centres (especially the NLC) before adjustment was one of consistent advocacy for workers' interest. In the period since 1988, this image has suffered significant reversals. It is in that sense that we can properly talk of a transformation of labour identity, of a corporate type, and at the NLC level. However, I will argue that while there is a co-occurrence with adjustment programme implementation, the factors that defined the state repression are not adjustment but the hegemonic project of successive military dictatorships. The Babangida regime was involved in a consummate *personal hegemonic* agenda. The Abacha regime is determined to completely re-invent the Nigerian body politic, and under the weight of state brutality, force the subordination of civil society. These objectives rather than the politics or the imperatives of adjustment, explain the transformation of the corporate identity of labour at the level of the NLC. Nevertheless, the politics of adjustment itself, its intensely anti-union rhetoric, the immanent preference for strong regimes that will ride roughshod over groups in civil society opposed to adjustment, gave a legitimacy to unions that otherwise might not have existed.

At the same time that we can see significant changes in the advocacy role of the Nigeria Labour Congress, a at base-level activism of labour leaves us with a competing interpretation. It is to this that I will now turn.

Industrial Relations Indices or Labour Politics Where it Matters?

The issue of reading labour identity from given macro-level indicators is fraught with danger. In the first place Nigerian strike data remains suspect (Adesina, 1992b). Second, we may make too much of strike statistics, especially when shopfloor militancy is treated as a prefiguring of revolutionary upsurge. Nonetheless, we find the data useful for our discussion but not so much that it allows us to make a direct inference concerning labour identity (it will not). Nevertheless, it gives us an insight into some important indicators of collective action and self-assertion of workers. More importantly, strike statistics allow us insight into dimensions of work-place struggles. A time series such as we have in table 1, below, spanning the pre-adjustment period and the period 1986 to 1995 provides a common basis for examining the changing pattern of such work-place struggles of workers. Since the issue of specification of class identity, at very high levels of abstraction, is tied to the interaction between capital and labour-power, enterprise level data affords us a glimpse of the persistence or otherwise of certain constitutive processes of labour identity. We are starting from the assumption that class is not the only identity which workers share. Nevertheless, occupational, class or enterprise identity are bound up in the issue of industrial action, which often defines the workers separate from those performing the global functions of capital.

Table 1. *Industrial Relations 1980–1995.*

Year	Trade Disputes	Work Stoppages	Workers Involved	Striker Days	Average Striker Days	Strike Propensity
	(1)	(2)	(3)	(4)	(4)/(3)	(2)/(1)
1980	355	265	221,088	2,350,998	10.63	0.75
1981	258	234	323,700	2,218,223	6.85	0.91
1982	341	253	2,874,721	9,652,400	3.36	0.74
1983	184	131	629,177	404,822	0.64	0.71
1984	100	49	42,046	301,809	7.18	0.49
1985	77	40	19,907	118,693	5.96	0.52
1986	87	53	157,165	461,345	2.94	0.61
1987	65	38	57,097	142,506	2.5	0.58
1988	156	124	55,620	230,613	4.15	0.79
1989	144	80	157,342	579,968	3.69	0.56
1990	174	102	254,540	1,339,105	5.26	0.59
1991	198	95	403,412	1,957,074	4.85	0.48
1992	185	92	127,546	396,619	3.11	0.5
1993	160	90	880,244	6,192,167	7.03	0.56
1994	175	103	1,537,890	234,299,461	152.35	0.59
1995	196	124	1,546,328	235,069,010	152.02	0.63

Source: FOS Annual Statistical Abstract. CBN *Annual Reports* several years.

For our analysis, I have drawn four sets of time series from official strike statistics. These are the number of trade disputes in a given year, the number of work stoppages (strikes), the number of workers involved in the work stoppage, and the 'man-days lost'. Rather than using 'man-days lost', I prefer 'striker days', since the days may actually not be lost, and those 'losing' the days do not have to be men alone. In addition, I have computed two further time series: 'average striker days' to give us an idea of the average length of the work stoppages, and 'strike propensity'. The latter measures the proportion of trade disputes that lead to work stoppage. These issues in strike statistics are discussed further in Adesina (1992b).

Figure 1. *Strike Trend in Nigeria (1980–1995)*

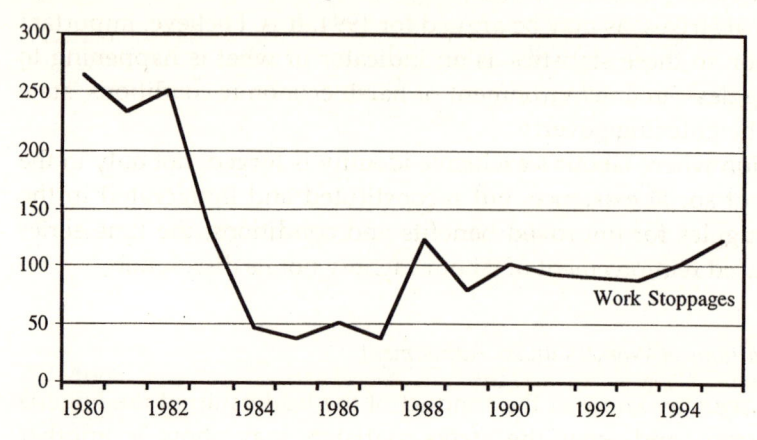

[Chart showing Work Stoppages from 1980 to 1994, declining from ~265 in 1980 to ~40 in 1985, then fluctuating around 100 through the 1990s, ending at ~120 in 1994.]

Figure 1 shows that apart from the steep decline in the period between 1983 and 1985, the trend in the period since structural adjustment was implemented has been generally on the increase. It would indeed seem that in spite of the hostile political environment for worker activism, especially since November 1993, strikes have not abated. Apparently, the decay in the NLC leadership has not had the negative effect that might be assumed.

Figure 2. *Trend in Number of Workers Going on Strike (1980–1995)*

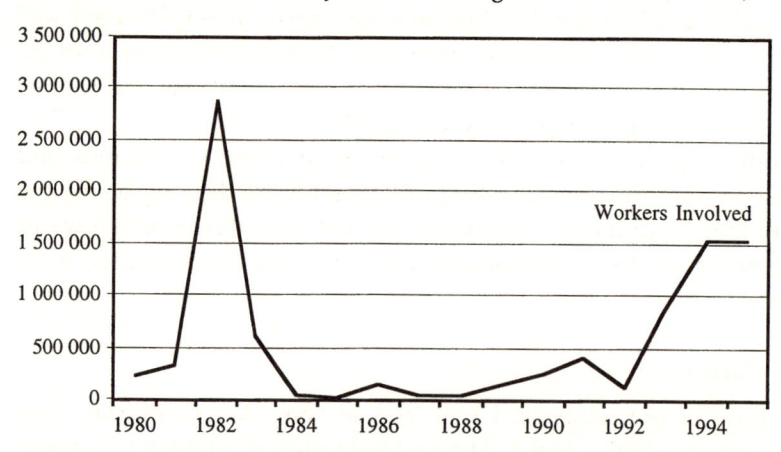

[Chart showing Workers Involved from 1980 to 1994, with a sharp peak of ~2,900,000 around 1982, falling to near zero by 1984, remaining low until 1992, then rising sharply to ~1,500,000 by 1994.]

Figure 2 brings the issue into sharp relief, when we consider that apart from the steep decline between 1982 and 1994, the overall trend between 1985 and 1991 was a relative increase. The trend since 1992 increased sharply. The import of this becomes clearer when we consider the total, recorded, striker days. The situation again, between 1982 and 1985 was of a relative decline, but the trend since 1986, and especially since 1992, has been one of virtual explosion in striker days. In 1994 and 1995 alone total 'days lost' averaged 234.6 million. Not only are total striker days virtually exploding, but the average length of strike action has also grown beyond what Nigeria can recollect in its history of recorded strike statistics. Yet, 1995 was hardly the year of 'political strikes' as may be argued for 1994. It is, I believe, important to pay attention to these statistics as an indicator of what is happening to workers' struggles—in an environment of harsh economic conditions, state violence, and heightening poverty.

In a situation where labour's exclusive identity is forged, not only in the daily routine of social existence, but reconstituted and invigorated in the context of struggles for improved benefits and conditions, the time series point to increased reinforcement of labour identity not its dissolution.

Changing Conditions of Workers under Adjustment

Beyond what we may know of the conduct of the leadership of the Nigeria Labour Congress, and what the strike statistics may show is another dimension that, even from the 'hawk's eye' view of things warrants attention. First, strike statistics will refer to those who are in employment, yet we know that labour market reform was critical to structural adjustment. The numerical flexibility translates into unemployment for many. Several studies on the early stages of the implementation of stabilisation programme show severe cutbacks in public sector employment. Less direct are the labour market consequences of low capacity utilisation, plant closure, etc. Theoretically, we know that the loss of employment will impact on aspects of the constitution of labour identity. For instance, long term unemployment will impact on the individual's self-appreciation as a worker. Relocation from the formal sector to informal sector labour market may activate the loss of labour identity and the privileging of other identities.

Furthermore, if poverty is deepening in the urban areas, for instance, and more of those in the formal (especially public) sector are dipping below the poverty line, these will have implications for the constitutive language of identity. Theoretically, this can create despair but it can also heighten resistance.

The Labour Market

For the purpose of our analysis, I will look at some labour market time series. These are in tables 2 and 3. The Federal Office of Statistics' national unemployment statistics are based on the ILO standard. This uses a household survey technique, asking respondents over a given age if they actively desired to work, actively searched for work, but could not find employment within (usually) the past week.

This definition of the unemployed while suitable for an industrialised economy becomes a problem in an economy like Nigeria's. This is because a substantial proportion of those in the active labour force are employed in the informal sector, or are self-employed in micro-enterprises, with low capital stock, or on farms and depending on the labour of household members. The

Table 2. *Registered Unemployed and Vacancies Declared (Lower Grade Workers)*

Year	Old Registration	Fresh Registration	Re-registration	Total Registration	Vacancies Declared	Placements
1982	15,688	70,157	51,570	106,496	19,943	7,557
1983	25,131	55,339	32,118	112,588	18,310	7,394
1984	30,670	50,108	40,167	120,945	14,612	3,865
1985	27,926	36,039	32,615	96,580	11,156	2,139
1986	27,210	31,273	26,675	85,158	13,050	2,378
1987	33,967	79,718	31,399	145,084	16,502	4,988
1988	66,625	30,003	19,534	116,162	14,154	2,506
1989	52,737	26,128	17,190	96,055	14,052	3,474
1990	55,043	20,355	14,354	89,752	7,637	1,917
1991	77,769	19,896	12,848	110,513	14,529	2,924
1992	66,812	12,693	11,002	90,507	10,103	2,494
1993	69,463	10,560	10,500	90,523	11,184	4,181
1994	68,930	10,022	7,437	86,389	9,893	3,481
1995	67,276	8,925	6,180	84,402	9,853	4,369

Source: 1984–1987 data from CBN *Statistical Bulletin* Vol. 3 No. 1 (June 1992). 1988–1991 data from CBN *1992 Annual Report*. 1992–1995 data from CBN *1995 Annual Report*.

definition of unemployed is therefore insensitive to underemployment or discouraged workers who gave up looking for a job because they are pessimistic about their ability to secure employment. While the problem of underemployment is general to most developing countries, the problem of discouraged workers is generally associated with weak labour demand in a recessionary economy like Nigeria. The FOS unemployment statistics will therefore underestimate the rate of unemployment.[1] While the FOS unemployment figure disaggregates for educational level of those classified as unemployed (those with secondary education posting between 70 per cent and 52.8 per cent rate of unemployment), it does not provide the data that we need for understanding such things as long-term unemployment, chance of

---

[1] For instance, the composite unemployment figure for 1995 was put at 1.8%, showing a steady decline from 3.4% in 1992, 2.7% in 1993 and 2.0% in 1994. Such unemployment rate is the envy of most OECD countries, and most unlikely for Nigeria. The World Bank (1995:3) shows that in the case of Ghana, while the official unemployment figure for 1988-89, using the ILO definition, was 1.6%, the rate of underemployment was about 24.5%.

Table 3. *Registered Unemployed and Vacancies Declared (Professionals and Executives)*

Year	Old Registration	Fresh Registration	Re-registration	Total Registration	Vacancies Declared	Placements
1984	706	1,324	484	2,514	657	26
1985	1,234	2,038	992	4,165	748	145
1986	2,295	2,329	1,499	6,123	606	148
1987	2,116	10,917	2,067	15,100	444	175
1988	9,013	3,646	3,616	16,293	591	281
1989	10,287	2,545	1,449	14,281	3,091	678
1990	6,436	2,853	893	10,182	3,695	986
1991	10,253	2,073	298	12,624	3,989	164
1992	21,324	11,195	1,666	34,185	3,347	141
1993	26,159	6,880	1,035	34,074	3,401	79
1994	27,191	5,456	1,365	34,012	3,731	78
1995	30,807	3,841	1,324	33,297	3,839	61

Source: 1984–1987 data from CBN *Statistical Bulletin* Vol. 3 No. 1 (June 1992). 1988–1991 data from CBN *1992 Annual Report*. 1992–1995 data from CBN *1995 Annual Report*.

re-employment, etc. For this information, we turn to the Ministry of Labour's labour exchange data. We should point out that the time series here is also likely to underestimate unemployment rate, since there is no incentive for registering at the labour exchange (for instance, payment of unemployment benefit).

Nevertheless, in using the time series as mainly indicative of the trend, a number of things begin to emerge from tables 2 and 3. For those classified as lower grade workers, while the total number of those on the exchanges' labour register declined over the period 1982 to 1995, so did the number of vacancies declared and placements (until 1990 before rising again). Those re-registering, and those newly registering showed an overall decline. The overall decline in vacancies posted with the labour exchanges shows weak demand in the economy. Quite instructive, however, is the problem of long-term unemployment as shown in the 'old registration' time series. The rate more than doubled under adjustment, and peaked in 1991. The erratic movement in the series does not suggest a steady decline.

The situation for those classified as 'professionals and executives' is grimmer. While declared vacancies for this category expanded, the number of placements rose into 1990 before nose-diving. Worse however, is that on the parameters of long-term unemployed and total rate of unemployment, things worsened under the structural adjustment regime.

Long-term unemployment increased 42-fold and the total rate of unemployment increased thirteen-fold.

Several studies have demonstrated the severe psychological impact of long-term unemployment on the unemployed. The category 'lumpen-proletariat' has an infamous record in most Left writings, and its equivalent in criminology. If the time series are to be believed in what they point to, (rather than what they affirm, since reliability of data remains a serious problem), then we can suggest that there will be significant changes in orientation and identity for those who fall in this category. In the absence of ethnographic findings, our conclusion remains speculative.

Labour and Poverty

The poverty impact of adjustment is something that has in the past few years come under empirical study. As we noted in the Introduction, Sub-Saharan Africa is the only region in the world where poverty is projected to grow into the next century. The so called africanisation of poverty, both rural and urban, is a phenomenon that is widespread. While in absolute terms the rural representation among the poor is high (the population distribution and real poverty are important reasons), the degree of poverty in the urban areas has also worsened significantly. Some recent World Bank studies in Nigeria point to a qualitative shift in the nature of poverty. The poverty unit within the World Bank Lagos Office has in the past fourteen months put the figure at not less than 50 per cent and growing. With over 50 per cent of the population living below the poverty line, food poverty has become a serious phenomenon. Households are presently consuming roughage that was previously food for small domestic ruminants (Todd, 1994). Surprisingly, though, the main World Bank report claimed that in the period between 1985 and 1992 the percentage of households living in poverty fell from 43 per cent to 33 per cent (World Bank 1996). However, the Federal Office of Statistics using the same data set from the same national survey of the household, put the national average of households living in poverty at around 79 per cent. Urban poverty is growing much faster than in the rural area.

Our own field study in south-western Nigeria supports the FOS results (Adesina, et al., 1996). Our results show worsening income inequality in both urban and rural areas (Gini index = 0.602), although income inequality was more pronounced in the urban areas (Gini index = 0.75). Using an income-gap index, we found a deepening crisis of household poverty. Poverty head-count for all households was 71.3 per cent, while the poverty gap (P_1) was 0.471, and P_2 = 0.227. However, wage-dependent urban households presented greater incidence of poverty, with a head-count of 83 per cent for those in regular wage employment, and over 84 per cent for those in unprotected waged labour markets.[2] Households with female heads were more represented among core poor households than male-headed households, although variation in welfare among female-headed households was much higher than among male-headed households. The important point we want to draw attention to is the increased vulnerability of wage-dependent households. The Bank itself acknowledged in a 1994 report on Nigeria (World Bank, 1994) that those on official minimum wage fell into poverty under adjustment, briefly recovered in 1990 and by 1992 had dipped below the poverty line again. The worsening public sector wage situation is a phenomenon that accompanied structural adjustment for most of the Sub-Saharan African countries (cf. Jamal, 1995; World Bank, 1995). By its own inadvertent admission, there is not much by way of economic growth to justify the excruciating pain of adjustment. Rate of growth in GDP per worker performed more poorly in the 1980 to 1993 period than in the 1965 to 1980 period. Out of 35 Sub-Saharan African countries only Mauritius, Chad, Uganda, and to a lesser extent Benin, posted *any* improved performance.

How does this deepening crisis of poverty impact on labour identity? As Jamal (1995) and Jamal and Weeks (1993) have argued, whatever the image of the African worker was that underscored adjustment programming (as dubious as it was), the adjustment programme had worsened the conditions of those in wage-employment. If poverty and labour market participation are indices of transformation of identity, then we can argue that such has happened to the bearers of labour-power in Nigeria as in much of Sub-Saharan Africa. However, this is not a transformation of identity in terms of moving from affluence into poverty. More careful studies of inequality and poverty, in the 1970s, show that the so called oil boom did not improve the welfare of most of those who depend on their labour power for subsistence (Jamal and Weeks, 1988). Nevertheless, the deepening crisis of poverty is altering the consumption pattern in a profound way. As the qualitative poverty assessment study shows (Todd, 1994) food poverty has become a major problem; but this is in terms of previous consumption of luxury goods. Indeed the paradox of adjustment is that those who lost out during the oil boom are still the losers under adjustment; only that the ranks of the former are being swelled by the new poor thrown up by adjustment. Our household survey, mentioned above, shows that 40 per cent of the households received less than 8.73 per cent of reported income, while our top 3 per cent received about 28 per cent of all reported income. If food poverty is increasing, and multiple labour market participation is becoming a preferred coping strategy, surely this will impact on worker-identity of a sort. However, there is very little to suggest that what we have is a transformation,

---

[2] For urban households with heads located in regular wage labour market $P1 = 0.556$, $P2 = 0.215$. For households whose heads are located in unprotected wage labour market, $P1 = 0.542$, $P2 = 0.279$.

which might suggest 'transformation into something else'. Rather, we will suggest that what we have is a deepening gap of perception between the rich and the poor; between the 'losers' and the 'winners' under adjustment.

Is Labour Identity Transforming?

The question that we must ask at this stage is: Is labour identity transforming? If by this we mean the traditional identity of those dependent on their labour-power for subsistence, then the response, one will suggest is 'No'. The labour militancy that the strike time series point to is not incompatible with the traditional identity of the working class; indeed, it is its distinct mark. To avoid heroic-myth-making, such macro-indicators of militancy do not necessarily translate into a teleological proletarian march. Even so, they portend some constitution of collective identity that separates this class from that of its dominators.

The increased poverty of the workers, at least public sector, must be understood as part of a widening of poverty in the society in general. Its impact on labour (-dependent) households is a diminishing quality of dietary intake, although a greater proportion of income is spent on food; greater social vulnerability in terms of access to education, health-care, and so on. None of these will suggest a transformation of labour identity, *per se*. Rather the working class is distinct in its separation from means of production, less discretionary control over the allocation of its labour time at work, and relative poverty in the society. What adjustment has done is deepen the vulnerability of those within the labouring classes.

Finally, the increasing subordination of trade union bureaucrats to the state is itself not an entirely new phenomenon in the Nigerian labour movement. If anything, the pedigree of the top leadership of the NLC after 1988, in the right wing of the pre-1976 trade union movement provided the clue to its behaviour. This by itself will not be an indication of a transformation of labour identity. It was Paschal Bafyau who led the renegade group of unionists in 1975 that served as the battering ram in the attack of the military regime on the trade union movement. What has changed, is in the virtual disappearance of a discernible corps of national union leaders willing to strike a course for labour regardless of the tenor of the regime in power. This, perhaps, is where we can begin to talk of the transformation of labour identity. The factors responsible for this shift have as much to do with adjustment, as they do with the neo-fascist agenda of the Babangida and Abacha regimes. Perhaps it can be argued that the deepening crisis of adjustment worsened the intra-dominant class bloc conflicts that underscore the specific form of military dictatorship under Ibrahim Babangida and Sani Abacha.

If the labour market gets increasingly tight and 'numerical' flexibility remains a recurring phenomenon, then we can expect that the phenomenon of long-term unemployment will affect the composition of the labour movement. The phenomenon of workers straddling multiple labour markets (moonlighting) in order to augment their income will affect the identity of those previously used to formal sector employment. The increasing retreat into the informal sector is another case in point. But to what extent do these suggest the transformation of labour identities, and 'Is it really new?'.

An area that I have not been able to capture more definitively—but where I believe we may be witnessing a sea-change in the privileging of non-labour identities of workers—is the aftermath of the annulment of the 1993 presidential election. At no time since the 1960s have we had this concerted mobilisation of ethno-regional identities by various factions of the Nigerian power elite. While this is not entirely new (Kukah, 1993), I believe that the virulent whipping up of primordial identities under the conditions of nascent neo-fascism, and the ethnicisation of social and political life, will have important implications for labour identity. Indeed, the mobilisation of regional and ethnic symbols in breaking the 1994 NUPENG strike, and in breaking collective resolve on several university campuses, during the 1996 ASUU strike, is indicative of a line that I believe requires more studied analysis. My 'frog's-eye' view of the ASUU experience suggests that the situation in 1992 is fundamentally different from that of 1996. The mobilisation of ethno-regional symbolism to break the strike represents a distinctly new factor. One must of course situate this in what looks like a determined effort to reconstitute the civil society and purge it of all forms of dissent or oppositional activities. The same will explain the refusal to hold the NLC elections. Now, if the mobilisation of ethno-religious identity against the strike was relatively new in its determined use by the state and the power elite, is it new to academia? I doubt this. Indeed, it is because of the persistence and the revival of such a phenomenon in the 'civil society' of the universities that the renewed mobilisation of these identities acquired so much resonance. The crisis in University of Lagos in the early 1960s, the recent crises in the University of Nigeria, Nsukka, and the Ahmadu Bello University amply demonstrate this. If it is not new, does it matter? That we may need time to discern.

To conclude on a tentative, if seductive, note: We know that the mode of domination, the language of oppression creates its alter-ego in the resistance by the dominated. We also know that class solidarity and identity is mobilised when the perception of unity of domination among the dominated subjects far out-weighs the linkages with the dominating subjects. What then will be the implications for labour identity, language of mobilisation and solidarity, if increasingly the structure of domination—even within the enterprise—is seen as defined by primordial identities? If, as the language of the process of reconstituting the civil society and the Nigerian body politic currently suggest, ethno-regional structuration will be the constitutive basis of social relations, what will be the implications? But then, what is new about that? Moreover, if there is something new about it, does it matter?

Racial, caste and gender structuring of hierarchy in the labour process is a distinct character of wage employment in much of the 20th century. The response of workers, as we have seen, is not to jettison class for the primordial, but to reconstitute class identity in the light of social structuring that derives from primordial identity. Again, we return to our starting point; that such primordial identities will become part of class.

Beyond this, however, is the need to understand that the same individual normally inhabits different social spaces, each with distinct (if different) identity. Where identity is concerned, an individual is Janus-faced. Rather than involving deception, this is defined by the social space that the human agency inhabits at the given time. Furthermore, the manifestation of apparently competing identities may represent contiguous social spaces rather than mutually exclusive spaces.

Bibliography

Adesina, J., 1990, "Labour in Nigeria's Development Experience", research report, Rockerfeller/CODESRIA Programme on Reflections on Developmenr, Bellagio, Italy.

Adesina, J., 1992a, *Labour Movements and Policy-Making in Africa*, working paper No. 1. Dakar: Codesria.

Adesina, J., 1992b, "Quantitative Alchemy and Strike Trend in Nigeria", in Otobo, D., (ed.) *Labour Relations in Nigeria Vol. 1*. Lagos: Malthouse.

Adesina, J., 1993, "Rethinking Worker Consciousness: Work, Class, and Culture", *Annals of the Social Science Council of Nigeria*, No. 5, January-December.

Adesina, J., 1994, *Labour in the Explanation of an African Crisis*. London: Codesria Books Series.

Adesina, J. (with) W. Ogunkola and B. Aromolaran, 1996, *Poverty and Labour Market Status: A Case Study of South-Western Nigeria*, Research Report. Ibadan: NISER/SSCN/IDRC.

Bates, R. H., 1981, *Markets and States in Tropical Africa*. Berkeley: University of California Press.

Adewumi, F. and J. Adesina, 1999, "Occupational groups", in Oyediran, O., and A. Agbaje (eds.) *Nigeria: Politics of Transition and Governance, 1986–1996*. London/Dakar: CODESRIA.

Elson, D., 1982, "The Brandt Report: A Programme for Survival.", *Capital and Class*, 16, Spring.

Elson, D., 1994, "People, Development and International Financial Institutions: An Interpretation of the Bretton Woods System", *Review of African Political Economy*, No. 62.

Faruqee, R., 1994, "Nigeria: Ownership Abandoned", in Husain, Ishrat, and Rashid Faruqee (eds.) *Adjustment in Africa: Lessons from Country Case Studies*. Washington, D.C: The World Bank.

Federal Office of Statistics, 1996, *The Nigerian Household 1995: Summary of Latest Results from the National Integrated Survey of Households*. Lagos: FOS.

Fine, B. and L. Harris, 1979, *Re-Reading Capital*. London: Macmillan.

Garba, A.-G., 1996, "What Can We Learn from Nigeria's Experience with the World Bank's 'Adjustment with Growth' Programme?", in NES, *Beyond Adjustment:*

Management of the Nigerian Economy. (Selected Papers of the 1996 Annual Conference). Ibadan: The Nigerian Economic Society.

Gray, R., 1986, "The Deconstruction of the English Working Class", *Social History*, Vol. 11, No. 3 (October).

Hassard, J., 1993, "Introduction", in Hassard, J., and M. Parker, (eds.), *Postmodernism and Organizations.* London: Sage Publications.

Jamal, V., 1995, "Changing Poverty and Employment Patterns under Crisis in Africa", in Rodgers, G., and R. van der Hoeven (eds.) *New Approaches to Poverty Analysis and Policy Vol. I – III.* Geneva: International Institute of Labour Studies.

Jamal, V. and J. Weeks, 1988, "The Vanishing Rural-Urban Gap in Sub-Saharan Africa", *International Labour Review*, Vol. 127, No. 3.

Jamal, V. and J. Weeks, 1993, *Africa Misunderstood or Whatever Happened to Rural-Urban Gap?* London: Macmillan.

Kukah, H. M., 1993, *Religion, Politics and Power in Northern Nigeria.* Ibadan: Spectrum.

Lal, D., 1983, *Poverty of Development Economics.* London: Institute of Economic Affairs.

Marx, K., 1976, *Grundrisse*, Harmondsworth: Penguin Books/New Left Review.

Nigeria Labour Congress (NLC), 1993, "The Position of the National Executive Council (NEC) of the Nigeria Labour Congress on the June 12 Presidential Elections", Port Harcourt, July 14–15.

Olukoshi, Adebayo (ed.), 1991, *Crisis and Adjustment in the Nigerian Economy.* Lagos: JAD.

Otobo, D., 1981, "The Nigerian General Strike of 1981", *Review of African Political Economy*, 22.

Otobo, D., 1992a, "State and Labour: The 1988 Ban of the NLC", in Otobo, D., (ed.) *Labour Relations in Nigeria Vol. 1.* Lagos: Malthouse.

Otobo, D., 1992b, "Organised Labour and Political Process in Nigeria", in Otobo, D., (ed.) *Labour Relations in Nigeria Vol. 1.* Lagos: Malthouse.

Rodgers, G. and van der Hoeven, R. (eds.), 1995, *New Approaches to Poverty Analysis and Policy Vol. I – III.* Geneva: International Institute of Labour Studies.

Stedman J., G., 1983, *Languages of Class: Studies in English Working Class History, 1832–1982.* Cambridge: Cambridge University Press.

Tabatabai, H., 1995, "Poverty and Inequality in Developing Countries: A Review of Evidence", in Rodgers, G., and R. van der Hoeven, (eds.) *New Approaches to Poverty Analysis and Policy Vol. I–III.* Geneva: International Institute of Labour Studies.

Therborn, G., 1980, *The Ideology of Power and the Power of Ideology*, London: Verso.

Todd, D., 1994, *Nigeria—Poverty Assessment Background Document: Qualitative Assessment Field Studies of Poverty Issues.* London: ODA.

Thompson, Paul, 1993, "Postmodernism: Fatal Distraction", in Hassard J., and M. Parker, (eds.), *Postmodernism and Organizations.* London: Sage Publications.

Toye, J., 1990, "Interest Group Politics and the Implementation of Adjustment Policies", paper presented at UNRISD/SIAS/CMI Joint Symposium, Bergen, 17–19 October.

Williams, G., 1994, "Why Structural Adjustment is Necessary and Why it Doesn't Work", *Review of African Political Economy*, No. 60.

World Bank, 1990, *World Development Report.* New York: Oxford University Press.

World Bank, 1991, *World Development Report: The Challenge of Development.* Oxford: Oxford University Press.

World Bank, 1994, *Nigeria: Structural Adjustment Program, Policies, Implementation, and Impact.* (West Africa Department, Country Operations Division), Report No. 13053-UNI, May 13. Washington, D.C.: World Bank.

World Bank, 1995, *Labor and the Growth Crisis in Sub-Saharan Africa.* (Regional Perspectives on World Development Report 1995). Washington, D.C.: World Bank.

World Bank, 1996, Nigeria, Poverty in the Midst of Plenty: The Challenge of Growth with Inclusion (A World Bank Poverty Assessment), May 31, 1996. Washington

Chapter 8

The Youth, Economic Crisis and Identity Transformation: The Case of the *Yandaba* in Kano

Yunusa Zakari Ya'u

Introduction

The economic crisis occasioned by the Structural Adjustment Programme (SAP) inaugurated by the government in 1986 has engendered a growing impoverishment of greater sections of the Nigerian society. This impoverishment has forced disadvantaged social groups in the country to seek for and implement some means of coping with the situation. Because the crisis affects different groups in different ways, social groups in the country have also evolved differentiated coping strategies and mechanisms.

One of the social categories most affected by the crisis is the youth. The collapse of social services and the increasing commercialisation of education have made it very difficult for many young people to remain in school. As a consequence, the number of school drop-outs is increasing. Simultaneous with this is a drastic decline in employment opportunities arising from the contraction of industrial activities and the employment embargo imposed by the government as part of its restructuring programme. There is also a sharp decrease in the rate of school transition from the secondary level to the university, throwing a large number of youths out of the educational system, most of whom remain largely unemployed.

For the young people who are able to continue to attend school, they are equally affected by the crisis, as their conditions of study have deteriorated. With the increasing burden of studies and lack of prospects for employment after graduation, they have to a large extent been drawn into the popular struggles against SAP and the campaign for the democratisation of the Nigerian political space. For example, students have been the vanguards of the major protests against SAP since 1987, in addition to providing the base for mobilisation for the protests which followed the annulment of the June 12, 1993 presidential election.

Lacking a readily available organisational platform, those sections of the youth outside the formal school system have not been able to evolve any large-scale organised system of either coping with the SAP-induced economic hardship—or challenging the programme as students have done. Nonetheless, in different cities, these youths have developed their coping strategies which are localised. In the processes of adjusting and coping with the new situation, the youth have undergone an identity transformation both at the level of consciousness and in their attempt to find a space in the new dispensation. This transformation has a very significant bearing on the continuing political contestations in the country.

One common feature of the adjustment and coping mechanisms of the youths outside the school system is the resort to violence. The organised form that this takes in Kano is called *Yandaba*. The *Yandaba* are gangs of unemployed youth who reject the poor conditions to which their social background has relegated them and by taking refuge in group criminal and violent activities. For most of the time, they live in secluded places (called *daba*) spending much of their time in petty hunting and experimentatons with different drugs, only interacting with the wider society for their food and other requirements, often in a violent way. A variant group of the *Yandaba* is the *Yan Daukar Amarya*, who generally share the same characteristics with the *Yandaba* but specialise in the abduction of women whom they rape.

Although the *Yandaba* do share a number of similarities with the *Yantauri* and *Yanbanga*, the three need to be differentiated. The *Yantauri* are people believed to be immune to harm or injury from iron or other metallic weapons such as knives (Dan-Asabe, 1991.) During the pre-colonial period, they were not only hunters but also a warrior class who defended their territories against attack from their neighbours. This meant that each community had its *Yantauri*. They have survived the social restructuring that colonialism and capitalism have engendered in the society, but no longer as a warrior class, even less hunters. They are now scattered in different wards of the city, often forming warring factions along historical lines. The *Yanbanga*, on the other hand, are professional political party thugs recruited by parties in the city. Most leaders of *Yanbanga* were *Yantauri* such as the famous late Sabo Wakilin Tauri. However, not all *Yantauri* are *Yanbanga*, just as not all *Yanbanga* were recruited from *Yantauri* background.

The *Yandaba* phenomenon itself in Kano is not a recent development. Yet, in its present form, content and outlook, it is completely different from what it used to be in the pre-SAP period. Specifically, SAP has brought certain fundamental changes in the perception of the individuals now attracted to the *Yandaba* phenomenon. These changes have created a new unique identity in the *Yandaba*, both in terms of their self-definition of themselves and in their attitude to the society. The resulting product is an individual whose approach in contesting a space in this difficult and seemingly hostile society is through the use of gang-violence. But SAP has also enlarged the reservoir from which those violent youths are recruited.

This chapter analyses the transformation of the *Yandaba* identity as moulded by SAP and its implication on the political processes in the country. In the course of carrying out the research for the chapter, a number of active and formerly active *Yandaba* cadres were interviewed. For confidentiality, most of the respondents are kept anonymous unless when specific assertions have been made, for which the respondent's permission was sought.

The Phenomenon of Adolescence Banding

The *Yandaba* phenomenon can be located within the framework of identity crisis experienced by adolescents but whose positive resolution has been hampered by some excruciating factors. Typically, adolescents between the ages of 10 and 20 tend to band together within their neighbourhood in loose associations, to pursue group activities, separate from adults and other age categories in the society.

Adolescence is a crucial contemplative stage in the development of the human personality. The adolescent is just about to become an adult with full responsibility of his own. He is therefore concerned with his future: what to do to make a success of it. Adolescence thus is the stage in which the individual has to answer many questions in order to develop his identity. As noted by Ryckman (1993), it is the period during which an identity crisis is normative. The resolution of this crisis entails the formation of a distinct identity with respect to the individual. Erikson has described this process of identity formation as:

> a process of simultaneous reflection and observation, a process taking place on all levels of mental functioning, by which the individual judges himself in the light of what he perceives to be the way in which others judge him in comparison to themselves and to typology significant to them, while he judges their way of judging him in the light of how he perceives himself in comparison to them and to types that have become relevant to him (Erikson, 1973:121).

Clearly then, identity formation is a social phenomenon involving the individual in a complex interaction with a definite social group. Because man feels insecure, he needs the approval of others to assert his identity. Consequently he is forced to seek for his identity within a group by acting in conformity with the group. He can tolerate this feeling of insecurity, as Fromm puts it "by being rooted in a group in such a way the feeling of identity is guaranteed by the membership of the group" (1991:191–92.) To that extent, the individual's identity is not definable outside the context of belonging to this group. Group or social identity then becomes the concrete manifestation of the individual's identity, which is to say that the individual's identity is expressible only in terms of norms, values, roles, expectations etc. of the group to which the individual belongs.

The phenomenon of adolescence banding served to situate the individual adolescent into the social milieu of his society and provided him the appropriate conditions for the formation of the socially acceptable individual identity. Individual adolescents joined the *Yandaba* groups because it not only offered them the opportunity to judge and be judged by others in their communities, it trained them to acquire the values and skills the society expected them to have in order to prepare them for an acceptable adulthood. It was a means of socialisation and a sort of a passing rite to adulthood.

In this respect, the typical adolescence 'gangs' were not only harmless groups but also provided certain social services to their neighbourhood. These included community work such as cleaning and clearing of the environment, protection of the neighbourhood especially against theft, leadership training and collective mutual assistance, such as during ceremonies or in bad times. Their activities also provided outlets for sporting and cultural events for community entertainment, with keen contest among various neighbourhood groups. In addition, they provided a means of enforcing community discipline among both youth and children. They stopped women from going out in the night or running away from their marital homes (within the context of a peasant patriarchal Muslim society, this was accepted as necessary). They were, therefore, not only tolerated but also accepted in the society, indeed respected.

Structurally, the adolescence gangs are an unstructured and diffused group. There was no definite membership and certainly no leadership in the formal sense. Enrolment was more or less automatic, with no clearly defined membership requirements or responsibilities. Consensus within the group was more on opinions and attitude considered acceptable to the larger community than to any unique group ideas. The community in turn allowed the groups a large measure of autonomy. The shifting nature of the membership and the transient nature of the phenomenon in the life of the individual were underscored by the gradual but eventual withdrawal of older youths from the groups. This withdrawal marked their graduation to adulthood and was usually accomplished by marriage.

Sociologically, the groups lacked the negativism of the delinquent gangs or the short-term hedonism that goes with street gangs. Retreat to drugs and sex, both elements of the sociology of the modern gangs, were absent. As a strictly male affair, the gangs respected the cannon of the community of parallel but complementary socialisation of different sexes as is common in orthodox Muslim communities. They do not have a perception of themselves as a group that is uniquely different from the rest of the community. They do not have attitudes or opinions that are fundamentally different from those of their communities and certainly do not see themselves in conflict with the dominant culture. If any thing, they are too much of conformists. They are not seen as deviants.

Participation in the group activities was purely non-utilitarian in the material sense. Other than acquiring the relevant skills and for socialisation into cultural values of the adult society, no one hoped to gain any material advantage from participation. The adolescence banding phenomenon, therefore, remained more of a bodily and moral expression than a source of material comfort. The incidence of theft and other illegal requisition of other people's properties were thus not associated with the groups even if individual members were involved (in which case the particular incidence was seen by both the community and the group as a deviant behaviour).

Finally, the adolescent banding phenomenon is basically apolitical. If the adolescents in the groups did recognise their conditions as wretched or that their society was oppressive, they did not see in group fraternity a framework to address these issues. Indeed by the logic of its role as a means of socialisation into the dominant values of the community, the adolescence banding phenomenon served to get the youth to not only adopt to their conditions, but also to accept without question the political imperatives of the society as given. It is from these adolescent gangs that the *Yandaba* recruited and turned them into violent gangs.

The Contemporary *Yandaba* Identity

Tajfel has defined "identity" as "an individual's knowledge that he belongs to a certain social group with some emotion and values significance of his membership" (1979:66–67.) To suppose, therefore, that there is something describable as "*Yandaba* identity" means that the *Yandaba* has a certain consciousness of himself as belonging to a unique group with certain attributes and attitudes that differ from those of others. This is true of the *Yandaba* today.

The contemporary *Yandaba* is acutely aware that he belongs to a particular group which sets him apart from others who do not belong. He accepts the responsibilities and commitments demanded of him by his membership of the group, and is ready to do anything including murder, to preserve and maintain his membership of the group. This group consciousness has helped in the development of a sectarian orientation in the contemporary *Yandaba*.

In contradistinction to members of adoleschence bands who have the same occupational aspiration with their parents, the *Yandaba* are largely unemployed school drop-outs whose aborted dreams of the future has nothing to do with remaining within the occupational confines or social status of their poor parents. They aspire, even if vaguely, to achieve a social status in society higher than that of their parents. In joining *Yandaba* gangs, therefore, they are at once rejecting the poor conditions that their social background defined for them and taking refuge in violent group activities directed at individuals vaguely seen as being a part of hostile society that has made life for them so precarious. It should, of course, be added here that not all of the contemporary *Yandaba* are from poor a background. There is now a sprinkling of children of the rich who form an influential (not in the numerical sense) layer of the *Yandaba* gangs.

Unlike conventional adolescent groups, the contemporary *Yandaba* gangs are not exclusively composed of adolescents. The age bracket has expanded both ways including boys as young as eight years old and adults of thirty-five years and above with families of their own. There are even instances of the son and father being both active at the same time in the *Yandaba* gangs (Liba, 1996). This means that the phenomenon is no longer in the transitory stage, as many older people have continued to remain active in the gangs. Sex barriers have also been broken down allowing females to integrate into the gangs (Liba, 1996). Indeed, in some quarters especially Fagge and Kofar Mata, there are *Yandaba* gangs composed exclusively of young unmarried girls who operate in complementary mode with their male counterparts. The entry of females into the gang structure is a subversion of a basic community value of the Hausa, Muslim society of Kano city.

The *Yandaba* mostly live on the fringe of the society in secluded places, spending most of their time in petty hunting and theft. "Market places, uncompleted or deserted buildings are their abodes, the hideouts of these teenagers who when not on an operation, live a communal life of sharing Indian hemp, dangerous drugs and *Burukutu* (a locally brewed alcohol)" (Ojudu and Zorro, 1988). Their life style is typically that of a strong group solidarity 'as each is ready to sacrifice everything, including his/her life in defence of (or revenge for) others'. They have deep aversion to formal authorities. To underscore this aversion to, or their rejection of formal authorities, they adopt a street culture of using drugs, gambling and sex. In a sense, therefore, the contemporary *Yandaba* phenomenon has some resemblance with the counter-culture of America and Europe of the 1960s and early 1970s.

Kenneth Westhues defines counter-culture as a "set of behaviours and values which radically rejects the dominant culture of society and prescribe a sectarian alternative" (1972:9). The *daba* (the hideout or hangout of the *Yandaba*) is the spatial location of "*Yandaba* counter-culture", the equivalent of the cultural communes of the counter-culture. In its relationship to the wider society, the *Yandaba* phenomenon meets Westhues' definition of counter-culture. From the perspectives of the *Yandaba* themselves, the alternative "culture" they project in rejecting the dominant one is a bohemian commune type in which virtually everything is to be done or enjoyed collectively. The excessive individualism of the wider capitalist society is repressed at least within the conclave of the *daba* and its operational terrains. Although hierarchy exists in the organisation of the *Yandaba*, this does not confer any special privilege to leaders in terms of either their material condition or living and eating habits in the *daba*. The predilection to keeping dogs which Musgrove (1974) observed as being part of the atributes of counter-culture communes is alos present among the *Yandaba*, although in their case, they use the dogs not just pets but also for hunting and as a means of defence against the police. The *Yandaba* phenomenon also features persons who are deeply alienated from their society and with psychologically troubled minds.

There are a number of other significant differences between the classic counter-culture and the *Yandaba* phenomenon. First, while counter-culture was largely spear-headed by the children of the middle class (Clark et al., 1991), the *Yandaba* phenomenon is dominated by the children of the poor. Dan-Asabe's survey (1991) concludes that most *Yandaba* have a poor background and that their parents were butchers, petty traders, donkey transporters, firewood sellers, leather workers, etc. It is only in its criminal dimension that the few children of the rich attracted to the *daba* are becoming an important segment of the phenomenon.

Secondly, the American and European counter-cultural movements had their base in the intellectual community, especially in the universities. The majority of the inmates of their communes were university students. Their critique and rejection of mainstream cultures had a deep intellectual dimension. The *Yandaba*, on the other hand, are recruited mainly from primary and high school drop-outs, lacking any systematic intellectual critique of the society they are rejecting. Indeed, a large percentage of these drop-outs are ex-pupils of traditional Qur'anic schools who came to the city in search of knowledge but who were forced to abandon their study at a tender age due to hard economic conditions and turn into street-begging from which they graduated into the *Yandaba* circles. A significant number of the *Yandaba* are not only semi-literate in the Western sense but also uneducated in the rudiments of Islamic knowledge. It is not surprising, therefore, that many of the *Yandaba* youths betray a hostile attitude to intellectualism.

Thirdly, as Winner (1977) observed, counter-culture was a rejection of the technologically complex Western societies which alienate, hence the emphasis on simple, non-technologically dependent living. In this regard, counter-culture had a sense of mission that is lacking in the *Yandaba* phenomenon. It hoped to build an alternative, even if only a utopian society. It was thus inherently, even though not overtly (actively) political. This qualification is necessary, given Kenneth Keniston's observation that the majority of the inmates of the counter-cultural communes were the alienated type who are "far too pessimistic and too firmly opposed to the system to demonstrate their disapproval" (1974:148). Although they were pessimists, in that they did not necessarily believe that the system could be reformed, they were making a political statement by dropping out of the mainstream culture. The *Yandaba* is only political to the extent that it interacts with the rejected society. It does not seek to remake the larger society. In fact, it has no vision of an alternative society to the one it is rejecting. Its basic demand on the society is to be allowed to live outside the formal authority and control of the larger society. Thus, while for counter-culture "dropping-out" was both a political and an intellectual decision, it has no such connotations for the *Yandaba*.

Additionally, while for counter-culture dropping-out was conscious, voluntary, and a self-imposed decision, for the *Yandaba* it is largely imposed by the economic realities of the country that have made it very difficult for them to have any other viable means of livelihood. For most *Yandaba*, the decision to join was not consciously taken. Keniston makes the following observation on counter-culture drop-outs:

> The decision to leave college was in none of our subjects conflict-free, light-hearted or hedonistic; deciding to leave college was for all the students we interviewed, a crisis in every sense of the word—a moment of intensified anxiety and stress, a turning point and a culmination of a long process of reflection and growing dissatisfaction (ibid.:193).

The contemporary identity of the *Yandaba* is completed by a predisposition to violence. Ojudu and Zorro have aptly captured the nature of the violence of the *Yandaba*, thus:

> ... [they] are not run of the mill thieves, they are bestial men whose goal is to inflict harm on their victims. They storm houses like para-troopers, inflict injuries on their victims, rape, sometimes kill and most often take nothing with them (1988).

It is important to note that their motive is not to steal but simply the act of violence itself. They do loot properties, but often after they have satisfied their desire for violence. The sight of fresh blood flowing from their victims has a strong fascination to them. Toughness in the sense of the ability to mete out violence and to take it calmly is the most cherished quality in their scale of values.

Although this violence is generally directed towards the society which the *Yandaba* perceive as oppressive, they have no systematic way of selecting their targets. Generally anyone who happens to be around the scene is a potential target. They are indiscriminate especially during inter-gang fights. Women are usually abducted and raped. A strand of the *Yandaba* that specialises in abducting women are called *Yan Daukar Amarya* (bride snatchers). The *Yandaba*, however, never deliberately attack members of their own immediate community (ward) unless in connection with perceived betrayal (Mohammadu, 1996.) Hence, they usually operate outside their wards. When they have to operate in the vicinity of their wards, it is usually either in inter-gang fights or in the protection of their community against attack by some gangs from elsewhere. Although they are generally feared and people abhor their "mindless" violence, their relationship with their immediate communities is symbiotic in that they protect the community against other

Yandaba gangs while the community offers them sanctuary against the police. Because inter-gang fights are very common and more destructive (there are hardly any cases of intra-gang fights), the violence of the *Yandaba* also consumes them. Yet, it is during such occasions that group solidarity and identity are at their highest.

Yandaba Violence and its Antecedents

The *Yandaba* phenomenon predated SAP. Its origin can be traced to the transformation of the *Yantauri* and *Yanbanga* through their incorporation into the political terrain of Kano City. The term "*Yandaba*" itself derived from *daba* which was associated with the camping place of *Yantauri* hunters whenever they went out hunting.

The origin and development of the *Yanbanga* phenomenon are closely related to the dynamics of Kano politics right from the struggle for independence. During colonial rule, the feudal class in Kano had become too exploitative and repressive towards the *Talakawa* (peasants). It was, therefore, not surprising that when the Northern Elements Progressive Union (NEPU) started its anti-colonial and anti-feudal struggle in Kano, it found wide acceptance among the *Talakawa*. But the message of NEPU was a threat both to the traditional aristocracy and the colonial authorities. Their responce to this threat was to launch a campaign of repression against NEPU using the Native Authority (NA) police and the *Dogarai* of the Emir (Emir's police). NEPU leaders and members were routinely arrested, detained, imprisoned, tortured and subjected to other forms of harassment, all in an attempt to curb the influence of the organisation among the *Talakawa* (Danbazau, 1981.)

At first, the NA was contended to use force to drive out NEPU from the political landscape. Paradoxically, however, the more repressive the NA became, the more the influence and acceptability of NEPU spread among the masses who saw in the party, the promise of liberation from the exploitative and oppressive system of the NA. The determination of the NA to wipe out NEPU became an obsession following the strong performance of NEPU in the 1951 local election in which NEPU won 12 out of the 26 seats in Kano, won another five in alliance with NCNC while the NA could only manage six (Dudley, 1968). The result of this election largely informed the decision of the NA to set up a rival political party to protect the interests of both the local aristocracy and the colonial authorities. Thus, in September 1951, the Northern People's Congress (NPC), which had been formed earlier as a cultural organisation, was transformed into a political party. The NPC immediately took over the responsibility of countering the influence of NEPU using the same instruments of NA police and the *Dogarai*, including of course the judiciary which was under the control of the NA.

When these failed to achieve the objective, the NPC had to look elsewhere to extend its repressive machinery. It was in this context that it cultivated a core of political thugs to terrorise NEPU members and supporters. These political thugs were to later acquire the name *Yanbanga* (a Hausa adoption of the English word "Vanguards"). In this early period, *Yanbanga* were mainly recruited from *Yantauri*. The use of these thugs by politicians to harass and intimidate their opponents became a source of frequent violent clashes between the supporters of NPN and those of PRP during the Second Republic.

After the 1966 coup that brought the military to power, these *Yanbanga* became dormant until 1979 when political activities were resumed. Each of the two dominant parties in the state, the National Party of Nigeria (NPN) and the People's Redemption Party (PRP) raised their own *Yanbanga* to continue the power struggle along the same lines as the NPC/NEPU contest of the earlier period. The role of the *Yanbanga* in the political struggle for Kano was to become even more crucial when internal party crisis created factionalism in the PRP, which was then the ruling party in the state. The July 10, 1981 rampage during which the Political Adviser of the Governor was killed is believed to have been carried out by the NPN thugs (Essien-Ibok, 1983)

Following the 1983 coup when the *Yanbanga* were disengaged again by their fleeing mentors, they found it difficult to re-integrate with the mainstream society. They were completely dependent on the politicians and now without other specialised skill or trade, they became unemployed. The economic crisis of the later years of SAP exacerbated their problems, and unable to find any legitimate gainful employment, they took to criminal activities, often unleashing violence on the society.

It is this predilection to violence of the ex-*Yanbanga* that the *Yandaba* now assimilated. Of course, many of the now older *Yandaba* started as *Yanbanga* during the Second Republic. From the *Yantauri*, the *Yandaba* inherited inter-ward rivalry, which has, with the new predisposition of the *Yandaba* to violence, become bloody. Once this violent aspect of the *Yandaba* became apparent to the society, they were now feared by the community. The most popular perception of the *Yandaba* by people is that "they (*Yandaba*) could unleash their terror on any innocent law-abiding citizen at the slightest outbreak of disturbance or disorder" (Kano State Government, 1991), being seen as "blood-thirsty".

While it is possible that the cinema through its showing of violent western films has had an influence on the violence of the *Yandaba* as both Dawakin Tofa (1994) and Wakili (1997) tried to show, it is obvious that the violence of the *Yandaba* draws its inspirational antecedents from both the *Yantauri* and *Yanbanga*. Their fixation with the need to prepare the body and toughen the mind to withstand all forms of physical exertion and the belief in the powers of traditional medicine to protect the body from injury from metallic weapons are all characteristic of the *Yantauri* which the *Yandaba* seem to have inherited. So are the inter-gang fights which are structured along the same historical lines as those of the *Yantauri*.

The attitude of the larger society towards the *Yandaba* ultimately led to the criminalisation of the *Yandaba* phenomenon. Having stamped them as criminals, the state set about to suppress them, using brute force. The irony is that the logic of criminality gave the *Yandaba* fresh impetus to the violence they unleash on society as they try to protect their space and autonomy. Because the police are ruthless with them when caught, they became more ruthless with their victims. Their daring acts and ability to "outsmart" the law-enforcement agencies made the *Yandaba* identity a major attraction to the increasing number of unemployed drop-outs who found in the *Yandaba* activities the possibility to live an adventurous life and take their revenge on society that has failed to provide a decent living for them.

Today, the dividing line between the *Yandaba* and other criminals is fast disappearing as *Yandaba* venture into other criminal activities. For example, recently a number of *Yandaba* were arrested for alleged involvement in armed robbery in the state. Indeed, now there is the growing tendency in Kano to use the label "*Yandaba*" for any group of people (indigenous) engaged in criminal activities. The entry of the children of the rich into the *Yandaba* phenomenon is crucial in this respect. They have access to cars, money and more sophisticated weapons (usually guns). Money allows unlimited access to women and drugs, especially cocaine (the children of the poor smoke Indian hemp generally) which is freely used in their domain. Cars make operations easy and swift, while guns simplify the violence, though in reality the typical *Yandaba* relishes his violence most when he uses the sword (dagger) or knife.

SAP and the *Yandaba* Transformation

Since the introduction of SAP in 1986 a number of important changes in the *Yandaba* phenomenon have occurred which, together, have led to the construction of a new identity for the *Yandaba*. It is now important to demonstrate how SAP has actually and concretely brought about these changes. Frank Musgrove's study of counter-culture (1974) demonstrated the relationship between economic changes and counter-cultural activities. In particular, he noted that every major economic change induces or produces some form of counter-culture. In this, the contemporary *Yandaba* phenomenon is strikingly similar to counter-culture for, in its essence, it is a product of the economic crisis engendered by SAP.

One of the most obvious changes in the *Yandaba* phenomenon is the sharp turn to violence it took after the economic crisis of the 1980s. The turn to violence is directly attributable to loss of the means of economic sustenance by the poor. Existing unemployment was compounded by massive retrenchment in both the public and private sectors. With the collapse of social services and inability of young people to secure any other legitimate means of livelihood, they are left in the street to fend for themselves by whatever means. It is not just the young people who have no jobs. The parents themselves have either lost their jobs also or their petty businesses have suffered. In the circumstances, the *Yandaba* structure provided the desperate youth with an organisational platform through which they could secure their livelihood even if criminally. Joining the *Yandaba* has, therefore, acquired an important utilitarian value as young people saw in it the possibility of securing their means of livelihood. Many ex-*Yandaba* interviewed said that they were attracted to the *Yandaba* hideouts because food they could otherwise not get was usually available there. Ironically, just as the *Yandaba* phenomenon has acquired a utilitarian value, it has also become criminalised because of its violence. The consequence is that in spite of acceptance by the society of the acquired utilitarian value of the phenomenon, it has withdrawn its recognition of what was once this community's means of socialisation of the youth. The *Yandaba's* community value has been undermined, as it no longer provides the youth with the opportunity to acquire the necessary skills and values for an acceptable adulthood.

Closely related to the acquired violence of the *Yandaba* phenomenon is the upsurge in the volume of the activities which is directly related to the growing number of unemployed youth. There is now hardly any part of Kano without the *Yandaba* gangs. The panel of investigation on the Kano October 1991 riot noted thus:

> Closely related to the issue of youth unemployment is the existence of notorious groups in almost every ward of the Metropolis of Kano known as *Yandaba* (Kano State, 1991:19).

More and more boys and girls who should otherwise be in school or in some gainful employment are drawn into the *Yandaba* gangs. But it is not only through the inability to remain at school or secure employment that SAP has forced young people into *Yandaba* gangs. A number of them were, in addition, forced into the *Yandaba* hideouts due to the housing crisis that hit the city from the 1980s. The rise in land value and in the cost of building materials meant that only the rich could build while the poor were progressively losing their homes. There is thus a shortage of sleeping space among the poor. In such a situation, it is more of a relief to the parents if the children, especially males, could on their own find alternative accommodation. This alternative accommodation for many is the *Yandaba* enclaves in which not only sleeping space is available, but also food and adventure, away from the control and authority of parents.

In fact the entry of *almajirai* into the *Yandaba* gangs has more to do with the issue of food and accommodation than with failure to secure employment. The livelihood of these kids who were mostly sent from rural areas to the city to acquire Islamic knowledge, depended on the Islamic concept of charity that enjoins the faithful to give to the needy from their wealth. The dilemma SAP has created for the society with respect to this is captured by Murray Last when he wrote:

> The economic crisis associated with the Structural Adjustment Programme has altered old priorities; the left-over food that could be given as alms to young Qur'anic students is much reduced in all but the most wealthy households, the casual jobs are even lower paid if valued in terms of what grain the wages might buy (Last, 1991:19).

The point is that there is hardly any food or charity the hard-pressed people can give to the *almajirai* and they have very little even to pay for the manual Labor that these *almajirai* provided. The option left for many of these young kids after much begging in the streets is to turn to the *Yandaba* gangs (Kano State Government, 1988a and 1988b).

Girls are drawn into the fold because SAP has affected them at two levels. First, like their male counterparts, their parents cannot afford the cost of educating them. Secondly, prospects for marriage which they could otherwise switch to in the absence of school have become precarious. The male youth, with no means of income of their own and their parents facing more or less similar hardship, cannot afford to marry as before. Again Murray Last put it eloquently: "Marriages are postponed for want of money, fewer wives are taken even by the well-to-do and divorcees find remarriage takes much longer" (1991:19). (Two of the terms of reference of the committee the Kano State Government set up on Women Affairs in 1988 were "to identify the cause of high rate of divorce... and to identify factors causing prostitution in the society" (Kano State Government; 1988c, 1988d)). The option thus open for these young girls is prostitution and no doubt, Kano, like any other city in Nigeria, has seen a rise in the population of prostitutes following SAP. But prostitution in the environment of the *Yandaba* requires similar toughness on the part of the girls to survive. From defending themselves from the attacks of *Yandaba* who rape and beat them, some of these girls come to be incorporated into the *Yandaba* gangs. The entry of women into the *Yandaba* phenomenon has added a new dimension to the operation of the *Yandaba*, as they use these girls as bait to lure their victims.

Another important change in the *Yandaba* phenomenon is the fact that adults now also take part in the gang activities. The fact that the phenomenon is no longer a transition stage to adulthood for many can be explained partly due to its criminalisation which has made the old *Yandaba* "activists" develop, as Robert Stabbing (1977:xvi) would say, a "feeling of being trapped in this deviant role by the force of penalty" that would appear when they try to establish themselves in non-deviant (non-*Yandaba*) circles. But it also has to do with their inability to find a gainful and legitimate space in the mainstream society that tallies with their expectations. For these post-adolescence *Yandaba*, the economic crisis which met them during adolescence made it impossible for them to resolve their adolescence identity crisis. The result has been to confirm Erikson's observation (1968:172–173) that such people develop negative identity in which they act in scornful and hostile ways towards roles offered as proper and desirable by the community. It is also in line with Keniston's observation (1971:74) that the achievement (resolution of the crisis) of identity becomes more difficult in a time of rapid change, which the SAP era is.

In the last few years, a number of riots resulting in the loss of lives and properties have occurred in Kano (e.g. October 1991, December 1994, May 1995). A large number of the *Yandaba* did take part in the looting that usually followed these riots (Kano State Government, 1995). These riots were however not directly organised by the *Yandaba*. They only seemed to have cashed on the situation to loot. The economic motive of their violence was illustrated by their targets. For instance, in the October 1991, riot about 558 shops and supermarkets were burnt, damaged and looted (Kano State Government, 1991). Similarly, in the 1995 riot, the rioting was concentrated in the commercial areas where shop owners battled with looters.

Successive governments in the state have tried unsuccessfully to curb the activities of the *Yandaba*. In spite of a massive crackdown and arrests, the menace seems to be on the increase. It is instructive to note here that police records on *Yandaba* show a steady decline of recorded cases from 1984 (Dawakin Tofa, 1994:46). While the police would like to present this as evidence of their success, the truth is that the *Yandaba* have become more adept at evading the police. What is more, many of the *Yandaba* once released from prison or detention go back to their gang activities. This is understandable, since time served in prison or in detention does not come with a means of livelihood. That indeed is the problem of the state solution to the *Yandaba* problem. Although various government reports recognised that the incidence of the *Yandaba* phenomenon is tied to youth unemployment, the government has not come up with an appropriate policy that would address the problem. The fact that policy prescriptions which derive from the tendency to view the *Yandaba* phenomenon as a deviant behaviour rather than a product of the economic crisis have failed to check the phenomenon, underscores the role economic crisis has played in the transformation of the *Yandaba* identity.

While SAP has brought a number of changes in the *Yandaba* phenomenon and especially intensified some trends, it is necessary to state that SAP is only a factor in the transformation of the *Yandaba*. Even before the introduction of SAP, the *Yandaba* had become a deeply rooted violent phenomenon. Its origin is more political than economic, in the sense that it was factional political struggles that led to the creation of the *Yanbanga*, who today constitute a significant component of the *Yandaba*. And its development and sustenance are due largely to political imperatives rather than to the effect of the brute force of economic necessity on the *Yandaba*.

Yandaba As a Political Force

The transformation of the *Yandaba* identity has also affected the way the *Yandaba* perceive the society in relation to themselves. Whereas their predecessors saw integration with the mainstream society as the ultimate aim, the new *Yandaba* see the society as not only oppressive but also as one that has to be violently confronted. Ironically, however, except for their disdain for formal authorities, the *Yandaba* do not generally pose or perceive their predicament in political terms. They seem to have very little awareness of the role of politics in their estrangement with society. Consequently, the state as an institution has never been the target of their violence. Even the police, the symbol of state authority that violently confronts them in their struggle for space, are not a premeditated target of *Yandaba*. Yes, they dislike members of the police force, and given an opportunity, they would not mind stabbing a policeman to death, but they do not deliberately set out to attack the police. It could be argued that this might be because they fear the counter-violence of the police, but it is more because, besides the therapeutic value of their violence, it has also a material motive which a police target cannot satisfy. You cannot get food by ransacking a police station or get money from an ordinary policeman walking on the street.

Yet the *Yandaba* gangs are a potential, if not already an established, political force in the political processes in Kano. Certainly, they are a political factor in the political configuration of Kano politics. To be sure, they do not see themselves as having any political agenda or project of their own. They despise the politicians as much as they despise the society that criminalises them. To understand the political significance of the *Yandaba*, it is necessary to understand the various forms, levels and motives of the exchanges that take place across the border that separates the mainstream society and the *Yandaba* enclaves.

The three elements of these exchanges across the border are confrontation, violence and the means of material sustenance. The *Yandaba* confronts the society in search of sustenance. In the process, violence is unleashed on the society with victims on both sides. Since the violence of the *Yandaba* has both material and utilitarian motives, and is characteristically apolitical, it can be bought by some people outside the *Yandaba* gangs who can meet their basic needs, and directed selectively to particular targets. This possibility has brought the *Yandaba* gangs into secretive liaison with both members of the business class and politicians. Because of the secret nature of these contacts, it is difficult to obtain concrete evidence on them, but it is widely believed that some businessmen, politicians and even some people in the traditional institutions do hire *Yandaba* to settle their personal/business quarrels/disagreements with their opponents or rivals. The reality of gang-ownership is an accepted one even if it is difficult to document it. Perhaps one of its indicators is the fact that members of the business and ruling class often employ *Yandaba* as their personal bodyguards or security guards.

The link of the political class with *Yandaba* is perhaps more obvious and operates at two levels. At one level, the *Yandaba* gangs provide a recruiting ground now for *Yanbanga* who have become an accepted part of the political party structure in Kano politics. Their general functions are to harass and intimidate the opponents of their patrons, terrorise constituencies where their patrons have no support/acceptability and create confusion and even stop elections if their sponsors cannot win either cleanly or through rigging. The second level is that they provide an army of mobilisers for campaigns and rallies. They also provide the retinue of paid-voters on election day, a common phenomenon in a political situation in which lack of faith and confidence in the political processes creates apathy among voters. The people are generally not keen on coming out to vote, leaving the politicians to look for hired-voters. This was most glaring in the 1996 local government elections. The majority of the voters in Fagge, Kano in particular were unemployed youth. One of the elected councillors was in fact alleged to be an ex-*Yandaba* cadre (Bashir, 1996). Today, to win election in Kano, you need money, thugs and the security agencies in that order.

But it is not only in these negative terms that the *Yandaba* are useful to the political class. In spite of their transformation into violent gangs, the *Yandaba* have been able to maintain a certain rapport with their immediate communities. In particular, they provide the bulk of the volunteers for the vigilante groups that protect the communities against thieves and attacks by *Yandaba* from other wards. They are still active in communal works in their respective wards. For these reasons, they are not only respected by the people of their respective wards but also listened to, thereby providing a base for political mobilisation within their wards. It is this support and understanding which communities have for their "own" *Yandaba* that make it difficult for the law enforcement agencies to effectively police the *Yandaba*. It is very difficult to arrest a *Yandaba* in his ward.

Yet, the inability of the state to crush the *Yandaba* in the face of economic hardship is potentially capable of leading to a general breakdown of law and order, which would be counter-productive to any political processes. Already there is a general feeling of insecurity. The state response is increasingly not only authoritarian in the way it deals with the *Yandaba*, but it also abuses the human rights of the *Yandaba*. One of the recommendations of the panel on the October, 1991 riots on how to deal with the *Yandaba* problem is that:

> A special tribunal or court should be set up to speedily try cases of *Yandaba*. A special unit of the law enforcement agency should also be set up to tackle the activities of those notorious groups. The court or tribunal suggested *above should be devoid of unnecessary legal technicalities* in order to facilitate trail and justice (Kano State Government, 1991:69: Emphasis added).

Even before this recommendation was made, the procedure outlined in it was more or less the practice of both the courts and police in dealing with the *Yandaba*. Many were summarily tried and jailed while a number of them suffered serious injuries and occasionally death due to torture by the police. Between 1990 and 1994, about 292 cases were tried by the court (Dawakin Tofa, 1994:49). Surprisingly this has not attracted the attention of the human rights community even though it carries along with it a miscarriage of justice. Innocent youth could be picked up on mere suspicion and before they could prove their innocence, they were either dead or had served an unjustified term in prison. What then would stop the state from using such a provision to frame those it considers a threat to its authority? The treatment of *Yandaba* by the state agents without recourse to standard legal procedure must be seen as politically dangerous to the struggle for democratisation, even if *Yandaba* are not consciously sympathetic to that struggle.

One rather curious political use of the *Yandaba* phenomenon is the attempt (and motive) to link its rise with the loss of authority by traditional rulers (Kano State Government, 1991). The argument being canvassed is that during the time that traditional rulers were in control of local government, it was not easy for criminals to operate since the traditional rulers "knew everyone". It is then suggested that traditional rulers should be given definite powers in the running of local government to ensure that crime is wiped out. The campaign for political relevance and more influence by the traditional rulers is playing up the fear the public have of the *Yandaba* phenomenon to push its own agenda. No doubt, in the current climate of insecurity and political confusion, such a campaign could appear altruistic to some but it would certainly remain a side distraction.

Given the large pool of unemployed youth in the city with whom the *Yandaba* share a common prospect for a bleak future, it is not difficult to see that such a situation could pose a serious threat to the authority of the state, if their anger is appropriately re-oriented towards a critical reassessment of their predicament in political terms. The *Yandaba* gangs could, and indeed did, mobilise large sections of unemployed youth. In all the riots in Kano, they have shown a capacity to hijack a protest by others and turn it into their own. This ability to lead the wider army of unemployed youth is, however recently, being seriously contested by a conscious politico-religious force—the *shi'ites*. Increasingly, they are gaining ground, partly, because of the resources at their disposal (which the *Yandaba* on their own do not have), partly because a large section of the unemployed have aborted ambitions in Islamic scholarship (the ex-*almajirai*) which the *shi'ite* movement appears to offer and partly because in the absence of concrete hope of a better future, religion offers a comprehensive, even if only in the hereafter, answer to the problems of human existence. The possibility and potential of the *Yandaba* gangs in playing a significant role in the struggle of the poor is affected by the religious groups, but its potential to be used by the oppressor class to maintain the status quo remains high.

Conclusion

The economic crisis has helped in transforming a portion of the non-violent, harmless adolescence groups that serve as a means of socialisation to adulthood into violent gangs of disillusioned youth who are ready to kill in order to survive. This transformation in the identity of the *Yandaba* has of necessity restructured the relationship between the *Yandaba* and both the state and the people. The state which hitherto had viewed the *Yandaba* phenomenon as a community issue in which it did not have to be involved, now seeks to violently suppress it. The ordinary people seem to be ambivalent toward it. While they abhor its violent nature and fear it as a destabilizing factor in community peace, nonetheless they feel that the *Yandaba* are part and parcel of the community, who still offer some useful services to the community. They thus feel a certain obligation to protect the *Yandaba* from the state. The rich and the politicians have found a use for them as security-guards and bodyguards and as a political campaign organ to influence voters and determine the outcome of elections.

Although central to this transformation is the role of the state in the restructuring of society through SAP and the subsequent criminalisation and brutalisation of the *Yandaba*, the *Yandaba*'s anger against society that they see as failing to meet their expectations, has not crystallised into a hostility against the state. The *Yandaba* identity is thus inherently apolitical. Lacking a political agenda of their own, they are now an army for anyone who can afford them. This means that even in intra-party disagreements there would be rival gangs to settle the disputes. Increasingly, elections both within parties and the larger society are being settled less by voters' choice than by the relative ability of contending political actors to deploy their thugs to complement money. The practice reinforces voter apathy in the city.

This portends the escalation of violence in the political processes. The evolution of a violent political culture is an inherent source of instability to the political development of the country. A more frightening prospect however is that given this disposition, the *Yandaba* could be used by anyone with a fascistic agenda to keep the population politically in check. Although the *Yandaba* despise formal authority, once such an authority is ready to provide them with food, money, drugs and the sort of environment they require, they could be deployed for whatever end by their patron. Already, in spite of their contempt for the police, a number of them are now "employed" by the police as informants on *Yandaba* and other criminals. They can certainly effectively police mass-based organisations. We perhaps only need to remember that Hitler came to power by mobilizing the discontent of the mass of unemployed German youth, whom he used to successfully smash all democratic forces. In other words, it is a disturbing tendency that the state is reinforcing its authoritarian disposition by somehow appropriating the violence of these gangs and the terror they generate in their urban neighbourhoods.

Bibliography

Bashir, M., 1996, Discussion, May 1996 at Fagge, Kano.
Clark, J. et al., 1981, "Sub-Cultures, Cultures and Class", in Bennett, T., et al., (eds.) *Culture, Ideology and Social Process*. London: The Open University Press.
Dan-Asabe, A. U., 1991, "*Yandaba*; The Terrorists of Kano Metropolitan?", *Kano Studies*, Special Issue, Kano: Bayero University, pp. 85–111.
Danbazau, L., 1981, *Tarihin Gwagwarmayar NEPU da PRP: 1951–1981*. Kaduna: PRP Research Directorate.
Dawakin Tofa, B. S., 1994, "A Sociological Study of *Yandaba* and Yan Daukar Amarya in Kano", unpublished M. Sc. Thesis, University of Jos.
Dudley, B. J., 1968, *Parties and Politics in Northern Nigeria*. London: Frank Cass.
Erikson, E., 1964, *Insight and Responsibility*. New York: Norton.
Erikson, E., 1973, "Identity, Youth and Crisis", in Ogilvy, J. A., (ed.) *Self and World; Readings in Philosophy*. New York: Harcourt Brace Jovanovich Inc. pp. 114–124.
Essien-Ibok, A., 1983, (ed.), *Political Repression and Assassination*. Kano: Research Unit, Government Office, Kano State.
Fromm, E., 1991, *The Sane Society*. Second edition. London: Routledge.
Kano State Government, 1988a, *Report of the Committee on Almajiri*. Kano: Kano State Government.
Kano State Government, 1988b, *Views and Comments of the Kano State on the Report of the Committee on Almajiri*. Kano: Kano State Government.
Kano State Government, 1988c, *Report of the Committee on Women Affairs*, Kano: Kano State Government.
Kano State Government, 1988d, *Views and Comments of the Kano State Government on the Report of the Committee for Women Affairs*. Kano: Kano State Government.
Kano State Government, 1991, *Report of the Panel of Investigation on Kano Disturbance*. Kano: Kano State Government.
Kano State Government, 1995, *Report of the Review Committee on the 1987 Kano State Social Policy*. Kano: Kano State Government.
Keniston, K., 1971, *Youth and Dissent: The Rise of a New Opposition*. New York: Harcourt Brace Jovanovich. Inc.
Last, M., 1991, "Adolescents in a Muslim City: The Cultural Context of Danger and Risk", *Kano Studies*, Special Issue, Kano: Bayero University Kano, pp. 1–21.
Musgrove, F., 1974, *Ecstasy and Holiness: Counter-Culture in the Open Society*. London: Methuen & Co.
Ojudu, F. and S. Zorro, 1988, "Kano's Terror Gang", *African Concord*, Vol. 2, No. 18 Lagos, pp. 27–29.
Ryckman, R. M., 1993, *Theories of Personality*. 5th edition, California: Brooks/Cole Publishing Co.
Stebbing, R. A., 1977, *Commitment to Deviance*. Connecticut: Greenwood Publishing Co.
Tajfel, H., 1979, *The Social Psychology of Minorities*. London: Minority Rights Group.
Wakili, H., 1997, Comments on the first draft of this paper.

Weshues, K., 1972, *Society's Shadow: Studies in the Sociology of Counter-Culture.* Toronto: McGraw Hill.

Winner, L., 1977, *Autonomous Technology: Technics-Out-of-Control as Theme in Political Thought.* Cambridge: MIT.

Interviews

Liba, M., 1996, Interview, April 1996 at Anguwa-Uku. Kara Mohammedu Liba is an ex-*Yandaba* and working as a labourer in NNPC Depot, Kano.

Mohammadu, T., 1996, Interview, March 1996. Mohammadu is an ex-*Yandaba* now working as a security guard at Bayero University, Kano.

Chapter 9

Youth Culture and *Area Boys* in Lagos

Abubakar Momoh

Introduction

One of the most trivialised and over-simplified subjects of study today is urban crime and violence, especially the phenomenon of youth crime and violence in urban areas. Four reasons account for this. The first is the *urban coalition thesis* which poses the rural-urban bias in a spatial and misleading way. In other words, the political economy of the creation of urban areas is often not studied within a proper theoretical framework. Second, the ideological basis of the delinquency and deviance of youth is not interpreted and understood within its relationship to the contributions of the existing political economy and in class terms. Third, urban youth problems are often abstracted from the sociology of the reproduction of class and generational categories both as subjects, and in the manner in which they are alienated and subordinated. In this regard, deviance acquires an intrinsic criminality. Part of the generational crisis between youth and adults has to do with the denial of self-perception and ideas of the youth as a social category. In this respect, they are forced to come under adult, male, and class dominance ruling. Fourth, the specificity of youth social behaviour, value system and attributes are seen as products of child growth or development that require guidance and supervision. This is where the delinquency and deviance theses arise from.

What results from all this is a misleading analysis and conclusion on the youth. The *Area Boys* question has been a victim of the foregoing shortcomings. Thus, although the phenomenon of *Area Boys* is pervasive and well known, very few studies have been conducted on it and those few studies have been very shallow and of limited value in enriching our understanding of the phenomenon.

Background to the Study

The youth constitute 43 per cent of the Nigerian population. In July, 1984 the federal government adopted a National Youth Policy which was reviewed in 1989. The stated objectives of the policy are:

- involvement and participation of Nigerian youth in the social, economic and cultural development of Nigeria;
- fostering of national and international understanding and unity among the youth;
- inculcating virtues of patriotism, discipline, selfless service, honesty and leadership in the youth, with a view to ensuring a purposeful sense of direction for the nation;
- provision of opportunities for vocational training for schooled and unschooled youth oriented primarily towards self-employment and self-reliance;
- encouragement of active complementary role of voluntary youth organisations in overall development of Nigerian youth (quoted in *Ten Years of Youth Work*, not dated: 1).

A cursory look at those objectives reveals that the federal government has no comprehensive and fundamental policy on youth. That policy itself, it should be noted, was put in place at the peak of the implementation of the Structural Adjustment Programmes, when urban violence and youth violence in particular increased profoundly. Unfortunately, it did not assuage the situation, for it was not seriously and concretely implemented. At best, the policy was an ideological, rhetorical and superficial declaration, which in both principles and precepts, meant very little to the youth.

There are three senses in which there is a relationship between the state, youth culture and *Area Boys*. First, the state is the domain of the ideological construction of specific identities, values and ideas that shape the culture of society and the way the youth is factored into that statist project is very significant for study, both in terms of its actions and responses. Second, the twin projects of statism (as expressed in state authoritarianism) and adjustment reforms are important to the study of urban youth crime and violence and the phenomenon of *Area Boys*. Third, the question of *Area Boys* opens up a terrain of discourse that raises such issues as the social responsibility of the state to citizens, the whole legal question of duty and obligation, the issue of antecedents and consequences of action, and the issue of loyalty and acceptable moral conduct.

In the literature and in popular discourses, the *Area Boys* phenomenon is seen as a crime and in a criminal sense, and the concept, it should be noted, is originally associated with Lagos which, as a centre of migration, having been the capital city and the industrial centre of Nigeria for a long time, has a national attraction for people and more especially the youth. An analysis done in 1989 showed that of a nation-wide sample population of 3,509 lifetime migrants, 384 came to Lagos; and 35.9 per cent of them fell within the ages of 15–29 (a youth category) (cited in Momoh, 1994:114).

For understandable reasons, crime has been very high in Lagos. The table below gives an insight into the crime rate in Lagos.

Table 4. *Crime in Lagos State*

Type of Crime	1989	1990	1991	1992	1993
Murder	44	59	05	08	114
Manslaughter	17	13	52	—	—
Attempted Murder	18	08	14	—	17
Suicide	32	28	15	01	07
Attempted Suicide	—	10	03	—	04
Rape	114	404	355	09	165
Armed Robbery	79	95	68	16	112
Kidnapping	44	85	48	—	57
Arson	105	44	29	52	16
Burglary	3,224	—	1,809	1,349	2,718
Total	3,677	746	2,398	1,435	2,310

Source: Police Annual Report, Force Headquarters.

But, *Area Boys* crime scarcely falls into any of these categories. Crime in Lagos Island, where the *Area Boys* are concentrated, is low (see Table 5). The basis for associating all forms of crimes with the *Area Boys* is not only partisan, but it is also ideological. However, that is what provides us leverage for studying *Area Boys* identities as they relate to their own social constructions and politics, and their general linkages and/or leverage in the context of politics in Nigeria. Put differently, *Area Boys* culture should be understood, not in the reductionist stigma of crime which it currently carries, but as part of the social and ideological contradictions of class politics played out in the urban context.

Scope of the Study

The research for this study was carried out in Lagos Island Local Government, which is one of the 20 local government areas of Lagos State. The revenue generated from Lagos Island alone is more than the total revenue generated by any selected three states of Nigeria put together. Most of the commercial houses in Nigeria have their headquarters there. It is the most urbanised LGA in Lagos State. The cost of living there is high and commerce or trade is the major activity. Lagos Island LGA covers Tokunbo/Freeman, Isale-Eko, Agarawu, Princess Street, Balogun Street, Ereko, Idumota, Adeniji-Adele, Olowogbowo, Epetedo, Massey Street, Martins Street, and Obalende among others. Because of the strategic commercial position of the LGA, it also has high crime attraction and/or potential. But whether this is traceable to *Area Boys* is one of the issues that this study has addressed.

The field work was restricted to three major areas, *viz.:* Isale-Eko, Agarawu and Massey. This is the heart of Lagos Island which houses all the skyscrapers, the Igbo traders' kiosks and the major markets. It, also, consists of the residences of some of the traditional Lagos settlers. Above all, it is the base of the original *Area Boys* and the source of the contradictions arising from *Area Boys* culture of drug addiction, violence and social activities. At the last census in 1991, Lagos State had a total population of 5,685,781. At that time, the State had twelve local government areas. The Lagos Island LGA had one of the smallest population sizes for an LGA, with a total population of 164,351 (of which 82,121 were males and 82,231 were females). The low population of the Island has to do with the fact that a substantial part of the land quarters offices, commercial houses and markets, apart from the fact that the land is compact and small.

Methodology

A combination of methods proved rewarding and enriching (as all methods complemented each other) in gathering the data for this study. These are: the use of questionnaire administration, using a 21-item interview schedule, extensive unstructured interviews with a select group of 'strategic' informants, and participant observation. We relied on strategic informants and assistants who are themselves *Area Boys*, or who have a good knowledge of the area covered by our research by virtue of being residents.

The total population of the *Area Boys* in Lagos Island LGA is put at 1,000. Some 350 questionnaires were sent out but only 106 were completed and returned. In some cases, the *Area Boys* demanded incentives to answer questions during the interview and to fill the questionnaires. Second, some of the *Area Boys* could not fill in the questionnaires themselves, even though some of them claimed to be literate and lettered. So, my field assistants in some cases, or some other persons, had to help them out. Most of the field work was done in November and December, 1996, a period which coincided with a lot of festivities and activities. Many of the *Area Boys* interviewed were in a good mood and therefore not hostile. The officials of the *Area Boys* Rehabilitation Centre and the police did not co-operate with, and assist, my field assistants, although officials of the Lagos Island LGA were co-operative.

Lastly, it should be stated that in terms of activities and domain of activities, area of residence is an important, but not the exclusive basis for *Area Boys* activities. In other words, there is no permanent delimitation of the area of activities of *Area Boys*, although a preponderant number of them conduct their activities in the streets around their abode. Hence, it is not all *Area Boys* in Lagos Island streets that are of Lagos Island origin or residence.

The Problem

Many crimes committed in Lagos and in virtually all of the states in South Western Nigeria today are attributed to *Area Boys*. Consequently, the *Area Boys* are not treated as human beings or citizens with shared values, attributes, expectations and aspirations. This prevailing perspective seems profoundly far-fetched. Thus, in this study, we seek to examine the social origins, the nature and characteristics of *Area Boys*, as well as their social activities and political role in society. The objectives are to answer the following questions:

- How did the *Area Boys* emerge and how can we characterise their social structure?
- Is there a link between urban crime and *Area Boys* activities?
- Is there a basis to question existing academic and ideological orthodoxies and stereotypes, respectively, on *Area Boys*?
- What is the relationship between state politics and *Area Boys*?
- How are the *Area Boys* organised, socially and politically, and how do they contest the terrain of politics?

From *Omo Area* to *Area Boys*: Identity Crisis and the Sociology of Criminalisation

Who are the *Area Boys* (and girls) both as a sociological category and as a conceptual variable? The misleading notion of *Area Boys* as deviants derives from the ideological bias in understanding them and the fact that field research on them has been seen as near impossible; seen as something akin to studying armed robbers or guerrillas. Hence, most writings on the *Area Boys* are based on arm-chair theorizing, relying on hearsay and simplistic empiricism. Such ideological bias may not be rectified by mere research findings. This observation, it must be noted, is not meant to suggest that we set out to venerate or romanticise the *Area Boys*. We are merely suggesting that correct questions must be posed and a correct approach should be adopted in investigating them.

What does the literature say of *Area Boys* (and girls) and under what conceptual matrix can we understand the *Area Boys*? How does their social history reconcile with that matrix? What are then the complex and intricate variables, agencies and circumstances that need to be factored into understanding the *Area Boys* and the transformation of their identities? Are the acquired identities of the *Area Boys* justified and who is responsible for the (new) acquired identities?

First, most of what is written on the *Area Boys* is more or less sensational news in newspapers and magazines. Any form of demonstration, revolt, violence, burglary, pilfering, robbery, armed robbery, is with reckless abandon attributed to the *Area Boys* (Momoh, 1994:100–104). It is therefore easy to see why state response through its security agencies is seen as being in order and not subject to question. According to Isamah (1994) the violence of urban centres has been due essentially to the economic hardships of the 1980s and 1990s and that the violence unleashed actually draws attention to the economic and social situation in towns. He argues that the violence of the urban centre is closely associated with the Structural Adjustment Programme. Isamah's views seem to be rooted in the frustration-aggression thesis. There is not necessarily such a correlation because a people may be frustrated and yet not aggressive or violent and vice-versa (Salami, 1994:80–81). The misleading view on this in the literature derives from the notion of frustrated youths as being principal players and principal apprentices of crime (Vanderschueren, 1996:100). Adisa sees SAP as detrimental for urban youth. He argues thus:

> Illegal roadside markets have become fertile grounds for petty thieves, day light robbery and activity. Those youth who survive the period of apprenticeship provided by the streets normally graduate into *Area Boys*, they grow into jobless youths with a penchant for "living in the fast lane", aspiring to a lifestyle of wealth and flamboyance which makes them easy targets for employment in the network of drug merchants where money flows fast and easy (1994:161).

The foregoing quote is highly misleading because it gives the impression that being a criminal youth automatically makes one an *Area Boy* or that being an *Area Boy* was the natural condition of the urban youth of Lagos. On the contrary, as Omitoogun (1994), who has done the most rigorous field study on the *Area Boys* to date, has noted, one can differentiate between Omo Eko (Lagos Boy), Omo Area and the *Area Boys*. He uses this to contrast the original social role and life of all Lagos youth with the current criminalised character that the *Area Boys* have come to acquire. He locates the criminalised form of the *Area Boys* in the fallouts of SAP (Omitoogun, 1994:203). This view partly tallies with our earlier view when we stated thus:

> The *Area Boys* as a social category became preponderant, popularised and organised from about 1986 when the Structural Adjustment Programme took its full course. Hence today, any form of crime or criminal activities in the entire South Western Nigeria is identifiable or traceable to the *Area Boys*. The *Area Boys* are the equivalent of "Yandaba" in Hausaland, they are also called Alaayes, Omo oni Ile (son of the soil or landlords), street urchins, "government pickin", untouchables, or all-right sir, (Momoh, 1994:98; Diouf, 1996:227).

Nevertheless, the limitation of Omitoogun's study has to do with four issues. First, he could not socially differentiate the stigmatised *Area Boys*. Second, he could not distinguish between their baseline identity and their acquired social characteristics and show the relationship between that and their role and (mis)uses in society. Third, he did not conceptualise the material and superstructural bases for the two contrasting conceptual uses of *Area Boys*, yet this remains cardinal to the understanding of *Area Boys*. It is at the heart of this that the ideological basis of *Area Boys* politics is reproduced and from therein the crisis of identity also originates. Fourth, his sample size was too small (45) given the area and institutions he had to cover; the Rehabilitation Centre, Agarawu, Onala and Oluwole areas, (and these are the areas with the highest concentration of *Area Boys* in Central Lagos). Also, his sample population had no female representation or 'Area girls', it was restricted to the male *Area Boys*. Furthermore, Omitoogun did not make any allusion to the 'Area fathers'. According to Obayori, the *Area Boys* are:

> ... merry, gay and deep-witted: the neighbourhood belongs to them, they belong to the neighbourhood, they know it like their palm.... they are half-educated, unemployed or semi-employed young men; those, who for one reason or the other, had to drop out of school, those who got tired of school routine and discipline, those who once had a trade but could not mobilise enough resources to acquire their instruments of trade or those who suddenly got tired of hanging out for the trickling income of their trade, just all sorts of young men who have problems conforming with the socially acceptable means of earning income (1996:15).

And in respect of their vocation, Obayori contends:

> Apart from petty thieves and "toll" (Owo ita) collection from traders and consumers in the "area" market via half-cajole (sic), half-harassment and clowning, when pressed, they also make money on the side producing fake documents .... Their taste too is a thing to be envied .... making upward of between N300 and N1,000 daily, they see themselves as Yankees who by one stroke of divine ill-luck were mistakenly born in Nigeria. To them (America) .... is where they rightly belong to (1996:15–16).

Historically, it is correct to say that it was a thing of pride to be called an *Area Boy*. The concept has its origin in Omo Eko (Lagos Boy) or Omo Area or Omo Adugbo (a boy of the community, locality or street). Hence, the youths of Central Lagos were identified with the streets or locality where they lived e.g. Lafiaji, Campos, Tokunboh, Freeman, etc. The two most significant cultural activities identifiable with Omo Area are Fanti and Eyo festivals. Once you belong to a particular street and you identify with it, the organised youths of that area naturally give you protection against molestation from youths from other streets (Omitoogun, 1994:202). In this way the youths of one community do not allow youths from another community to raid their spinsters or beat up their weak ones unchallenged. Sporting competitions such as table tennis and soccer were played between one group of street youths and another, and the basis of selection into a team depended on this camaraderie and a spirit of community. Sports and cultural activities were the defining characteristics of Omo Area. As Omitoogun has correctly observed:

> Neither education nor wealth is a barrier to social interaction among boys from the same area, although, age is. Omo Eko all enjoy the blissful life; a penchant for parties, lavish dressing and other ostentatious display of wealth, when there is any (Omitoogun, 1994:202).

Eminent Lagosians such as Dr. Wahab Dosunmu, Second Republic Minister of Works and Housing, Bola Tinubu, a Senator in the aborted Third Republic, and Prince 'Demola Adeniji Adele, past Chairman of Lagos Island Local Government, belong in the 'Omo Area' category. Adeniji Adele himself had said that the 'Omo Area' are the real *Area Boys* of Lagos as against the fake *Area Boys*, the hoodlums. He described himself as being part of the real *Area Boys* noting that the real *Area Boys* are *responsible, respectable and well-to-do indigenes of Lagos Island* (Omitoogun, 1994:203). This view lays bare the contradictory and conflictual relationships which exist between so called real and fake *Area Boys*, which has to do with changed values and economic means. The basis of moral and cultural consensus had changed, generational differences and the expectations of each other had also changed. The culture of the so called Omo area disregarded economic means, but the culture of the *Area Boys* was fundamentally predicated on social atomism, lack of access to economic means, the idea of hoodlums, drug addiction and so on, although these were not the defining basis or origin of the so called fake *Area Boys*. Put simply, the *Area Boys* as different from 'Omo area' did not seek crime, even though what society claims to be a crime is now *factored into their traits and social characteristics*.

The transformation of the 'Omo Area' to *Area Boys* has been blamed on the introduction of SAP and the contraction of the labour market. This was said to have forced them into becoming drug *strikers*, who retailed drugs to consumers on behalf of dealers and some of whom, in the process, become users and even addicts (Omitoogun, 1994:203; Adisa, 1994:161). The argument is that the transformation of the social identity of 'Omo Area' into *Area Boys* has to do with changing economic conditions. But with this came the criminalisation of that identity: whether one was rich (and very few were) or poor, being *Area Boy* alone became an anathema because the reason for being an *Area Boy* was seen no longer in cultural terms but in economic and deviant senses. But more often than not the organic link between *Area Boys* and crime is not convincingly made and crime is seen to acquire, in the literature, a social expression identifiable with the poor and not the elite (Odekunle, 1979; Ndiomu, 1994). It is for this reason that the politics of *Area Boys* and its criminalisation has consequences for class politics and class ideology. The relationship between 'Omo Area' and *Area Boys* is one of contempt and tokenism, it is therefore alienating and apologetic. The contradiction between both patterns of relations is often conflictual and at times cooperative, depending on what is at stake. But for the most part the *Area Boys* are at the receiving end.

More often, the *Area Boys* are associated with crime and violence, but the social and ideological context of their violence is not well studied to explain whether their violence can be criminalised on the weight or strength of the type of crime committed and the purpose, reason and objective for committing the crime. For instance, while it is true that the state views consumption of drugs as a crime, sleeping under a bridge or an uncompleted building is not seen as a crime. Moreover, drug consumption (cocaine, heroine, marijuana, etc.) is not restricted to the poor. This raises the fundamental issue of justifiability in constitutional law.

As Campbell (1985) rightly stated, the criminalisation of drugs, such as marijuana, took place at the same time as the trade in them. In other words, it was only when such drugs moved from use to exchange values that they became criminalised. Who are the merchants of drugs, including the ones consumed by the *Area Boys*? They are the rich, who mostly do not fall into the category of *Area Boys*. Two points need to be made. First, we are not denying that *Area Boys* do not commit what, by law, constitutes a crime; rather, what we question here is the status of the ideology that informs such law. Second, the very fact that the dominant culture of the *Area Boys* is rooted in drug addiction, automatically creates an aura of criminality around them.

The table below gives a summary of violent crime in Lagos metropolis.

Table 5. *Standard Score on Violent Crime in Lagos Metropolis (1990–1992)*

Area	A	B	C	D	E	F
Ajegunle	-0.33	0.3	-0.48	0.48	-0.87	-0.38
Apapa	2.45	2.73	0.94	2.68	1.84	2.99
Ebute-Metta	-0.75	0.20	-0.70	-0.70	-0.79	-0.92
Eko (Lagos Island)	-0.09	0.81	-0.13	0.27	-0.71	-0.07
Ikeja	0.06	-0.25	1.32	-1.2	0.34	-0.03
Ikoyi	0.73	0.02	-0.62	0.11	0.85	3.43
Ilupeju	0.54	-1.27	0.98	0.06	1.23	0.34
Iponri	-0.61	-1.19	-0.49	0.06	-0.83	-1.01
Ketu	-0.76	-0.31	-0.21	-0.05	-0.93	0.5
Mushin	-0.80	1.36	-1.18	-0.89	-0.87	0.81
Ogba	1.59	0.00	0.48	1.25	0.22	0.92
Onikan	-1.43	-0.55	-0.03	-0.40	-0.33	-0.59
Oshodi	-0.56	-0.27	-0.98	-0.47	-0.55	-0.94
Shomolu	-1.00	-1.27	-0.93	1.40	-0.7	0.55
Surulere	0.68	1.25	1.60	0.09	-0.40	0.10
Victoria Island	0.68	0.68	1.77	-0.93	2.19	0.98
Yaba	-0.42	-0.50	-1.36	-0.36	0.32	-0.79

A = Murder, B = Grievous Harm and Wounding (GHW), C = Assault, D = Rape, E = Robbery, F = Total (composite) score,

Source: Mukoro quoted in Adisa (1994:158).

A cursory look at Table 5 shows that Eko (Lagos Island), which is our area of focus for this study, has relatively low violent crime rates in virtually all the sub-heads. Thus, while the *Area Boys* are stigmatised as being violent criminals, recorded crime rate in the area in which they live and operate, does not prove that to be correct.

There are so many reasons that make the violent crime thesis against *Area Boys* spurious. First, in some cases where *Area Boys* extort money from Igbo traders, they are mostly instigated by the landlords i.e. the contradiction between Lagosian landowners and the Igbo commercial class. Second, before *Area Boys* unleashed their violence, they often put their potential victims on notice e.g. Hausa money launderers, Igbo traders or even Yoruba strangers from the hinterland (Ara Oke). Indeed, some of those people had problems with the *Area Boys* at the onset because they had contempt for them and refused to accept the reality of their existence. Third, *Area Boys* become violent mostly against the law enforcement agents, such as the Police, agents of the National Drugs Law Enforcement Agency (NDLEA) and Rehabilitation Centre officials, who they see as enemies and not friends. In this sense, they perceive their violence as defensive. Fourth, *Area Boys* do not rob shops or engage in the crime of stealing because they know they could be very easily identified, as a result of their living within the locality.

When it is realised that SAP itself cannot be implemented without the authoritarian disposition of the state, it is easy to see why the *Area Boys* sometimes resort to violence to defend, protect or promote their interests. Contingent to every class is a functional notion of violence. On the other hand, the increasing culture of military rule and its attendant militarism, which condones lawlessness such as extra-judicial killings, rule by decrees and so on, is a specific form of violence unleashed on society. Therefore, the violence of the *Area Boys* is, in a sense, a specific response to the violence embedded in militarism. For instance, many of the *Area Boys* interviewed are unhappy with the culture of militarism, detention without trial, extra-judicial killings (such as the killing of the Dawodu brothers in Central Lagos in 1989), and so on. How violence is defined in this case is a political question, in the Fanonian sense (see Fanon 1967:27–28).

The basis of criminalizing the *Area Boys* has an essential implication, it involves the debasement and dehumanisation of the *Area Boys*, as human beings and as people with objective material interest and shared aspirations. The stigma of deviants and criminals only helps to deny them the baseline identity of human beings and citizens. Their self-perception, aspirations and expectations are caricatured, in order that they could be trivialised. This, however, relates to what we call the crisis of identity. This crisis has implications for (a) generation (b) class (c) ideology and (d) economic contradictions.

One crucial point that should be noted is that many of the *Area Boys* who are caught in a criminal act are more often than not sent to the rehabilitation centre rather than to prison. This implicitly gives meaning to the fact that the state recognises that the "crime" of the *Area Boys* is of a special type.

Social Structure of *Area Boys*

Omitoogun identifies three categories of Area Boys: the educated elite, the nouveau riche with dubious sources of income and the rock bottom or poor Area Boys. The first category is made up of Area Boys of Lagos Island who, although well educated, find it difficult to leave the slum of Lagos Island in spite of their status. In this group too are other not-too-well-educated but successful men, engaged in legitimate business. They prefer to 'dignify' Lagos Island with their presence rather than to relocate or leave it. The second group mostly earn a living through drugs and such related trades, including forgeries and illegal visa transactions. Most of such people are based in Agarawu (the core of our case study area) where the sale of cocaine and marijuana (agbana, a Yoruba word for light or fire) flourishes. The third category is made up of the never-do-wells who like a good and ostentatious life-style, but are handicapped by lack of education and wealth (Omitoogun, 1994:204).

Our social construction of the *Area Boys* includes the 'Area fathers' and 'Area girls'. It will also be useful to know how and why the *Area Boys*, thus conceived, became what they are, in terms of their status and origins. For instance, some of the so called never-do-wells necessarily took to being *Area Boys*, not because they have higher taste, but because they have no sustaining means of livelihood. For example, when we asked about the educational background of our respondents, we got the following responses: primary six 12.2%; West Africa School Certificate 51.8%; Junior Secondary School (JSS III) 3.6%; Tertiary Institution 14.1%; uneducated 14.1%; and No Response 0.99%. On the issue of those who dropped out of school, of the 34 respondents who answered this question 67.6% dropped out for financial reason; 5.8% dropped out as a result of repeated failure; 17.6% dropped out as a result of lack of interest; 2.9% dropped out as a result of expulsion from school while 5.8% indicated No Response.

So, it is quite clear that majority of our respondents dropped out of school due to financial difficulties. When asked why they took to the streets as *Area Boys* and girls, a total of 89 respondents answered this question thus: as a means of livelihood 48.1%; to get money for drugs in order to prevent jonessing/withdrawal 35.8% and No Response 16.0%. From this, one point becomes discernible, the *Area Boys* mostly come from poor background. In respect of how they earn a living, respondents answered this question thus: protecting lives and property for money 32.0%; working for 'big men' to extort money from the people 34.9%; winning contract to cause trouble and beat up people 11.3%; through criminal deception and fraud (also popularly called 419) 3.7% and No Response 12.2%.

When asked whether they were proud to be *Area Boys*, about 18% of the respondents said "Yes", while about 75% answered "No". About 7% did not respond to the question. Furthermore, when asked whether they saw the activities of the *Area Boys* as a crime or mere fun, 51.8% responded by answering that it was a crime while 33.9% said it was not and 14.1% did not respond to the question. This lays bare the fact that the *Area Boys* did not seek criminality nor do they believe in what they are doing as being a natural or decent way of living. There are some aggressive activities that are not necessarily violent or criminal in nature. The *Area Boys* cannot be stigmatised as criminals, merely because some of them are violent or because the state said they are. The best way to proceed, therefore, is to decriminalise the *Area Boys* phenomenon by posing it primarily as a social problem.

The female *Area Boys* or the 'Area girls' constituted 32.1 per cent of our total sample population, while the male *Area Boys* constituted 67.9 per cent. This shows that there is need to shift focus to the gender dimension of the discourse of the *Area Boys* phenomenon. Previous studies just give the impression that there are only male *Area Boys*. How did the 'Area girls' come to join this social group? What do they do? We shall return to these questions shortly.

The 'Area fathers' are in a technical sense the grown-up, or older category of *Area Boys*. Their misdemeanour is similar to that of the *Area Boys*, but it differs from them in one principal way, namely, that the 'Area fathers' have been in the streets for a longer time than the *Area Boys*. They have responsibilities, such as taking wives and children, to cater for and they rely very heavily on their income from the *Area Boys* who make returns and pay homage and tribute to them from their own meagre earned incomes. The 'Area fathers' are usually at loggerheads with the *Area Boys* when it comes to sharing money. It is the belief of the former that the latter are reckless and have few or no responsibilities to cater for. The latter often protested as a result of such treatment which culminates in conflicts. Top politicians normally get in touch with the 'Area fathers' to pass on money or items such as draughtboards, table tennis and football equipment's to the *Area Boys*. The police and community leaders often talked to the 'Area fathers' and the *Alagbara Adugbo* (Area champion or leader of the *Area Boys*) in order to keep peace or forestall trouble.

Hierarchically, the *Alagbara Adugbo*, (always a male) is made the head of the *Area Boys* in his locality, by virtue of being the strongest and bravest of the *Area Boys*. In this respect an *Alagbara Adugbo* is most likely not to be hooked on drugs, because those hooked on drugs are normally very frail and weak, and mostly engaged in jonessing and withdrawal syndrome. Once an *Area Boy* or girl drops out of school for reasons of lack of finance or expulsion, he/she would not like to go back to home. Almost invariably, they take to living either with the 'Area fathers' (who are most likely to have a rented house), or in the streets, garages, stalls, uncompleted houses, under bridges, and so on. These then constitute their hideouts. To have leverage and penetrate the social ladder, new entrants into the *Area Boys* circle work for the 'Area fathers'. It is important to note that some of the 'Area fathers' have up to three wives. These wives are most likely to be 'Area girls' or 'graduates' of that social category. The ideology of fend-for-yourself more often than not governs their relationship with their husbands, who have no visible or steady sources of income. Our data indicates that 62.2 per cent of our respondents were from polygamous homes, while 34.9 per cent were from monogamous homes. This social background may well be instructive on the attitudes of the wives of 'Area fathers' to the principle of fend-for-yourself.

The *Area Boys* mostly do menial jobs, such as informal guards or watchmen protecting lives and property, washing cars, serving as bus conductors, touts in garages, janitors, vendors at public buildings, market places, and motor parks, retailers of drugs, servicing people and touting at market places, embassies and public offices. For example, they 'help' visa applicants to queue at embassies; they front for Lagos landlords who have problems with Igbo (tenant) traders, they provide security for night crawlers or people who are stranded at odd hours. They plant nails in roads to deflate tyres of motorists in order to collect illegal tolls. They dig up roads in order to cause a traffic jam (go slow), all in order to extort money from motorists, especially during the rainy season when there is flooding, they guide motorists as to which part of the street to take and how to avoid getting into a ditch or big pot-hole. Added to this, some of the *Area Boys* snatch bags and ornaments, pick pockets and so on. Others engage in 'responsible begging' for money or financial assistance from the public (a.k.a. *Fine Bara*). The 'Area girls' mostly queue up at embassies as early as 4.30 a.m. for their female clients, mostly Lagos business women who may want to travel abroad. They also serve as food vendors, drug sellers and shop keepers. The point must be made that the *Area Boys* and girls do not break into houses or market stalls; in any case, security in Central Lagos is very high because of its commercial importance and some of the *Area Boys* even serve as vigilantes or security guards. Most of the crimes of the *Area Boys* are committed in the streets and during the day-time and not at night.

The *Area Boys* that we interviewed and administered questionnaires to mostly fall within the age bracket of 12–35. The breakdown of the ages of our respondents is thus: below 15 years, 0.99%; 15–25 years, 46.2%; 26–35 years, 37.7%; 36–45 years, 13.2%; and 46 and above 0.9%. Only one respondent refused to state his age.

It is noteworthy that although the concept of *Area Boys* has its origin in *Omo Eko*, in terms of the ethnic origin of the *Area Boys*, however we discovered that many of our respondents were not originally from Lagos or Lagos State. In terms of state of origin, those from Lagos constituted 26.4%; from Ogun 22.6%; from Kwara 14.2%; from Ondo 5.6%; from Oyo 14.1%; from Osun 4.7%; from Anambra 1.8%; from Kano 1.8%; from Imo 1.8%; from Rivers 1.8%; from Abia 1.8%; from Kaduna 0.9%; from Sokoto 0.9%; and Igbo 0.9% (the respondent did not indicate his state of origin in Igboland).

The implication of this is that it is not only original indigenes of Lagos that constitute the social category of *Area Boys*. This also suggests that the often projected correlation of *Omo Eko* with *Area Boys* is highly problematic. One point that needs to be stated, however, is that, in a fundamental respect, how we define citizenship affects how we view the citizenship status of the *Area Boys*. Are the *Area Boys* Lagosians? In the first place, only 74 out of 106 respondents answered the question on state of origin and that is highly suggestive. Of those who answered it, 46.2% said they were born in Lagos and have lived there ever since; 5.6% said they have lived in Lagos for between 5–10 years; 1.8% said they have lived in Lagos for between 11–15 years; 7.5% indicated that they have lived in Lagos for 16–20 years; 8.4% said they have lived in Lagos for over 21 years. About 4% did not respond to the question, perhaps because they do not have an idea as to when they came to Lagos, for how long they have lived in it or perhaps because they are embarrassed by the question.

We asked our respondents how long ago they became *Area Boys*. The details of the answers given are as follows: 1–5 years, 16.98%; 6–10 years, 39.62%; 11–15 years, 16.98%; 15–20 years, 5.66%. This shows the close link between the introduction of SAP and the emergence of *Area Boys* and girls. It is also note-worthy that many of them became *Area Boys* from about the on-set of the era of adjustment reforms.

Many of the respondents did not indicate when they became *Area Boys*. This may be indicative of their self-perception of what they are doing as being wrong when viewed against their previous cultural mode of activities as *Omo Eko*. It should also be noted here that although the *Area Boys* have deference and respect for prominent *Omo areas* (indigenes) such as Wahab Dosumu, Adeniji Adele and Dr. Fadipe, these people seem to have contempt for them and interact with them only for the utilitarian value they have; especially politically. For example, Adeniji Adele (popularly called 'Princess' by the *Area Boys*), is generally acknowledged to be generous. When the wives of an 'Area father' or *Area Boy* give birth, he is said to often give some token sum to facilitate the child's naming ceremony. He also buys games equipment, such as table tennis tables, for the *Area Boys*, in addition to employing some of them in his company, Crown Fisheries. When he served as the Chairman of the Lagos Island local government, he facilitated the recruitment of many *Area Boys* as inmates of the Rehabilitation Centre. As it is, while the Omo area can become an *Area Boy*, however, the chances of an *Area Boy* being reintegrated as Omo area are very slim, because of the social stigma he/she has acquired. This social stigma is essentially as a result of their mode of living which is rooted in drugs and menial jobs and indecent means. In a sense, this also makes the distinction between Omo area and *Area Boys* a class question.

Drugs and Youth Culture

One of the major defining characteristics of the *Area Boys* is that most of them use drugs (cocaine, heroin, marijuana, etc.) either as occasional users or addicts, or as peddlers. The interviews suggest that nearly all *Area Boys* who lived in the streets use or are hooked on drugs. Initially it was the male Omo area (not *Area Boys*) who were involved in the drug business, they merely sent some of the *Area Boys* (especially the girls) abroad as carriers, with drugs concealed in innocuous places and using all sorts of tricks to beat immigration and customs officials. This relationship was initially based on the *Area Boys* trust in their partners, and the knowledge that the Omo area would not betray or double-cross them in the deals. Over time, however, the 'Igbo 419', criminal class began to join in the drugs trade and they are often involved in double-dealing and out-manœuvering the *Area Boys*. Some of these Igbo traders have shops in Central Lagos where they merely retail goods as a front for their main trade in the illicit drugs business. The *Area Boys* often raided such shops when they were out-manoeuvred by the Igbo drug barons; but the ordinary on-lookers often misinterpreted this as a mere attack on Igbo traders without knowing the genesis of the problem.

The trafficking of drugs abroad brought quick money and even transformed the lives of some of the *Area Boys*. Many of them began to take interest in the trade, but only a few of them could travel abroad. Those who could not travel abroad stayed home to retail the drugs for barons as strikers (Adisa, 1994). They sold the drugs in grams or in pinches. Selling in grams is more profitable than selling in pinches, because of the high rate of turnover of sales to the strikers. Some barons (especially those *Area Boys* who made money from successful drug courier trips abroad) began to use the drugs and some of them, in the process, got addicted to them. Some of those who used them said they wanted to be high, and to boost their morale in pursuing their daily activities. Many of those who got addicted to cocaine, heroin and morphine, claimed that they became addicted because they were in search of the original drugs, as many of them, hitherto, did not know the difference between the genuine and fake drugs, especially as some dealers and producers began to fake the drugs by substituting them with yam powder (elubo), or the fever relieving drug Alabukun, generally called 'performer' by the *Area Boys*. To the *Area Boys* a 'performer' is any drug other than cocaine, heroin, morphine, etc., which can have the same effect on them as those hard drugs. These are often cheaper than the real drugs. After taking or tasting those fake drugs (performers) the *Area Boys* tend to somehow crave for the real stuff, and in the process they become hooked, exhibiting all the characteristics of addicts.

Data gathered from 77 respondents indicates that 12.2% were drug sellers on the streets and 60.3% were drug addicts. When asked why they took to being drug dealers or drug addicts, 16.8% said it was as a result of the money involved; 67.5% said it was as a result of peer group influence, and 14.2% said that it was as a result of frustration. Some of the parents or relations of the *Area Boys* often bring them back home after they get hooked on drugs in order to rehabilitate them privately. However, after spending a lot of money, and if the condition of the addicted *Area Boys* has not changed, the parents or relations often abandon them. Some of such addicts steal and sell the trinkets and valuable items of their parents/relations. Once abandoned, they revert into gangs and live in uncompleted and or abandoned buildings, garages, or under Lagos fly-over bridges. It is usually members of this group that mostly harass commuters and citizens for money in the streets.

The Rehabilitation Centre (RC)

The RC is located on Adeniji Adele road in Lagos Island. It was established in 1993 and was formerly named the Lagos Island Local Government Women Resource Centre. The emergence of drug addicts and growing phenomenon of *Area Boys*, and their continued harassment of members of the public in streets, mainly as a result of the influence of and the need for hard drugs, informed the decision of the Lagos Island Local Government and Mrs. Maria Sokenu, the then Managing Director of the People's Bank of Nigeria, to establish the RC. It served both drug addicts and the *Area Boys*.

It is important to note that the RC was more of a political, rather than a social, response to the *Area Boys* question. This is in the sense that it was established only when the *Area Boys* became a strong and organised political force in the resistance to SAP policies. Anti-SAP protests began around 1988 and the *Area Boys* were actively involved. Thus, it became expedient to contain the *Area Boys* and somewhat neutralise them politically by reducing their numbers in the streets. The RC served a political purpose in this respect. At its inception, Mrs. Sokenu co-ordinated and personally took charge of all activities in the centre, such as feeding, provision of health-care services and training programmes in artisan jobs such as carpentry, bricklaying, tailoring, and so on. Moral and religious instruction was also given in the centre, in addition to medical and psychiatric attention to addicts suffering from withdrawal syndrome.

We tried to find out what the *Area Boys* know about the RC. A majority (48.1%) of our respondents said that they are aware of the existence of the RC. Quite interestingly, most of our respondents are drug addicts, and 75% said they were willing to be rehabilitated at the RC. When asked to assess the efforts of the RC, 54.7% of the respondents said the RC was trying.

The RC is structured such that inmates have an executive among themselves with the most well-behaved, and strongest, appointed as the leader. Inmates are brought to the centre through contacts with former inmates, the local government council and the Yaba Psychiatric Hospital and Social Welfare Home. The *Area Boys* who go to the RC do so not necessarily because they steal, but because they are drug addicts or a potential political threat to the state's so called security.

There are so many problems at the RC such as over-crowding, poor sanitary conditions, lack of enough security personnel to check and curtail excesses of inmates, lack of funds to provide adequate infrastructure and equipment for the training of inmates, and lack of adequate medical facilities to treat sick inmates. It was learnt that many inmates who either got bored, or experienced a feeling of maltreatment, high-handedness and lack of proper socialisation, escaped into the outer society to return to their life as *Area Boys* and girls.

Area Boys, Politics and Democracy

There are two senses in which what can be termed as the *Area Boys* politics should be understood and examined. The first is as politics created in the context of the state. In this sense, it is dependent and subordinated politics. For example, this is how we should analyze the role of the *Area Boys* in the struggles against militarism and in favour of the winner of the June 12 1993 presidential elections. The second is in respect of the autonomous political sphere which the *Area Boys* seek to appropriate or create for themselves. This is evident in the social and political construction of their daily lives and in their struggles against SAP.

Can *Area Boys* have a sense of politics that is correct and altruistic? Should they be allowed to express political views? Has their transformed identity from Omo area to *Area Boys* denied them any political right? First, it should be noted that the militarism of the Nigerian state is rooted in structural violence and the *Area Boys* are a cardinal product and target of such violence. Second, SAP has thrown up authoritarian political regimes and this means that the economic terrain, and by implication also the political terrain, has to be contested (Beckman, 1991). If the *Area Boys* are a product of adjustment reforms in a social sense, then in a political sense it means they have a lot at stake and therefore cannot afford to be apolitical. Third, the history of the *Area Boys* in street politics, and in cultural festivities, such as the *Fanti* and *Eyo*, make them relate with both traditional and secular authorities and have a leverage as what can be called 'street parliamentarians'.

In other words, in spite of everything else, the *Area Boys* have their own impression of politics and their political interests. For example, they see their plight, in the main, as occasioned by the state's abdication of its social responsibilities to them. To that extent, as citizens, they do not believe they owe the state much. When asked whether the actions of government have benefited the *Area Boys* in their communities, 67 per cent of the respondents that answered the question said No.

In the aborted Babangida transition programme, many of the *Area Boys* were recruited as political thugs to beat up opponents or to serve as bodyguards for politicians (Momoh, 1996: 25). When asked whether they would take part in a violent action for a just cause; 46.2% responded in the affirmative, while 48.1% said No. Yet many of the *Area Boys*, in their organised forms within localities, joined in the Campaign for Democracy (CD) call to struggle for the reversing of the annulment of the June 1993 presidential elections believed to have been won by Chief M.K.O. Abiola. It seems that M.K.O. Abiola was the personal attraction as he was said to dole out money freely to *Area Boys* whenever he was around Central Lagos. Thus, the *Area Boys* vandalised the shops of Igbo traders (who insisted on selling their goods even in spite of the stay-at-home call by CD) and the shops of such prominent people as Okoya Thomas, owner of Eleganza Company, who is believed by the *Area Boys* to be adroitly anti-Abiola. When asked about their perception of Igbo and stranger traders in Lagos, our respondents answered as follows: they are exploiters 40.5%, aliens 5.6% and partners 51.8%. Yet when asked whether they believed the June 12 struggle, which was meant to install Abiola as president, was a just cause, 46.2% answered Yes, 49.0% answered No, while 3.7% did not respond. But quite contradictorily, when asked whether they took part in the struggle for June 12; 89.6% answered Yes, 5.6% answered No and 4.7% had No Response. Most of those who joined in the struggle for June 12, it became clear, did so as a group—the break-down of the responses is thus: those who joined as individuals 10.3%; those who joined as a group 82.0%; and those who did not respond 7.5%.

It should be stated that the *Area Boys* were very active during the civil disobedience call of CD and their action went a long way to make the struggle very effective in Lagos. When asked whether they believed their actions could bring changes to Lagos State; 57.5% said Yes; 39.6% said No; and 2.8% had No Response. It should be stated that the social life of the *Area Boys* is such that makes them meet and interact on a daily basis and in that process also discuss matters of common and/or beneficial interest, including tasks and responsibilities.

Since the killing of the Dawodu brothers in 1989, *Area Boys* struggles against state politics and policies had taken the form of anti-SAP protest, in 1989 and 1992; and quite a number of the *Area Boys* were killed as a result of this. In the anti-SAP protest, *Area Boys* formed an alliance with the students, especially those from the University of Lagos, who often mobilised them. In 1992, when the leadership of NANS engaged in anti-SAP protest, they tried to prevent the *Area Boys* from looting and burning. However, when they got to the neighbourhoods under the control of the *Area Boys*, not even the police could contain them. In the end, six *Area Boys* were shot dead. Obayori noted that "[t]hose shot were said to be *Area Boys* seizing the opportunity of the protest to loot" (1996, 14). Following the call by the Campaign for Democracy (CD) for mass protest as a result of the annulment of the June 12, 1993 election, the *Area Boys* heeded the call. They not only manned their traditionally controlled areas in Lagos Island, but went to the Mainland and other areas to mobilise people for the cause.

On July 5, 1993, the *Area Boys* joined a mass of people to march to M.K.O. Abiola's house. On their way they were attacked by the police on the Agege motor road, at Mushin. The students who led them appealed to them through their leadership not to be violent. They were however disappointed when on getting to Abiola's house, after the speech-making exercise and address by Abiola, he did not give them money (egunje) (ibid:19). They then returned to their bases in the hope of burning buses (danfo) but were talked out of this by the students. They eventually settled for a bonfire using petrol and tyres.

On July 6, 1993 the *Area Boys* embarked on a looting spree, especially in shops of Igbo traders who resisted the call of the CD. They also burnt some public buildings. The army intervened with a shoot-at-sight order after Sir Miscall Otedola refused to heed the instruction of General Sani Abacha, then Chief Army of Staff that "law and order" must be "restored to Lagos at any cost". Many people were killed in the process. As Obayori observed, "Abacha officially backed up the killings and sent out more troops on the morning of 7th (July) to complete the job" (1996:14).

Finally on November 10, 1993, on the eve of the judgment of the Federal High Court on the status of the Interim National Government (ING), the *Area Boys* once more mobilised themselves and went to Abiola's residence at Ikeja. This time they had lunch and were happy. Then on November 11, they began to mobilise for protest. The student leaders of the University of Lagos cautioned them not to be violent. They refused, and instead, attacked the students at the Yaba-Jibowu fly-over.

Since General Sani Abacha assumed the reins of power on November 17, 1993, he has engaged in an orchestrated repressive policy against the *Area Boys*. It is in this respect that the Rehabilitation Centre (RC) is seen more as an alternative prison rather than a rehabilitation place. This is what makes the RC acquire more of a political character than a social one. Indeed, to complement this, *Area Boys* are now being sent to proper jail. Under Colonel Olagunsoye Oyinlola, then Lagos State Governor, seven *Area Boys* were paraded before the press on March 26, 1994, by the Task Force on Environmental Sanitation, they were tried and sentenced to jail, without legal aid and without the option of a fine (*ibid*:20). At present, under Colonel Mohammed Marwa, the Lagos State Governor, his "Operation Sweep" has brought untold harassment and attack on the *Area Boys*. They are now constantly raided, hounded and thrown into detention without trial. The whole objective of "Operation Sweep" is to cleanse Lagos State of so called hoodlums, robbers and crime.

The *Area Boys* do not believe in military rule because of its highhandedness, intolerance, and exclusionary nature. When asked about their view on the success of the Abacha transition to civil rule programme, 8.4% said it will succeed, while 88% said it will not succeed. At the time of the fieldwork, the five registered political parties are seen to be seriously lobbying the *Area Boys* for support and assistance in their campaigns to mobilise voters for the 1997 local government elections. The parties mostly use contacts and points people; the 'Area fathers', rehabilitated and jobless *Area Boys* have been the most amenable in this regard. It is apparent that in their current *lumpen* form, the politics of the *Area Boys* will be dictated by the logic of the interest of the Omo area and top politicians in Lagos to whom they show deference and respect. Their political consciousness has not moved beyond spontaneity and fatalism, because of their lack of enduring links with political organisations and movements. We must not dismiss, however, the politics of the *Area Boys* because it has potentials for self-expression and the possibilities for self-actualisation and liberation. The challenge is how to harness this into wider forms of popular struggles. The relationship of the *Area Boys* to the CD supports our claim in this regard.

Although the *Area Boys* are spatially organised (in streets, and neighbourhoods) and socially cohesive in the way they go about the pursuit of reproducing their material lives, they have, however, not internalised a clear-cut political consciousness, even though they are politically informed and do freely discuss politics and matters relating to democracy. The social space which the *Area Boys* construct for themselves creates an avenue for a new mode of politics and it is a terrain that can be exploited for deconstructing statist and hegemonic politics based on dominant class interest, as ramified and expressed in pluralist political parties and transition to civil rule.

The *Area Boys* have a culture of politics which requires study and examination in both its ideology and activism. Such a culture of politics follows a tradition of the quest for emancipatory politics ably conceptualised by Wamba-dia-Wamba (1993, 1994) which sees politics as what is defined or what takes place outside the context of the superstructure and the state. But to appreciate that the *Area Boys* have their own mode of politics will require re-humanising and decriminalizing the essence of their social being, as well as reconceptualising them as a people organised as an interest group. Diouf calls it heterodox practices, thus: "... youth have set about promoting new solidarities and producing new parameters, confronting the state, parents, and educators—or simply ignoring them" (1996: 234).

There is, clearly, a renewed state offensive against the *Area Boys* through the Lagos State Government's "Operation Sweep" project, which is operated by a combined team of the police, army, state security services and NDLEA officials. Between September, 1996 and January 1997, no less than 200 *Area Boys* have been arrested and detained. Operation Sweep operates like a lawless and parallel state machinery. They have been supported in less than six months with over N300 million by the state and the federal governments, which gave them 30 vehicles for their operation.

Conclusion

There are four basic issues that underline our argument in this study and which can, indeed, be posed as four contradictions: urbanite, class, ideological and generational. First, the *Area Boys* phenomenon is a product of urban contradictions and uneven development. Second, it is rooted in class contradictions, because most of the *Area Boys* are the urban poor and victims of a class society. Third, the *Area Boys* issue is a reflection of generational contradictions between a preponderantly adult and well-to-do Omo area and the youth, *Area Boys*. These generational contradictions mediate with the other contradictions to give full expression and meaning to the understanding of the *Area Boys* phenomenon. Fourth, the *Area Boys* question is ideological, because it is rooted in a theory of social atomism and urban anonymity. It dehumanises people and criminalises them, without establishing the causative agent. In this regard, the youth are seen as deviant or delinquent and the state as benevolent and charitable to them (e.g. through the RC.) This is thoroughly misleading because the state is a class agent and the producer of urban contradictions. It is the marketer of the ideology of criminalizing the *Area Boys*. And the state's goal in doing that is to caricature or trivialise the urban youth crisis in order to dismiss it most simplistically.

Our research findings can be summarised as follows. First, although the economic crisis, especially SAP, is central to the production of the *Area Boys* phenomenon, it is however not the singular cause or explanation for the conditions of its reproduction. There is need to seek explanation also in the regime or a culture of violence introduced in the form of militarism. Second, and this is a corollary of the foregoing, most *Area Boys* have a dominant youth culture associated with drug addiction, but drug addiction does not necessarily translate into violence or robbery/stealing. Indeed, most of the stealing that occurs in Lagos Island is not done by *Area Boys*. Third, there is no correlation between crime and violence in studying the *Area Boys*. Thus, although they may be violent at times, the objective of *Area Boys* is not often to use violence to commit crime, but to rectify what they perceived as a problem, which is at times economic and at other times political or social. Fourth, although the *Area Boys* sometimes steal or engage in crime, the criminalisation of the *Area Boys* stigmatises them and obfuscates their true character. For instance, the *Area Boys* did not set out to steal or be vandals even as *Area Boys*, they set out to earn a living through visible and known means in the streets. They became petty thieves and pick-pockets only as a last resort. It is dominant state ideology that attributes all crimes and robbery to the *Area Boys*. Any *Area Boy* caught stealing in his traditional area is often subjected to punishment or discipline by his colleagues in an organised manner. Punishment often meted out ranges from flogging to beating the floor with the bare fists.

Fifth, *Area Boys* as human beings, have a consciousness of good and bad and of a sense of responsibility. Thus, although they may not be disposed to good virtues due to their objective material being, they however still uphold those virtues as worthy of dignifying their humanity. Their attitude to the Rehabilitation Centre supports this claim. Sixth, there is need for society to humanise the *Area Boys*, for in this way, it will be easy to appreciate the merit of their expectations of the society and their politics. To deny the politics and culture of *Area Boys* in society in the context of a non-statist political culture is to deny the multiple contradictions that serve as composite in-put to generate a national culture of politics. The baseline identity and the defining basis of *Area Boys*, in the first place, is their humanity. To deny this in the analysis of the contradictions that they get enmeshed into, as a result of urban crisis, is to reify them, vulgarise them, commoditise them or make them inanimate objects.

The goal of the state, and the dominant class and adult generational forces seems to be to make the *Area Boys* scapegoats of the society. The dominant ideology on urban youth in Nigeria is not only doubly suspect and dubious, it is also a product of the ideology of defeat and fatalism. It is worth emphasising that the transformation of the cultural Omo Area identity to the criminalised *Area Boys* identity is not simply an economic question, but also an ideological one. The sub-human and caricatured way researchers and the state alike have treated the *Area Boys* is a product of an ideological divide. The response of *Area Boys* in both their mannerisms and social actions, including violent ones, is in part meant to contain state violence, action and class politics. This is because the conflicts that they engage in with the state, and therefore for civil society, are at the heart of the reproduction of their material lives. That not much has been done to deconstruct the dominant discourses on *Area Boys* does not by itself accord self-evident truth or scientific status on those discourses. The hatred of the ruling class and the middle class for this "non-class" will not do.

Finally, we must not allow the *Area Boys* phenomenon to acquire the status of a lamentable social mystery; rather we should see it as a perversion and a negative fallout of human civilisation from which we must seek scientific explanation. And this explanation is not located in the *Area Boys* themselves, but in an totally perverted social heritage and parasitic political economy.

I acknowledge with thanks the assistance of my informants many of whom prefer to remain anonymous and also of my able field assistants, Surajudeen Mudasiru and Taiwo Hundeyin, who are graduates in Political Science, Lagos State University. Mr. Mudasiru is a self-professed *Area Boy* and I benefited immensely from his experience and guidance in the course of undertaking this research.

Bibliography

Adisa, J., 1994, "Urban Violence in Lagos", in Osaghae, E., et al., (eds.) *Urban Violence in Africa: Pilot Studies*. Ibadan: IFRA.

Beckman, B., 1991, "Empowerment or Repression? The World Bank and the Politics of African Adjustment", *Africa Development*, Vol. XVI, No. 1.

Campbell, H., 1985, *Rasta and Resistance: From Marcus Garvey to Walter Rodney*. Dar-es-Salam: Tanzania Publishing House.

Diouf, M, 1996, "Urban Youth and Senegalese Politics: Dakar 1988–1994", *Public Culture*, Vol. 8, No. 2.

Fanon, F., 1967, *The Wretched of the Earth*. Middlesex: Penguin Books.

Isamah, Austin N., 1994, "Structural Adjustment, Social Alienation and Urban Violence", in Albert, I. O. et al., (eds.) *Urban Management and Urban Violence in Africa*. Ibadan: IFRA.

Momoh, A., 1994, "Population and the Political Economy of Urban Crisis: The Case of Lagos", in Ibrahim, J. et. al., *Population Space and Development in Nigeria*. Paris: Club du Sahel.

Momoh, A., 1996, "Vigilantism in the Era of Transitions in Africa: The Case of South Africa and Nigeria", paper presented at the Social Science Research Council Conference on Transitions in Africa, held in Niamey; June 4–6.

Ndiomu, C. B., 1994, "Crime and National Survival", *Orita*, Vol. XXVI, Nos. 1 & 2.

Obayori, F., 1996, *June 12 in Perspective (Five Critical Essays)*. Lagos: Lumumba Memorial Book House.

Odekunle, F., 1979, "Juvenile Delinquency and Adult Crime", in Akeredolu-Ale, E. O. et al., (eds.) *Social Problems and Criminality in Nigeria*. Lagos: Federal Ministry of Health and Social Welfare.

Odekunle, F., 1986, "The Legal Order, Crime and Crime-Control in Nigeria: Demystification of False Appearances", *Nigeria Journal of Policy and Strategy*. June.

Oki, Ololade J., (ed.), n.d, *Ten Years of Youth Work 1982–1992*. Lagos: Federal Ministry of Education and Youth Development.

Omitoogun, W., 1994, "The *Area Boys* of Lagos: A Study of Organized Street Violence", in Albert, A. O. et al., (eds.) *Urban Management and Urban Violence in Africa. Urban Management and Urban Violence in Africa*. Ibadan: IFRA.

Police Crime Statistics, 1989–1993, *Police Annual Report*. Lagos: Force Headquarters.

Salami, A. T., 1994, "Urban Violence: The State of Theory, Implications for Contemporary Urban Management in Africa", in Albert, I. O. et al., (eds.) *Urban Management and Urban Violence in Africa*. Ibadan: IFRA.

Vanderschueren, F., 1996, "From Violence to Justice and Security in Cities", *Environment and Urbanization*, Vol. 8, No. 1.

Wamba-dia-Wamba, E., 1993, "Democracy, Multipartyism and Emancipative Politics in Africa: The Case of Zaire", *Africa Development*, Vol. XVIII, No. 4.

Wamba-dia-Wamba, E., 1994, "Africa in Search of a New Mode of Politics", in Himmelstrand, U. et al., (eds.) *African Perspectives on Development*. London: James Currey.

Chapter 10

Structural Adjustment, Students' Movement and Popular Struggles in Nigeria, 1986–1996

Said Adejumobi

Introduction

At no time in the Nigerian post-colonial history has the level and dimension of the socio-economic crises been so profound as under the regime of structural adjustment (SAP). Virtually all the social sectors were hard hit, either entering a comatose state or declining substantially in performance (Adejumobi, 1995, 1996; Odumosu, 1996). Education was a major victim of the social sector crisis engendered by SAP. The policy prompted a downsizing of education on the state agenda, emphasising cost recovery and rationalisation in educational enterprise and seeking to align the acquisition of knowledge with the demands of industry. Thus, the tendency on the part of the state under SAP, shifted from *caring for education* to the exercise of political control on education.

This situation gradually transformed the educational institutions from being "citadels of learning to battlegrounds," where the various actors or social groups within the system—students, teachers and non-teaching staff, had to stand in defence of their organisational rights, protect the welfare of their members and sometimes enter the arena of popular struggle to expand the democratic space at the national level, which they consider to be organically linked to their struggle at the micro-level. Indeed, as Beckman and Jega (1995) rightly noted, organised interests which contest relations of domination in their respective arenas, will inevitably come up against the state and will have a stake in the political solutions which will facilitate the pursuit of their interests. The students' movement in Nigeria represents the best tradition in this regard.

From 1981, with the onset of the economic crisis, the students' movement launched not only a consistent and sustained campaign for educational reforms, but also sought to forge alliances with democratic groups, trade unions, and professional organisations in order to have a common and broader platform for the struggle against political misrule and challenge the unpopular policies and programmes of the state. The struggle for the re-democratisation of the country gradually gained ground, with the return of the military on the political scene in Nigeria in November 1993. Increasingly, the popular identity of Nigerian students, as represented by their association, the National Association of Nigerian Students (NANS) lies in their culture of popular struggle and resistance. Thus, the students' movement in Nigeria has been variously described as the "barometer of public opinion", "the vector of social change" "the conscience of the society" and "voice of the voiceless". In other words, NANS is viewed as the vanguard of the interest of the masses or dominated social groups and classes in Nigeria.

On the other hand, the state and the dominant class perceive the student movement as an "irritant", "saboteur" or "anarchists", which must be daily controlled and if need be, ruthlessly suppressed. The state under SAP, with a heightened authoritarian profile, came to regard the students' movement as one of the vested interest groups which constitute an obstacle to the implementation of SAP, and all tactics must be deployed to attenuate its political strength and alter its popular identity. These tactics include repression, infiltration, co-optation and decimation. All these measures have far-reaching and sometimes contradictory consequences on the students' movement and the course of its popular struggle.

This chapter examines the impact of adjustment reforms on education in general, and Nigerian students in particular and the implications of this for the changing role of the students' movement in popular struggle. Also, it seeks to unravel how the contradictions provoked by SAP gradually engendered various forms of identity recomposition among the students, and the implications of this for the course and future of popular struggle by the students' movement.

The Sociology of Education and the Theory of Students' Popular Struggle

In most parts of the world, students have a virile culture of popular struggle and resistance, which transcends the boundaries of the political divide and ideologies of states. The examples are legion, starting with the historic May 1968 riots in France, spearheaded by students and which eventually led to the fall of De Gaulle's presidency. From the mid-1960s, in the United States of America, students were at the fore of the popular protests against the continued participation of the U.S. in the Vietnam war, demand the recall of American troops from the war. As it turned out eventually, Vietnam became America's "Waterloo" in foreign policy (mis)adventure in the 20th century. In Latin America, most of the universities, especially in the 1970s earned the reputation of being "political universities" as they became the hotbeds of popular revolts and rebellion (Ayu, 1986).

In countries like Brazil, Peru, El Salvador, Nicaragua and Uruguay, students' movements, either alone or in coalition with other interest groups and organisations, challenged the tyranny and political dictatorship which characterised the political life of these countries. In China, students have been in the vanguard of the campaign for liberal democracy. The Tiananmen Square incident of 1989 in which protesting students were killed and maimed by the state, represents one of such effort. In Africa, students participated actively in the decolonisation project, as exemplified by the activities of the West African Students Union (WASU). In the post-colonial era in Africa, students have continued to play active roles, either in making political claims on the state, influencing public policy, dislodging unpopular and despotic regimes, or in recent times, urging for the democratisation of the polity. For example, in Benin Republic in 1990, the Central Union of Students (CUE) was quite instrumental in the political agitation against the IMF. policies in the country and in the call for political reforms. The association played an important role in the process leading to the convocation of the National Conference in Benin Republic. In Zambia, the students were also part of the broad alliance—the movement for multi-partyism and political liberalisation in the country. In Nigeria, as we shall analyse presently, the students' movement constitutes a critical hub of the democratic movement in the country.

Yet, in spite of the rich culture of popular struggle and resistance by students' movements world over, studies on students and their struggles remain essentially narrative, with little effort to capture the phenomenon in theory and understand the sociology of students' revolts and resistance. In other words, little has been done to unravel the questions: Why do students engage in popular struggle? And why students? Why not the working class (i.e. trade unions and professional groups)? What are the role and purposes of education in the advocacy for social change and how does this impact on students' activism?

Conventional explanations on student struggle can be subsumed under three main categories. These are the "youth culture", the "external influence" and the "social crisis" theses. The "youth culture" theory holds that students, being an active segment of the youth population, are socially sensitive and often driven by impulse and emotions. They possess unbounded energies which, at the slightest provocation, usually result in demonstrations, riots and revolts. The group as a "transitory social category" (Momoh, 1992) or "presumptive elite" (Marvick, 1965), tend to revolt against what endangers their present interest or the interest of the social class which they will soon graduate into (the middle class). It is the latter which defines their involvement in popular struggle. Thus, the struggle of the students is conceived as simply generational, to be de-activated as soon as they grow into adulthood and join the middle class.

The "external influence" theory suggests that students are a manipulable group. They are often directly instigated into political action by external forces, which usually include their teachers and the politicians. As Darlington Iwarimie Jaja (1992:35) argues "student power is employed and motivated by academics and politicians". Indeed, this is the usual position of the state on students' revolts, hence, its usual attack on teachers, especially the university teachers who are often accused of "teaching what they are not paid to teach" (see Mohammed Panel Report, 1978). This position often provides an ample opportunity for political blackmail and vendetta by the state against its perceived foes or opponents.

The third explanation is the "social crisis" theory. In this regard, students' uprising is conceived as a national response to socio-economic and political crises in the society (Yusuf, 1992; Momoh, 1992; Albert, 1995). Given the historical antecedents of the students in popular struggle in the colonial era, they have come to interest themselves in the question of political power and its management. Their actions are therefore often directed towards problems of corruption and profligacy of the leadership, economic mismanagement and political misgoverning, the deteriorating living standards of the people, and the problems in the educational sector.

While the latter explanation may be tenable, it does not answer the question: why students? Is there a linkage between schooling, political consciousness and activism? What are the role and purposes of education in social consciousness/political conscientisation and the advocacy for social change?

In the sociology of education, three major positions are discernible on the role and essence of education in social change. In the liberal and positivist tradition, schooling and education are considered as *politically neutral* forces for social change. They are only active and relevant in the realm of economic and social progress and not in political actions. Education stimulates economic and social progress by serving as a source of manpower production and technological innovation, hence economic growth, and also provides a means of social advancement for individuals through access to better employment, income and social status. Thus, education is a technical endeavour, with the curriculum designed to emphasise the features of "objectivity", "scienticism" and "facts". It is an absolutely de-politicised enterprise.

On the other hand, the phenomenologists argue that knowledge and education are socially constructed and they are social processes which are defined by reality. In other words, schooling and education are subject to social and political influences and the school curriculum is also influenced by these realities (Young, 1971). Although the phenomenologists admit the social basis of knowledge and education, they neglect or fail to deal with the issue of how and why reality is constructed in particular ways and the nature of power configuration which holds sway in such reality, and how such forces resist subversion.

From the radical or the Marxist position, schooling and education are not a neutral enterprise, rather, they are a political act, for the creation and recreation of specific forms of consciousness that enable social control to be maintained by the dominant class, without recourse to overt mechanisms of domination (Apple, 1979; Dale, et al., 1976; Bowles and Gintis, 1976; Sarup, 1978, 1982; Harris, 1982). The school is a potent, yet subtle instrument of ideological legitimisation through the forms of consciousness it reproduces and the socio-economic system it justifies and legitimises. Thus, in enhancing their hegemony and ideological dominance, the ruling classes, as Antonio Gramsci noted, often seek the control of knowledge-preserving and producing institutions of the society, which are mainly the schools (Bates, 1975). In essence, the school curricula are essentially mechanisms of political quiescence, consensus and social control (Apple, 1979).

Although schooling and education are designed to institutionalise dominant values, norms and belief systems, and preserve the social order the relationship, however, between the school as an institution, knowledge forms, the teacher or educator and social realities, often engenders a contradiction, in which the school may be gradually transformed into a citadel of political conscientisation and social consciousness, which facilitates political actions. First, teachers as workers, are confronted with their own objective material/class conditions and social realities which invariably affect the content and knowledge forms which they produce and transmit. For instance, in countries like the Philippines and Nicaragua, knowledge forms and the curricula have been influenced or modelled to include courses like "liberation theology", which have implications for political conscientisation and social actions. In other words, knowledge and ideas are never free from the interests of the actors involved in their production and transmission.

Secondly, in bringing knowledge and training to bear on social reality for the students, particularly at the tertiary level, students are made to develop critical consciousness, which has far-reaching consequences for them, especially in third world countries characterised by gross social inequalities, impoverishment of the people and savage underdevelopment. This consciousness, as Edwin Madunagu (1982) noted, always strives to express itself in concrete actions. Thus, education sometimes stimulates the students towards what Madan Sarup (1978) referred to as practical dereification, a meeting point between ideas and praxis. The school and education, therefore, in the view of scholars like Paulo Freire, Amilcar Cabral and Franz Fanon are arenas of political and ideological contestations and struggles, which serve as instrument for social change and human liberation. The role played by Nigerian, and indeed African students, in the liberation struggles in Nigeria and other African countries suggests that this is the perception and object of education in Africa. It is within this context that we can situate the popular struggle of Nigerian students. The struggle, as Ekpein Appah (1988), a former student union activist puts it, is a case of the "gown coming to town", a realignment of ideas, social reality and praxis.

SAP and the Crisis in Education

The 1970s in Nigeria were characterised by a period of large-scale expansion in the educational sector. Apart from the introduction of the universal primary education programme (UPE), the number of post-primary and tertiary institutions increased tremendously, in response to the increasing demand for education in the country. Table 6 depicts the increased enrolment over the period 1970–1984. As the table indicates, while Primary, Secondary and University enrolments were 3,515,827, 310,054 and 7,297 respectively in 1969/70, by 1980/81 these had increased to 13,777,973, 1,999,324 and 76,197 respectively; representing an increase of 391%, 644% and 1044% respectively. The expansion of the educational sector was partly facilitated by the increase in revenue of the Nigerian state, arising from the oil boom of the 1970s.

As the receipts from oil began to dwindle, especially from the late 1970s, a regime of financial austerity was introduced, which imposed serious strains on the educational sector. For example, in 1978, the Nigerian Universities Commission (NUC) increased the meal charges for students from fifty Kobo to one Naira fifty Kobo (N1.50k) per day and the accommodation fee from thirty Naira (N30) to ninety Naira (N90) in the universities. It was these increases which precipitated the 1979 students' protest and demonstrations, named the "Ali must go" crisis.

Although the educational base was expanded, as more tertiary institutions were created under the Shagari administration, mainly out of political exigencies there was, however, no corresponding increase in the federal allocation to the education sector under the regime. The education budget, as percentage of the total federal expenditure, was 8.3%, 8.6%, 8.6%, 7.4% and 8.2% in 1979, 1980, 1981, 1982 and 1983 respectively, which continually fell short of what was allocated to a sector like defence (Adekanye, 1993). The trend was not reversed with the inception of the Buhari regime, rather it was exacerbated. Public expenditure on education was slashed significantly under the regime. The education budget, as percentage share of the total public expenditure, plummeted from 8.2% in 1983 to 6.4% in 1984 and further to 5.4% in 1985. In other words, as the economic crisis deepened in Nigeria, there was a gradual de-prioritisation of education on the state agenda.

Between 1980 and 1990, federal expenditure on education, as percentage of the Gross Domestic Product, averaged only about 1.1% (Odumosu, 1996), which falls grossly below the 15% rate recommended by the United Nations Development Programme (UNDP). The nature and dimensions of the crisis

Table 6. Educational Enrolments in Nigeria 1969/1970–1983/84

Year	Primary		Secondary General		Polytechnics/ Institutes of Technology		Universities	
	Number	Index	Number	Index	Number	Index	Number	Index
1969/70	3,515,827	100.0	310,054	100.0	13,645	100.0	7,297	100.0
1970/71	3,894,539	110.8	343,313	110.7	15,203	114.4	12,055	165.2
1971/72	4,391,197	124.9	339,722	109.6	15,953	116.9	14,371	196.9
1972/73	4,662,400	132.9	452,372	145.9	12 515	91.7	20,804	285.1
1973/74	4,889,857	139.1	498,744	160.9	12,117	162.1	20,469	280.5
1980/81	13,777,973	100.0	1,999,324	100.0	42,895	100.0	76,197	100.0
1981/82	14,311,608	103.9	2,508,794	125.0	52,858	123.2	90,418	118.7
1982/83	14,676,608	106 5	2,905,023	145.3	60,496	142.0	99,237	130.2
1983/84	14,387,271	104.4	3,065,678	153.3	59,585	138.9	113,158	148.5

Source: Cited in Tijani M. Yusuf (1985) "Education and Manpower Development: The Nigeria Case" University of Maiduguri 7th Convocation Lecture, p. 27.

in the education sector assumed more deleterious proportions with the inception and implementation of SAP.

In analysing how SAP affects education in Nigeria, it is pertinent to start with the basic philosophical underpinning of SAP and its implications for a social sector service like education. SAP conceives of the economic crisis in Africa as a public sector crisis. That is, the public sector is at the heart of the stagnation and decline in growth in Africa (World Bank, 1994.) The state investments in public sector activities, including social welfare services, are believed to be too expansive, consuming enormous public funds, with small returns both financially and in efficient performance (Adejumobi, 1997). In addition, most of the debts incurred by the state particularly external debts, are believed to have been contracted either on behalf of a public sector agency or to undertake some public sector activities. Indeed, the World Bank estimates that the public sector share of the total external debts of developing countries is about 6%. (World Bank, 1995). In order to halt this drift, SAP seeks to address the problem in two major ways. The first is to substantially reduce the size of the public sector, checkmate public expenditure and down-size the state. The second is to seek to open up public sector activities, including social welfare services, to private sector participation through a process of liberalisation and the privatisation of these services.

According to the World Bank, social sector services like education deserve to be subjected to private participation and market rules, because they are essentially private goods, which yield direct benefit to the consumers. The private rate of returns is considered to be much higher than the social rate of returns on these services, hence, the need to charge economic rents on them and keep the prices of these services above normal efficiency levels. (Adejumobi, 1996, 1997). Table 7 illustrates this.

Table 7. *Rates of Return on Investments in Education in Sub-Saharan Africa*

	Primary	Secondary	Tertiary
Social Rate of Returns	24.3%	18.2%	11.2%
Private Rate of Returns	41.3%	26.6%	27.8%

Source: World Bank (1995) *Priorities and Strategies for Education. A World Bank Review.* Washington: World Bank, p. 22.

As the table indicates, the private rate of returns on education in Sub-Saharan Africa is far higher than the social rate of returns, which means that the benefit which accrues to the consumers of education is far more than the social good this brings to the society as a whole. For higher education in particular, the World Bank argues that the private rate of returns which is put at an average of 30 per cent (World Bank, 1989:81), far exceeds that of any other region of the world, and doubles the social rate of returns on it. In essence, the World Bank continues, it would be most imprudent and irrational to insist that the state must continue to bear the burden of financing tertiary education. The World Bank therefore recommends that the role of the state in higher education should be redefined, private sector participation encouraged, and sources of funding should be diversified to include the payment of school fees. (World Bank, 1994:34). To quote the World Bank:

> To relieve the financial burden imposed on public institutions by increasing enrolments, the World Bank study advocates sweeping reforms in the ways such institutions are funded. For example, *students should be required to pay a greater share of their education costs, public subsidies for non-instructional expenses, housing and meals for instances should be sharply reduced, if not eliminated altogether...*, higher education institutions should be encouraged to pursue higher income generating activities (World Bank, 1994b:34, emphasis mine).

The above is the exact position adopted by the neo-liberal economic policy of SAP on education in Africa.

The SAP package therefore affects education in three important respects. First, through its contraction of public expenditure on social security and services, state funding on education in real terms, tends to shrink considerably. Second, in conceiving education more as a private good, it constitutes one of the areas where the principle of the market is to be applied through the liberalisation and commercialisation of the sector. Third, the other policy measures of SAP, which include currency devaluation and interest rates deregulation with its adverse effects on the rate of inflation in the country, tend to have negative consequences for the welfare of both staff and students in the educational institutions and also on the provision of infrastructures and learning materials and equipment in schools, which usually have a high import content.

On the effect of neo-liberal economic policy on education, Madan Sarup surmises that:

> The main objective of Government policies now is to restructure the educational system. This is done by halting the movement towards comprehensive education, by downgrading the public sector in education, starving it of resources, and shifting resources to the private, independent sector. With the cuts in state expenditure, the reduction in the teaching force, the worsening of pupil-teacher ratios, the bias of the education system is getting even wider (Sarup, 1982:113).

This situation of a deepening crisis in education under a regime of SAP generates a serious contradiction. It reproduces various forms of resistance by staff and students in the schools, with the staff struggling against their deteriorating welfare and working conditions in the work-place and the students embattled by their despicable living conditions and their poor facilities and learning environment. Between 1986 and 1994, teachers at all levels of education in Nigeria—primary, secondary and tertiary, had to embark on industrial actions, several times, to press for improved conditions of service and better working environment. Perhaps, the most profound of these actions was that undertaken by the university teachers, under the aegis of their union—the Academic Staff Union of Universities (ASUU). ASUU had to go on strike about four times during this period. Regrettably, Nigerian academics who hitherto constituted part of the middle class were among the social strata pauperised and assigned to join the teeming population of the "new poor", who struggle for survival through multiple modes of livelihood and "moon-lighting". (Mustapha, 1992, 1995; Asobie, 1993). This process, as Yusuf Bangura (1994) noted, led to a gradual de-professionalisation of the academics with frustration, alienation and incessant strike actions as results.

For the students, their welfare conditions were not less appalling. Many could hardly afford a decent meal. There was acute water shortage, epileptic power supply and un-hygienic, but over-crowded accommodation in most tertiary institutions. Hunger and general deprivation, as Isaac Albert (1995) noted, tend to unite the students together under SAP. Both the Committee for the Defence of Human Rights (CDHR) and the Civil Liberties Organisation (CLO), two leading human rights groups in Nigeria, have documented the ruins left of primary and secondary education in Nigeria under SAP (*Victims*, 1991; CLO, 1994). On the linkage between SAP and the crisis in education, NANS has this to say:

> The crisis of the education sector itself is a reflection of the crisis-ridden, neo-colonial capitalist economy with production geared primarily for *profit* and not the satisfaction of the *needs* of the people. The capitalist ruling class has continued to shift the burden of the crisis onto the back of the working people and the youth—particularly under Structural Adjustment Programmes, in form of retrenchment, wage freeze, commercialisation of vital social services, and so on (NANS, n.d., emphasis in original).

In summary, education entered into severe crisis under SAP in various respects. Public expenditure on education declined in real terms and continued to lag behind other less productive sectors like defence. Learning and research materials became depleted to dangerous proportions and the living standards of both staff and most students were grossly devalued. Furthermore, a culture of authoritarianism gradually crept into the educational institutions, especially at the tertiary level, under SAP. There are three angles to this incipient despotism in the campuses. First, due to declining financial resources, the ability of the school authorities to meet the basic welfare needs of both staff and students began to decline. Many school administrators chose to adopt strong-arm tactics to suppress those demands. Second, given increasing financial dearth, there was blatant corruption and mismanagement by most Administrators of tertiary institutions, who saw such posts as an avenue for financial upliftment for themselves. Authoritarian rule was required to instill fear in the community and cover up such frauds. Third, the general atmosphere of militarism which constitutes the flip side of SAP, was gradually being reproduced in the tertiary institutions. As such, the appointment of "despotic" sole administrators gradually became a norm in the management of universities. The essence was to reproduce the values of "commandism" and a "machine-like" structure, a replica of the military formation, in the universities. All these played a crucial role in transforming the educational institutions from being a market place of ideas and knowledge, to an arena of political contestations, repression, struggle and resistance, under SAP.

NANS and Popular Struggle under Adjustment Reforms

The National Association of Nigerian Students (NANS) was formed in July 1980 at a meeting of students' representatives and activists across the country, held at the Yaba College of Technology, Lagos. Its formation was a sequel to the proscription of the former students' movement, the National Union of Nigerian Students (NUNS) in 1978 by the Obasanjo regime, after the nation-wide students' unrest of that year.

After its formation, NANS major goal was to seek for reforms in the educational system through launching the NANS Charter of Demands in December 1982. The major objective of the charter is the democratisation of all levels of education in Nigeria. The concept of democracy in education, according to NANS, is hinged on three factors. These are adequate funding of the educational institutions from the primary to tertiary level, to the extent that every Nigerian is well educated (not just the ability to read and write). Second, is on the relevance of education to those receiving it and third, is the enthronement and consolidation of the democratic culture in schools, in terms of participatory decision-making and the autonomy of the institutions. (NANS, 1982).

Furthermore, the charter also relates the problem of democratisation in education, to the undemocratic nature of the economy and polity. The Character of the economy, according to the charter, is one that is biased against the mass of the people, as it perpetuates gross social inequalities, mass poverty and is ruled by foreign capital. On the polity, the charter notes as follows:

> Pervading the society too is the absence of democracy and wanton violation of the constitutional rights of the people. We believe the aim of democracy is not just the four yearly electoral ritual .... The various Governments should see democracy beyond the form of western democracy. Socio-economic justice should form the basis of democracy. (NANS, 1982:12–13).

In perceptively understanding the linkage between the problems of education and those of the political economy, NANS saw the need to advance its struggle beyond the frontiers of the campuses and schools, and to forge cooperation and alliances with mass democratic organisations and professional groups. Thus, the association established a fraternal relationship with the Nigeria Labour Congress (NLC) then led by Hassan Sumonu, consolidated its traditional relationship with ASUU and was to have a good and close working relationship with human rights organisations and democratic groups like the CDHR, the CLO, and the umbrella democratic organisation, the Campaign for Democracy (CD), which were later to emerge. Interestingly, most of these organisations emerged partly in response to the deepening crises in the society, economy and polity under SAP. NANS was a prominent member and major actor in the CD and the latter's struggle, against the Babangida regime particularly between 1992 and 1993.

The NANS charter of demands constitutes the background and a something of a working paper for the struggle of students, both on the campuses and at the national level, in subsequent years. For example, the campaign for academic reforms (ACAREF) which was launched in April 1991 was adapted from the charter, and the pursuit of ACAREF was central to the students' protests and demonstrations of 1991.

The frequency and intensity in the incidence of students' popular protest and resistance tend to deepen, just as the crisis in the Nigerian political economy escalates under SAP. On this, NANS noted that:

> The people of Nigeria have witnessed consistently and almost on a yearly and continuous basis, protests, demonstrations, and other forms of crises. However, none has been as endemic and perennial as the crises in institutions of higher learning. *Between 1985 to 1992, for instance, there occurred over three hundred major uprisings in various schools in the country. In fact, only an Ostrich would argue that the crises in the educational institutions are not direct manifestations of the collapsing socio-economic structure of our time* (NANS, September 24, 1992, emphasis mine).

At the national level, students' upheavals became an annual ritual. Although NANS was frequently banned during this period the association, however, continued to operate actively, insisting that it did not need the recognition of the government, but that of the Nigerian people and that it must exist not on the terms of the state, but on its own terms. Indeed, what NANS demonstrated during its struggle, was that an organisation with a sense of mission, correct tactics and sufficient will, can earn the right not just to exist, but exist on its own terms. (Kura, 1993; Maiyegun, 1992.)

NANS' struggle, during the Babangida era, was not only directed against SAP, but also to its political Siamese twin—the transition to civil rule programme. NANS argued that a transition to a civil rule programme constructed on a SAP economy, cannot give birth to democratic politics, rather, it would engender creeping dictatorship and incipient fascism (Solidarity, 1990). The programme was therefore considered as a package of diversion and fraud, embellished in a welter of contradictions, which was bound to fail.

For NANS, both SAP and the transition to civil rule programme of the Babangida regime, were to be vehemently opposed, if the campaign for educational reforms in Nigeria was to be meaningful. Consequently, NANS struggle during this period which was waged with resilient vigour was directed at these issues.

Considerable documentation has been done by other scholars on the role of the students' movement in popular struggle under SAP, precisely between 1986 and 1991, it therefore needs no rehash (Mohammed, 1986; Yusuf, 1992; Shettima, 1993; Momoh, 1992, 1994; Mustapha, 1993; Bako, 1994; Beckman and Jega, 1995; Albert, 1995). What we shall do is to highlight the developments for the period covered in extant studies, and to critically analyse in some detail those which are not, particularly between 1991 and 1994. Also, we shall in the next two sections of the chapter analyse the developments which occurred between 1994 and 1996, when NANS became enfeebled and demobilised and its aftermath.

The 1986 students' protest was not, in the strict sense of it, an SAP-inspired uprising, at least in terms of its manifest causation. However, its latent or remote causes have to do with the excruciating policies of the Buhari and the Babangida regimes, which were associated with the IMF/World Bank conditionalities.

The crisis started at the Ahmadu Bello University (ABU), Zaria in the attempt of the local students' Union to contain the high-handedness and arbitrary rule of the Vice Chancellor, Ango Abdullahi. Ango Abdullahi was reputed to be a very autocratic Vice Chancellor, who in his around six-year tenure in office, expelled and suspended about 160 students. (ASUU, 1986:11). Although there was a constellation of factors contributing to the crisis, the immediate cause of it was that the Students Union, following the directive of NANS, sought to commemorate the 1978 "education jihad", in memory of their colleagues slain during the popular uprising. For the event, the students duly sought and obtained permission from the school authority to stage a peaceful rally, which they did on April 21, 1986. A regulation at the ABU forbade male students from entering female hostels, but this was done during the rally, which the Vice Chancellor construed as an affront to his authority and the laws of the university. Consequently, some student union leaders were rusticated, while some others were suspended. Outraged by the school authority's decision, the students organised a rally on May 22, 1986 in solidarity with their dismissed colleagues. In response, the Vice Chancellor invited the police to quash the "revolt". The clash which ensued between the police and the students, left four students dead, including a female student.

The callous killing of the ABU students on their campus by the police, ignited a wildfire of mass demonstrations, riots and violence in most tertiary institutions in Nigeria. The students, who engaged the police in street battles in the major cities like Lagos, Ife and Kaduna were actively supported by different groups of people—commuter drivers, motor park-touts, the unemployed, the workers and market women. This brutal action of the police was also condemned by most organisations and interest groups in the civil society.

However, the decision of the Federal Government on the crisis, was not to assuage the aggrieved students, but rather, to impose punitive measures on the students, their teachers and the organisations sympathetic to the cause of the students, like the Nigerian Labour Congress (NLC). For example, some universities and polytechnics were shut down for over six months for their role in the crisis (e.g. Obafemi Awolowo University, lle-lfe, and Kaduna Polytechnic), Students Union activities were suspended on all campuses, NANS was proscribed, ASUU disaffiliated from the NLC, through Decree 17 of 1986 and some labour leaders were arrested and detained for about two weeks.

The 1988 and 1989 nation-wide students' demonstrations and protests were directly related to the SAP policies of the state. The former were against a three kobo hike in the price of fuel by the Nigerian National Petroleum Corporation (NNPC). The protest started at the University of Jos on April 11, 1988 and quickly spread to other higher institutions across the country. The action, as usual, was joined by non-students, who saw it as an opportunity to express their bottled up anger against the economic policies of the state. A national crisis seemed imminent. By April 18, 1988, over 19 universities, five colleges of education, and seven polytechnics had been closed (*The Guardian*, May 2, 1988:9). In addition, the power to re-open those institutions was vested only in the President, General Babangida, which suggests the seriousness of the situation, while, some repressive measures, like the mass arrests and detention of union leaders and activists, followed.

The 1989 students' protest, which was later christened the "Anti-SAP" riot of 1989, was meant to challenge the "criminal insensitivity of the Babangida regime to the worsening plight of the people", which was caused by SAP. Similarly, through the protest NANS sought to demonstrate its "categorical rejection of the package of diversion and fraud called the transition programme which the regime smartly contrived to confer political legitimacy on SAP" and also to show disaffection with the collapse of the educational system in Nigeria (Solidarity, 1990:6).

Prior to the crisis, the NANS leadership under Salihu Lukman canvassed alternative policy options to SAP, the transition programme and the crisis in the education sector. These included, the freezing of debts repayments, and an embargo on further external borrowing, the nationalisation of the commanding heights of the economy, the constitution of a mass-based constituent assembly which would elect an interim democratic government that would initiate and manage the transition to multi-party democracy, and the granting of greater priority to social sectors like education and health, rather than defence and the ECOMOG military adventure in Liberia. However, the Babangida regime insisted that it would have nothing to do with a banned organisation.

The 1989 protests are one of the most profound and well co-ordinated popular uprisings by NANS. Virtually all parts of the country were touched by serious disturbances, especially the cities of Lagos, Ibadan, Ife, Zaria, Port Harcourt and Kaduna. The crisis shook the Babangida regime to its very foundation, such that it had to quickly respond to it with a mixture of stick and carrot. The latter took the form of SAP relief measures. These included, the directive to the National Directorate of Employment to create 65,000 jobs, the Federal Ministry of Works to create 10,120 new jobs, 20 million Naira was given to each Federal University, the People's Bank was created, workers allowances were increased, the students in tertiary institutions were to be awarded N500.00 each as a bursary, and import duties and tariffs on vehicles were reduced in order to assuage the transport problems in the country. As regards the former, a cycle of repression of NANS leadership and the assault on student unionism continued.

In 1990, the focus of resistance was against the World Bank loan of $120 million negotiated by the Federal Ministry of Education on behalf of federal universities in Nigeria. The loan was to be for staff training, purchase of equipment and books and physical rehabilitation. However, attached to the loan in the tradition of World Bank adjustment lending, were tough conditionalities and policy prescriptions for educational reforms in Nigeria. These included, the introduction of school fees as a means of raising revenue from non-governmental sources, staff and course rationalisation and the phasing out of sub-degree programmes in Nigerian universities. As Sabo Bako (1994) argues, the object of the loan was to subject university education in Nigeria to the iron law of deregulation, privatisation, rationalisation and direct global control by international capital. To be sure, the World Bank itself admits that the essence of such loans is to create a framework for the liberalisation and eventual privatisation of higher education in developing countries. To quote the Bank:

> Higher education lending will be directed to countries prepared to adopt an education policy framework which stresses a differentiated institutional structure and a diversified resource base with greater emphasis on private provision of services and private funding (World Bank, 1994:35).

As expected, NANS reacted sharply to this development. It condemned the conditionalities of the loan as being "not only horrible and inconceivably immoral, but they will totally destroy the already collapsing educational system in Nigeria". NANS was joined by other progressive forces and organisations like ASUU, the CDHR and the CLO in berating the conditionalities. According to the CLO, "the implementation of those criteria would render the vast majority of the population unable to acquire university education." (*Liberty*, 1990). NANS therefore directed all its branches to take appropriate steps to forestall the implementation of those conditionalities in their respective schools.

Agitation against the World Bank loan started at ABU, Zaria with the students presenting their demands for a rejection of the loan to the university authorities and subsequently, organising lecture boycotts and protests. The protest was soon to take a national dimension as universities like Obafemi Awolowo University (OAU) Ile-Ife joined the trail. However, the nascent crisis was stalled, when a new configuration beset the political scene in Nigeria, with the aborted Orkar coup of April 1990. The students had to make a tactical retreat in the struggle, for two main reasons. First, the Orkar Coup changed the mood of the nation and became the issue of national focus and attention. Second, in order to avoid being wrongly implicated in the coup, which serve as a convenient basis for unleashing terror on the NANS leadership, there was need for a retreat.

In 1991, NANS resumed its opposition to the economic and political policies of the Babangida regime. At its Senate meeting of April 27, 1991 at the University of Ilorin, NANS reviewed the state of the nation and that of education in particular and came up with a ten point demand. At that same meeting, NANS launched the ACAREF, which was to inform some of its demands. The NANS demands included, a declaration of a state of emergency in the educational sector, immediate payment of a N2,000 bursary loan to students of higher institutions, immediate recall of all suspended or expelled student activists and leaders, right to independent student unionism, free education at all levels, a halt to panicky closure of campuses when students and staff make legitimate demands, adequate funding of education, and greater participation of students in the administration of their institutions.

NANS at the Ilorin meeting issued a 30-day ultimatum to the Federal Government to meet its demands or face a nation-wide protest. Before the expiration of the deadline, concerted efforts were made by the state through threats, blackmail and intimidation to cajole the students into submission and divide their rank and file (see *Tell*, June 3, 1991; *Liberty*, Vol. 2 No. 2. 1991). For example, Abdulkarim Adisa (then) a colonel and Governor of Oyo State warned the students to desist from the planned protest, or government would meet force with force and that the "outcome will be very bloody". In order to give flesh to the government threat, the Inspector General of Police, Aliyu Attah, directed all state police commands to be on the red alert and "deal decisively with any demonstrations". Consequently, armoured tanks and an avalanche of regular and mobile policemen were deployed to strategic locations outside the campuses of tertiary institutions.

The government strategy seems to have paid off as some schools dissociated themselves from the planned protest, while some others were indifferent to it by the expiration of the deadline on May 26, 1991. NANS itself was not oblivious of the internal weakness and dissension within its fold, hence, it expressed its readiness for dialogue with the government before the expiration of the deadline. The government declined the offer. In spite of the tardiness and poor preparation of NANS for the protest, nevertheless, the protest was carried out in schools in Ilorin, Ife, Jos, Ibadan, Abeokuta and Katsina Ala. (*Labour Militant*, 1991).

In May 1992, another round of popular protests and demonstrations by students, rocked the country. The rationale was basically economic—arising from the excruciating social hardships which SAP continued to wrack on the lives of the people and also the deplorable condition of education in Nigeria. Specifically, the further devaluation of the Naira on March 5, 1992, which prompted an increase in the prices of goods and services, the fuel crisis of April 1992, the profligacy and extra-budgetary spending of the Babangida regime on wasteful sundry pet projects like the Better Life Programme, the National Guard and so on, were the major issues at the heart of the 1992 struggle (NANS, September, 24 1992).

At its 26th Senate meeting on April 25, 1992 at the University of Port-Harcourt, Rivers State, NANS, having appraised the situation in the country, empowered its secretariat (then) based at the University of Lagos to declare a nation-wide strike (i.e. protest) should the government continue to ignore the plight of the Nigerian people. Subsequently, the Secretariat later declared 13 and 14 May 1992 as days of national protest by Nigerian students. This took place and even extended into weeks in some cases. As usual, the government responded with a heavy dose of repression.

In 1993, there was no major student uprising, despite the fact that this was a very crucial year for the country politically, in terms of the June 12 1993 presidential election annulment. Two reasons account for this. First, there was the ASUU strike which went on for four months, between May 3–September 9, 1993. This kept most universities shut and the students off campus. Secondly, when the students resumed in October 1993, the pressure on the students' movement especially, from the final year students on the need to maintain peace on the campuses in order to be able to bring the lingering academic session to an end, was widespread. In other words, the situation in the various schools seemed inhospitable for a political action.

However, this does not suggest that Nigerian students or NANS were passive or indifferent to the sociopolitical developments in the country. They were not. While the ASUU strike lasted, NANS gave its full support to it, which it considered to be in the overall interest of educational development in Nigeria. In a statement on the strike, NANS described as unacceptable the lack of seriousness of the government in resolving the chaotic situation on the campuses and condemned the obnoxious steps being taken against the university teachers in their patriotic struggle (like the purported dismissal of all the teachers). NANS warned that it would engage the state in a frontal contest if an amicable settlement was not reached soon (see CLO, 1993:139). Indeed, the pressure from NANS and other interest groups in the civil society made the state eventually back down and accede to ASUU demands.

On the political level, NANS at the end of its 12th Annual Convention held at ABU, Zaria on February 6,1993 issued a communiqué in which it claimed to have "derecognised" the Babangida Junta from January 3, 1993, (which was the regime's earlier stipulated hand-over date) and called on all progressive forces in the country to join hands with the CD in its struggle to save the nation from an imminent calamity imposed on it by a "cabal of bandits". (NANS, February 10, 1993). Also, NANS reiterated its call for the convocation of a sovereign national conference. To be sure, Nigerian students actively participated in and were indeed, the backbone of the CD activities during the June 12 struggle in 1993, although such was not done overtly at the level of the organisational platform of NANS.

Furthermore, in the heat of the June 12 struggle, a NANS Senate meeting was held, quite discreetly, in Enugu in July 1993 at which it was resolved that advertisements should be placed in national newspapers condemning the annulment of the June 12 election, re-stating the correctness of NANS' position in dismissing the Babangida Transition to Civil Rule Programme as far back as 1987, deploring the crisis in the education sector and the role of despotic Vice Chancellors on the various campuses.

With the lingering June 12 crisis, some pro-democracy activists, possibly out of despondency, began to advocate for a radical coup, that is, a quick intervention by a progressive arm of the military to resolve the political impasse, since according to them, it was the military which created the problem, it must also be central in resolving it. NANS, in a press statement rightly cautioned against this new tendency. NANS correctly argued that "the fate of this country should not be sought in extra-civil society forces like the military of whatever ideological variant, because the military in the third world is by and large counter-revolutionary". Later events were to vindicate NANS' position.

As the Interim National Government was contrived by the Babangida regime in August 1993, NANS decried the political arrangement simply as a fraud and vowed never to recognise it or have anything to do with it. The political contrivance was soon to fall with ignominy, in November 1993.

With the inception of the Abacha regime on November 17,1993, NANS, in a press release, expressed regret that the military once again had to intervene in Nigerian politics due to the greed and opportunism of the "newbreed" political class. NANS warned that the "return must be very brief" and advised the Abacha regime, to "resist the temptation of repressing students and activists of change".

In 1994, the students' movement regained its momentum in popular agitation and struggle. First to be addressed was the issue of the introduction of school fees. By the beginning of the year, most states like Ondo, Oyo, Ogun, Imo, Anambra, Edo, Kebbi, and Abuja had either introduced or increased the school fees charged in the primary and secondary schools and in some tertiary institutions. For example, in Anambra State, the increase in school fees in primary and secondary schools was over 400 per cent, while at the Ibadan Polytechnic, in Oyo State, it was over 800 per cent in tuition fees, in precise figures from N420 to N3,600, while accommodation fees went up from N170.00 to N650.00 (CLO, 1994). After a review of the situation, NANS directed that all students in the country, should resist the introduction of school fees through sustained protests and demonstrations. These protests took off in places like Ondo and Edo States and in apparent fear of a possible escalation of the crisis, the National Council on Education (NCE), which is the highest decision-making body on education in Nigeria, met and decided that state Governments should rescind the decision to introduce higher school fees.

On the political front, NANS' focus was on two major issues in 1994. These were the National Constitutional Conference (NCC) being planned by the Abacha regime and the pro-democracy struggle of June-August 1994 meant to revalidate the June 12 mandate. On the former, NANS after its 31st Senate meeting held at ABU Zaria in its communiqué dissociated itself from the conference and charged Nigerian students not to participate in the discredited jamboree, which would only enhance the "ignoble sustenance of the obnoxious status-quo". NANS called for the dissolution of the Constitutional Conference Commission and the restoration of a people-oriented government that would emanate from the Sovereign National Conference. (NANS, 1994:2).

The renewed pro-democracy struggle of 1994 was triggered off by the arrest of M.K.O. Abiola, (winner of the June 12 1993 presidential election) on June 23 1994, after he declared himself President of the Federal Republic of Nigeria in Epetedo, a suburb an area of Lagos State on June 11, 1994, a day after the one year anniversary of the annulled election. Pro-democracy organisations like the National Democratic coalition (NADECO) and the CD and trade unions, particularly the National Union of Petroleum and Natural Gas Workers (NUPENG) and the Petroleum and Natural Gas Senior Staff Association (PENGASSAN) took the lead in the struggle to terminate military rule in Nigeria and actualise the June 12 mandate.

The efforts of NUPENG and PENGASSAN in the 1994 pro-democracy struggle are highly commendable and their (strike) action most profoundly felt. In order to support the cause and complement the efforts of NUPENG and PENGASSAN, a NANS Senate meeting was summoned for Auchi Polytechnic. The meeting resolved that students nation-wide should take practical actions ranging from lecture boycotts to demonstrations to support the cause. The NANS directive was heeded and well carried out in the universities of Ile-Ife, Ibadan, Calabar, Benin, Edo and Delta State and in some colleges and polytechnics. For example, at the Delta State University (Delsu), Abraka, the students on July 20, 1994 stormed and seized the state radio station and made a broadcast on the "state of the nation" to the people, calling for the unconditional release of M.K.O. Abiola and demanded that the military should formalise arrangements to hand over power to him. At the University of Benin and the Edo State University, the students while on rampage in the cities of Benin and Ekpoma respectively, attacked and vandalised the properties of Samuel Ogbemudia, and Tony Anenih both in Benin and burnt the house of Augustus Aikhomu at Ekpoma. These three were considered to either be supporters of the Abacha regime or have played a crucial role in the June 12 election annulment. Ogbemudia was (then) Abacha's Minister for Labour and Productivity, Tony Anenih, the Chairman of the defunct Social Democratic Party (SDP) who apparently negotiated away the victory of his party at the June 12 polls, and Augustus Aikhomu, was Vice President of General Babangida whose regime annulled the June 12 election. In order to contain the popular protests and strikes from both students and labour, the Abacha regime had to unleash unprecedented terror on these groups.

Beyond the national struggle, local students' union in the various campuses and schools also had to contest relations of domination in their respective schools. Such occurred at the Lagos State University 1992/93, University of Agriculture, Abeokuta between 1992 and 1994, the Ibadan Polytechnic in February 1994, Katsina Polytechnic in June 1994 and the Institute of Management and Technology, Enugu in May, 1994. The most recent were the mass demonstrations carried out by primary and secondary school students in Edo State in October 1996, over the increase in tuition fees. School fees in secondary schools were increased from N200.00 to N1000.00 representing 500 per cent increase. During the action, the students burnt down the police headquarters in Auchi, and chased away the policemen at the station (*see P.M. News*, October 31, 1996). The State Government responded to the crisis with a slight reduction of the tuition fees from N1000 to N700.

In summary, popular protests and resistance by the students' movement both at the national and local levels reached an unprecedented height, both in scale and magnitude, under a regime of economic crisis and structural adjustment. Such efforts became inextricably linked with the struggle to expand the democratic space both at the national and local constituency level—the schools and campuses. However, NANS' struggles gradually took a detour especially from 1995, as we examine shortly.

Things Fall Apart: Repression, Co-optation and Factionalism in NANS

By 1995, the strength and vitality of the students' movement and its capacity for popular struggle had begun to wane, with the state deploying a mixed strategy of repression, incorporation and co-optation to factionalise and decimate NANS. The method adopted against NANS was similar to that used for NUPENG and PENGASSAN which Samuel Ogbemudia described as operation "Find, Fix and Finish" (The 3FS), which was meant to annihilate all voices of opposition. Perhaps, the only difference in the case of NANS, is that it was incorporation and co-optation, rather than repression which proved to be the most useful methods in the decimation of the association. In other words, by 1995 things had begun to fall apart for NANS, with the association bedevilled by internal wrangling and bickering, greed, opportunism and a loss of focus and direction.

We shall discuss presently, the three dimensions of the state's strategy in weakening the students' movement. Repression appears to be the most visible and a daunting weapon used against NANS. Between 1986 and 1994, no less than 1,000 students were arrested and detained, over 300 killed and maimed, many wounded and over 600 rusticated and suspended as an aftermath of the various protests and demonstrations carried out during the period. A brief overview will suffice. After the 1985 students' protest, NANS leaders was arraigned before the miscellaneous offences tribunal, while in 1992, Olusegun Maiyegun, the NANS President was kidnapped and detained for 19 days. He was later charged along with some other pro-democracy activists with treason, due to their role in pro-democracy activities. During the 1989 protests, the death toll was officially put at 300 (including non-students) (Momoh, 1994:53), while about 90 students were killed and maimed during the 1994 uprising particularly in Benin and Ekpoma. In 1991, no less than 200 students were arrested, including the NANS leaders and were detained under extremely inhuman conditions. Indeed, both Mahmud Abdul Aminu, the NANS President and Bamidele Aturu, an activist, wrote to the Nigerian public on the inhuman conditions of their detention. The write up was entitled "Before we Die". In the same year, about 150 students were expelled from the universities of Ibadan, Jos, OAU, Ife, University of Agriculture, Abeokuta and College of Education, Katsina, and over 50 suspended. 13 students were put on trial for arson at the University of Jos.

Added to this, was the frequent banning of NANS and the restrictions on students' union activities on the campuses and the persistent closure of the institutions of higher learning in the country by the state.

The most vicious of the state's assaults on the students' movement was the promulgation of the Students' Union Activities (Control and Regulation) Act, otherwise known as Decree No 47 of 1989. The decree was meant to vitiate the strength and unity of NANS and completely demobilise it. The major highlights of the decree include the making of students' participation in union activities a voluntary one and by implication making the payment of union dues by students voluntary. It also empowered the Governing Council or the Vice Chancellor to proscribe any association or society in higher institution, granted the Minister of Education the power to expel or suspend any student whenever he considered such action to be in the "public interest" or for "public safety" and power to the President to proscribe any student union or association in the institutions of higher learning, when such was deemed as being inimical to the "interest of defence, public safety, public order, public morality or public health".

The repressive measures of the state, such as the decentralisation of student unionism, and its being made voluntary, the ban on NANS, frequent arrest and detention of its leaders, and the militarisation of the campuses, however, produced a contradiction. These adversities, according to Anthony Olusanya, a former NANS Senate President, invigorated the association (NANS) and contributed significantly to the unalloyed and undiluted solidarity among the students. (Olusanya, interview, December, 1996). But the point to be stressed is that in the long run, those measures were detrimental to the health of the students' movement.

Besides repression, other state tactics for weakening NANS were through infiltration, promotion of divisions and dissension within the association, through bribery and co-optation of its members. This was a usual practice of the state, except that it became more pronounced and pervasive under the Babangida regime, which used it, among other weapons to dislodge the opposition. NANS itself was not unaware of this fact. As Nasir Kura, a former NANS President noted:

> As it is also well known, from time to time, one of the main tactics fascist governments employ to weaken the opposition is to cause division and confusion within their organisations. This is particularly marked in this regime's policy towards patriotic bodies, especially those whose leadership and membership have refused to succumb to "settlement" (Kura, 1993:3).

The formation of splinter groups or parallel organisations mostly sponsored by either the school authority or the state, became a norm in most campuses and even at the national level, especially where the authentic leadership of the union remained uncompromising and incorruptible. For example, at the Lagos State University in 1992/93 there was the establishment of a group called the "peace activists" allegedly sponsored by the school authority to act as a counter-force to the local students' union, during the crisis in the university. In 1994 at ABU Zaria, the school authority under the Vice Chancellorship of Professor Daniel Saror chose to annul the students' union election ostensibly because the winner of the election Mr. Adoji Omale, was not the "choice" candidate of the University authority.

At the level of NANS leadership, the tendency to create division in the association was also rife, but such was effectively checkmated by the leadership. For example, in April 1993, a group led by Adebowale Esho, the President of the University of Ibadan Students' Union, claimed to have passed a vote of no confidence in the NANS National Executive Council led by Nasir Kura, for its "undemocratic behaviour" and sought to organise what he called an "All Nigerian Students Conference" to deliberate on the issue of the "democratisation of NANS" (Esho, 1993). The group was alleged to be in close interaction and working relationship with the Ministry of Education and indeed, held a meeting with the (then) Minister of Education, Professor

Ben Nwabueze, where Esho promised that NANS would henceforth desist from being confrontational to the government. Esho's efforts to bring factionalism into NANS were, however, rebuffed, when the NANS Senate, which met on April 23–24, 1993 at the OAU, Ile-Ife, decided to suspend him from the Senate of NANS, for anti-union activities. Esho was to later apologise for his misdeeds and pleaded for leniency from the union.

With the inception of the Dennis Inyang-led leadership from 1994, NANS appeared to have finally succumbed to the politics of co-optation and "settlement", which was the dominant method of ensnaring oppositional groups by the state under militarism. The NANS leaders' stance on major national issues was quite suspect, or at best controversial, hence, it was accused of complicity and collaboration with the Abacha regime. Three incidents tend to substantiate this allegation. First, Dennis Inyang was nominated as a delegate by the Abacha regime to the NCC, although he declined the offer, however, the Senate President, Bashir Muktar, went on air via the Nigerian Television Authority (NTA) "Tonight at Nine" national network programme, to castigate Inyang for this decision, stating that the decision was unilateral and did not represent the wishes of the Nigerian students. Muktar expressed his willingness to take up the offer on behalf of Nigerian students if Inyang refused. The action of Muktar was quite shocking to the general public, who saw it as very unusual for NANS or any of its officials to use a state platform like the NTA to express itself or speak in such manner in favour of the state. Undoubtedly, state patronage was at play.

Secondly, in June 1994 the NANS Senate met at the Auchi Polytechnic and directed that mass demonstrations and protests should be organised by the local branches in support of the pro-democracy struggle of that period. As we earlier noted, this was done in some branches especially, Delta, Edo, and Ekpoma, albeit with heavy casualties of arrests and killings. However, the NANS leadership did not issue a single statement condemning the repressive action of the state nor did it make any effort to secure the release of those arrested. (Student Rights Concern, 1995.)

Thirdly, the Dennis Inyang leadership sought funds from, and organised a "Save Education Campaign" (SEC) in Abuja in 1995 in collaboration with, the National Council for Women Societies (NCWS) led by Mrs. Laila Dongoyaro. NCWS is generally believed to be a state-sponsored association, with heavy state funding. Two questions were raised on this activity. First, why was the campaign held in Abuja? Why was it not held on the campuses of the various institutions? Why the collaboration with the NCWS? Indeed, the critics of Dennis Inyang' leadership saw the SEC as a fund transmission belt from the state via the NCWS to the NANS leadership. It was a form of "settlement".

On the apparent complicity of the Dennis Inyang leadership with the Abacha regime, Akinsola Enisan, a former public relations officer of the OAU students' union remarked as follows:

As soon as Dennis Inyang became the President of NANS, he sat over the liquidation of the throne of NANS. NANS then became a tool in the hands of the military. Dennis' romance with the state was no longer news as the N300 million save education campaign was organised by him under the auspices of the National Council of Women Societies. Those who stole our money, and destroyed our educational system were invited to donate money and so Aso Rock and Maryam Babangida Centre at Abuja became the alternative secretariat of NANS (Enisan, 1996).

The allegations of a "sell-out" against the NANS leadership prompted a wave of agitation by student activists and local unions for the convening of a NANS Senate meeting to review the situation. But this was delayed till June 10, 1995. The trajectory of the events which followed, led to the holding of two NANS conventions, one at the Ogun State University, Ago-Iwoye and the other at the ABU Kongo Campus. These conventions produced two different sets of leaders; the Ago-lwoye convention elected Miss Comfort Idika as President, while the ABU convention chose Babe Kasala as President. Thus two factions were born in NANS. The Idika faction held another election in December 1996, with Ropo Ewenla emerging as President, while for the Kasala faction, its convention held at Edo State University, Ekpoma, on December 14, 1996 ended up in a fiasco and produced three new factions within the group.

The factionalism in NANS, as Wale Okuniyi, a student activist and former President, Lagos State University Students' Union admits, has completely incapacitated the association, made it a "lame duck" union in combating the state in popular struggle and also squandered the good will and credibility of the association before the Nigerian people. (Okuniyi, interview, December, 1996).

Identity Recomposition and the Decline of Popular Struggle

As NANS became weakened and largely demobilised, new forms of group and social identities and centres of power began to emerge or take centre-stage on the campuses, which are mostly independent of and antagonistic to the ideals of NANS. These groups which are mainly esoteric and sectarian in nature came to serve as new sources of security, identity, social and psychological ego for many students. The groups include ethnic associations, religious groups and social deviant or counter-culture groups like the secret cults. The latter (i.e. secret cults) have become the most pronounced with their proliferation and domination of the social space on the campuses, such that they now serve as the base of social recruitment or allegiance for students aspiring to students' union position. Yet, the object of the secret cults in contemporary times is not grounded in any understanding of national sociopolitical issues or in addressing local problems or in intellectual development, rather, it is embedded in the ideology of repression, opportunism, and violence. Most higher institutions in Nigeria today have become excellent centres of violence, where gun-shots, arson, and a general culture of fear and intimidation are perpetrated by the secret cults.

But the raging questions are: How did the secret cults come to substitute for the students' union? And how did they become so powerful? Secret cults have long existed in tertiary institutions in Nigeria and they are as old as the history of university education in the country. The first secret cult, the Pyrates Confraternity, was formed in 1952 at the University College, Ibadan, as a protest group against the evils of colonialism and its tendencies as manifested in the campus. Its members, led by Wole Soyinka, were highly disciplined and held dear the ideals of fairness, equality and justice in their activities. By the 1970s a splinter group had emerged from the Pyrates Confraternity, which constituted itself into a new secret cult called the Buccaneers Confraternity. The number of secret cults were at a minimum, until the mid 1980s when SAP began, with its consequential social dislocations, hardships and general atmosphere of political repression and militarism in the society, including the university campuses.

The reasons for the proliferation of secret cults on the campuses, are both internal (i.e. to the cults themselves) and external. The internal reason lies in the perennial internal struggle for power, positions and the urge for reforms in the respective cults. This often leads to break-aways and the formation of many new groups.

The external reasons for it are two. First, is the complicity of the university authorities in, overtly or covertly, supporting and abating the activities of the cults, who often encourage and manipulate the group as a counter-force against, and so as to suppress, the students' unions. The case of the University of Lagos seems quite instructive. In March 1994, the students' union led by Omoyele Sowore after many futile appeals to the university authorities to control the dangerous activities of the cults, sought to checkmate the cults themselves. In the ensuing scenario, Sowore was seriously attacked by the cults and had to be hospitalised for some time. Surprisingly, however, Sowore and some other students' union leaders and activists were later suspended and rusticated by the university authorities, and also arrested and detained by the police. The victim was made to become the accused.

Secondly, in the absence of an umbrella students' union, at least a potent one, there seems to be no organisation to articulate, negotiate or defend the collective interest of the students, who therefore seek succour and protection in these new identities and groups (Alubo, 1996). More importantly, the crisis of social livelihood which SAP imposed on most students led them in search of new sources of material support, which unfortunately, the students' union with dwindling resources cannot provide. However, the secret cults appeared to be a ready alternative, whose members often parade wealth and affluence. The social background of the members of the secret cults has been transformed drastically from the middle of the 1980s, their members are now mostly made up of children of very wealthy parents and those in positions of power and authority in the country. In other words, the cults are made up of students who have the material wherewithal to support their colleagues in distress, but such colleagues first have to be initiated into the cult.

In terms of the perpetration of violence on the campuses, two reasons tend to account for this. First are the frequent rivalry and clashes among the groups mainly for supremacy and territoriality. A cardinal philosophy of cultism is that "those who are not with me, are against me" and that "two captains cannot sail in the same boat", hence, the endemic suspicion, rivalry and frequent clashes among the groups. Secondly, the culture of militarism which permeated the society under SAP reproduced itself in the universities. The secret cult, because of its clandestine character, happened to be the social agent most amenable to perpetrating this culture of fear and intimidation on the campuses. In any case, some of its members, seem to have inculcated from their parents who are in power, the values of organised violence and oppression.

These organisations (i.e. cults) which largely have a perverted focus, as our extensive field research revealed, cannot be the harbingers of any noble cause either at the local or national level. Instead, they will continue to reproduce and perpetuate on the campuses, the contradictions of a nation with a societal morass, political tyranny and economic injustices.

Conclusion

The struggle of the students' movement (NANS) under adjustment reforms, is best situated within the context of the struggle of the civil society against the social and class contradictions and inequalities provoked or accentuated by SAP. NANS was the most consistent pressure group, which continually articulated the problems of the masses and the educational sector and frontally confronted the state, in protests and demonstrations, on an annual basis from 1986–1994. During this period, local students' unions also sought to expand the democratic space on the campuses, by contesting relations of domination in the various schools.

However, the dialectics of the politics of the implementation of SAP, was such that the state, especially under the Babangida regime, laid "land mines" and "ambushes" for civil society, by unleashing crude militarism and other tactics on it (i.e. civil society), aimed at dismantling and destroying the civil associations and social movements, opposed to adjustment reforms. The Nigerian Labour Congress (NLC), the Nigerian Bar Association (NBA), the Nigeria Union of Journalists (NUJ) and many others, became victims. NANS was to later fall prey to this ploy.

The "crowding out" of the students' union from the social and political space in the schools, threw up, and left the arena for, new forms of identities—ethnic, religious and cult groups. These groups which are embedded in sectarian politics and lacking a national focus or interest in progressive national or local cause or ideals, are likely to compound the social crisis in the schools, as events are presently unfolding. This scenario of apparent disarray and confusion among the students in particular and the civil society in general, appears to be conducive to and profitable for the governing class, in its project of perpetuating neo-liberal economic policies and military dictatorship in the country.

Clearly, the societal contradictions reproduced in the changing identities from unionism to cultism in the schools, are those in which there is the transcendence of brawn over brain, force over reason and militarism over knowledge.

In reclaiming its role in the popular struggle, Nigerian students will have to rebuild and rejuvenate NANS. This requires ending the opportunism, factionalism and greed which permeates its present crop of leaders.

Bibliography

Academic Staff Union of Universities, 1996, *ASUU and 1986 Education Crisis in Nigeria*. Ibadan: ASUU.

Adejumobi, S., 1995, "Adjustment Reform and Its Impact on the Economy and Society", in Adejumobi, S., and A. Momoh, (eds.) *The Political Economy of Nigeria under Military Rule: 1984–1993*. Harare: SAPES Books.

Adejumobi, S., 1995, "Structural Adjustment and Multinational Corporations in Nigeria: Impact and Implications", *Development and Socio-Economic Progress*, 64, 27–41.

Adejumobi, S., 1996, "Structural Adjustment, Privatisation Policy and Infrastructural Services in Africa: With Examples from Nigeria and Ghana", research report submitted for the project "African Perspectives on the Structural Adjustment Programme", Dakar, Senegal.

Adejumobi, S., 1997, "The Privatisation Policy and the Delivery of Social Welfare Services in Nigeria", Mimeo.

Adekanye, B., 1993, "Military Occupation and Social Stratification", *Inaugural Lecture*, University of Ibadan.

Albert, O. I., 1995, "University Students in the Politics of Structural Adjustment in Nigeria: Between Liberalisation and Oppression", in Mkandawire, T. and A. Olukoshi (eds.) *The Politics of Structural Adjustment in Africa*. Dakar: CODESRIA. pp. 374–392.

Alubo, O., 1996, "On Campus Cultocracy", *The Guardian*, January 26: A8.

Appah, E., 1988, "The Town and the Gown", *The African Guardian*, May 2:23.

Apple, M. W., 1979, *Ideology and Curriculum*. London: Routledge and Kegan Paul.

Asobie, A., 1993, "The Pauperisation of the Nigerian Petty Bourgeoisie" in Nnoli, O., (ed.) *Deadend to Nigerian Development*. Dakar: CODESRIA. pp. 180–202.

Ayu, I. D., 1986, *Essays in Popular Struggle*. Oguta: Zim Pan-African Publishers.

Bako, S., 1994, "Education and Adjustment in Nigeria: Conditionality and Resistance", in Diouf, M. and M. Mamdani (eds.) *Academic Freedom in Africa*. Dakar: CODESRIA. pp. 150–175.

Bangura, Y., 1994, *Intellectuals, Economic Reform and Social Change: Constraints and Opportunities in the Formation of a Nigerian Technocracy*. Dakar: CODESRIA Monograph Series. 1.

Bates, T. R., 1975, "Gramsci and the Theory of Hegemony", *Journal of the History of Ideas*, XXXVI, 36.
Beckman, B., and A. Jega, 1995, "Scholars and Democratic Politics in Nigeria", *Review of African Political Economy*, No. 64, 167–181.
Bowles, S. and H. Gintis, 1976, *Schooling in Capitalist America*. London: Routledge and Kegan Paul.
Civil Liberties Organisation, 1993, *Annual Report on Human Rights in Nigeria, 1993*. Lagos: CLO.
Civil Liberties Organisation, 1994, *Annual Report on Human Rights in Nigeria, 1994*. Lagos: CLO.
Dale, R., et al. (eds.), 1976, *Schooling and Capitalism*. London: Routledge and Kegan Paul.
Enisan, A., 1996, "NANS: Facts and Fiction", *This Day*. July.
Esho, A., 1993, "Why we pass a vote of no confidence on the NANS Executive Council", April 2, Mimeo.
Federal Government of Nigeria, 1986, *Report of the Commission of Inquiry into the Student Crisis at the Ahmadu Bello University, Zaria*. Lagos: Federal Government Printers.
Federal Government of Nigeria, 1989, *Students Union Activities (Control and Regulation) Act*. Decree No. 47 of 1989. Lagos: Government Printer.
Harris, K., 1982, *Teachers and Classes: A Marxist Analysis*. London: Routledge and Kegan Paul.
Iwarimie-Jaja, D., 1992, "The Role of Student Power in Nigeria", *Philosophy and Social Action*, Vol. 18, No. 4, pp. 28–36.
Jega, A. M., 1994, *Nigerian Academics under Military Rule*. Stockholm: Department of Political Science, University of Stockholm.
Kura, N., 1993, "NANS is As Intact As Ever", Text of a Press Conference Held at the *University of Lagos*, May 20.
Madunagu E. 1982. Problems of Socialism: The Nigerian Challenge. London: Zed.
Maiyegun, O., 1992, "We Are Not Asking for Recognition", *Sunday Punch*, June 7.
Marvick, A., 1965, "African Student: A Presumptive Elite", in Coleman, J. S., (ed.) *Education Political Development*. New Jersey: Princeton University.
Mohammed, A. S., 1986, "The Aftermaths of the Ahmadu Bello University Students' Crisis of May 1986", *Review of African Political Economy*, No. 37, pp. 97–103.
Mohammed Panel Report, 1978, *Report of the Commission of Inquiry into the Nigerian Universities Crisis*. Lagos: Federal Ministry of Information, Printing Division.
Momoh, A., 1992, "Students and Democratic Struggle in Africa", *Philosophy and Social Action*, 18:4, pp. 37–46.
Momoh, A., 1994, "Interest Groups, Militarism and the Transition to Civil Rule in Nigeria (1987–1993)", *Indian Journal of Politics*, Vol. XXVIII, Nos. 3–4.
Mustapha, A. R., 1992, "Structural Adjustment and Multiple Modes of Social Livelihood in Nigeria", in Gibbon, P., et al. (eds.) *Authoritarianism, Democracy and Adjustment: The Politics of Economic Reforms in Africa*. Uppsala: SIAS.
Mustapha, A. R., 1993, "Ever Decreasing Circle: Democratic Rights in Nigeria", in Nnoli, O. (ed.) *Deadend to Nigerian Development*. Dakar: CODESRIA.
Mustapha, A. R., 1995, "The State of Academic Freedom in Nigeria", in Diouf, M. and M. Mamdani (eds.) *Academic Freedom in Africa*. Dakar: CODESRIA. pp. 103–120.
National Association of Nigerian Students (NANS), 1994, communiqué of the 31st Senate meeting of NANS held at A.B.U. Zaria. March 19.
National Association of Nigerian Students (NANS), 1994, text of a press conference on the state of the nation, March 14.

National Association of Nigerian Students (NANS), 1993, communiqué of the 29th NANS Senate meeting held at Obafemi Awolowo University, Ile-Ife, April 24–25.

National Association of Nigerian Students (NANS), 1993, communiqué at the 12th NANS convention held at A.B.U. Zaria, February 6.

National Association of Nigerian Students (NANS), 1993, "NANS Shall Exist on Its Own Terms", text of a press conference at University of Lagos, May 5.

National Association of Nigerian Students (NANS), 1992, "Unending Crisis on Campuses: The Issue Is That of Our Rights to Express Ourselves".

National Association of Nigerian Students (NANS), 1992, communiqué of the Emergency Senate of NANS held at University of Benin, June 27.

National Association of Nigerian Students (NANS), 1992, "Nigeria: A Sinking Ship?", Communiqué of the 26th NANS Senate meeting held at the University of Port Harcourt, Rivers State, April 25.

National Association of Nigerian Students (NANS), 1991, "The Campaign for Academic Reforms [ACAREF]", April 27, (mimeo).

National Association of Nigerian Students (NANS), 1991, communiqué of the extraordinary Senate meeting of NANS held at the University of Benin, June 15.

National Association of Nigerian Students (NANS), 1991, communiqué of the 25th Senate meeting of NANS held at the University of Lagos, November 23.

National Association of Nigerian Students (NANS), n.d., "For the Immediate Resolution of the Education Crisis in Ondo State and Nigeria".

National Association of Nigerian Students (NANS), 1982, "Nigerian Students' Charter of Demands", (mimeo).

Odumosu, O., 1996, "Structural Adjustment and Its Impact on Social Services in Nigeria", in Fadahunsi, A., and T. Babawale (eds.) *Beyond Structural Adjustment: Towards a Popular Democratic Development Alternative*. Lagos: Fredrich Ebert Foundation. pp. 122–144.

Sarup, M., 1978, *Marxism and Education*. London: Routledge and Kegan Paul.

Sarup, M., 1982, *Education, State and Crisis: A Marxist Perspective*. London: Routledge and Kegan Paul.

Shettima, K. A., 1993, "Structural Adjustment and the Student Movement in Nigeria", *Review of African Political Economy*, No. 56, pp. 83–90.

Students Rights Concern, 1995, "NANS in Crisis?", (mimeo).

World Bank, 1989, *Sub-Saharan Africa: From Crisis to Sustainable Growth*. Washington D.C: World Bank.

World Bank, 1994a, *Adjustment in Africa: Reforms, Results and the Road Ahead*. Washington D.C: World Bank.

World Bank, 1994b, *The World Bank Annual Report 1994*. Washington D.C: World Bank.

World Bank, 1995a, *Priorities and Strategies for Education. A World Bank Review*. Washington D.C: World Bank.

World Bank, 1995b, *African Development Indications. 1994–95*, Washington D.C: World Bank.

Yesufu, T. M., 1985, "Education and Manpower Development: The Nigerian Case", *Convocation Lecture*, University of Maiduguri.

Young, M. F. D., 1971, (ed.), *Knowledge and Control*. London: Collier-Macmillan.

Yusuf, A. A., 1992, "From the Citadels of Learning to Battleground: An Exploration of 'Students' Unrest' in Nigeria", *Indian Journal of Politics*, Vol. XXVI, Nos. 2–4, pp. 63–83.

Newspapers and Magazines

African Guardian, 1988, May 2:9.
Labour Militant, 1991, September-November.
Liberty, 1991. Vol. 2 No. 2.
Liberty, 1990. Vol. 1 No. 1.
P. M. News, 1996. October 31.
Solidarity, 1990, Vol. 1, No. 1.
Tell Magazine, 1991, June 3. 37.
The Guardian, May 2, 1988:9
Victims (CDHR Newsletter), 1991, Vol. 2, No. 4.

Interviews

Olusanya, Interview, December, 1996.

Contributors

Jimi Adesina is a Senior Lecturer in the Department of Sociology, and a member of the Centre for Econometric and Allied Research, University of Ibadan. He obtained his doctorate from the University of Warwick. He has published extensively on the Nigerian working class and generally on the transformation of labour processes in Africa. He is the author of *Labour in the Explanation of an African Crisis*, 1994.

Said Adejumobi is a Lecturer in the Department of Political Science at the Lagos State University, Ojo. He did his post-graduate studies at the University of Lagos. He is widely published in the area of political economy and has contributed to many books and reputable journals on Nigerian politics. He is the co-editor of *The Political Economy of Nigeria under Military Rule 1984–1993*, 1995.

Jibrin Ibrahim holds a doctorate from the University of Bordeaux, France, and was a Reader in the Department of Political Science, Ahmadu Bello University, Zaria before he left to join the Centre for Research and Documentation (CRD), Kano. He has written extensively on democratisation processes in Africa and on ethnic and religious conflicts in Nigeria. He co-edited *Democratisation Processes in Africa: Problems and Prospects*, 1995. He is also the editor of *Expanding the Nigerian Democratic Space*, 1996.

Attahiru Jega obtained his doctorate from Northwestern University, Evanston, Illinois, USA, and is a Senior Lecturer in the Department of Political Science, Bayero University, Kano. He has contributed to many publications on Nigerian politics and economy, especially on the military and democratisation in Nigeria, and on the role of professional groups under structural adjustment. He is the author of *Nigerian Academics under Military Rule*, 1994.

Abubakar Momoh is a Lecturer in the Department of Political Science, Lagos State University, Ojo. He did post-graduate work at the University of Lagos. He is widely published in national and international journals, and has also contributed to many books on the Nigerian political economy. Together with Adejumobi, he co-edited *The Political Economy of Nigeria under Military Rule, 1984–1993*, 1995.

Ibrahim Mu'azzam did his post-graduate studies at Ahmadu Bello University, Zaria, and lectures in the Department of Political Science, Bayero University, Kano. He has contributed to many works on Nigerian politics, and on political philosophy generally. He has been a keen observer and researcher of the question of secularism and the dynamics of religious conflicts in Nigeria.

Abdul Rauf Mustapha obtained his doctorate from St. Peter's College, University of Oxford. He held the position of a Reader in the Department of Political Science, Ahmadu Bello University, Zaria until recently when he left to join the University of Oxford as a Fellow based at Queen Elizabeth House. He is widely published in edited books and reputable journals on the agrarian question and the state in Nigeria, as well as on the dynamics of ethnic and communal relations and their implications for democratisation.

Charmaine Pereira holds a doctorate in Psychology of Education from the Open University, Milton Keynes, England, and lectured in the Department of Sociology, Ahmadu Bello University, Zaria, for a couple of years. She has contributed to books and journals on gender issues and in the general area of psychology.

Yunusa Zakari Ya'u lectures in the Department of Electrical Engineering, Bayero University, Kano. He did his post-graduate studies at both the Ahmadu Bello University, Zaria and the Obafemi Awolowo University, Ife. He has been a keen observer of and commentator on the Nigerian political processes under economic crisis and structural adjustment. He has contributed to many academic publications, in addition to having written over one hundred newspaper feature articles. He is also the co-author of *The Populist Factor in Nigerian Politics*, 1995.